Hi Gary

Thanks for your interest in this book. The main feature of the book is the short summaries at the beginning of each chapter designed to provide "need to know" information for your potential customers. Customers will become "more knowledgeable customers" as a result of providing questions... your technicians will have... Plus: to have a copy of this as a quick reference book for your field to your feedback it useful

Gary Bennett

BUGS BE GONE
Pest control in homes and other buildings

By Gary W. Bennett, Ph.D.

Professor of Entomology and
Director, Center for Urban and
Industrial Pest Management

Purdue University • West Lafayette, IN

ACKNOWLEDGEMENTS

Bugs Be Gone is a book inspired by Bennett (Bennie) Parr, a retired pest management professional (PMP) who saw the need for a consumer guide for insect pests in and around homes and other buildings. Although this author had been thinking for years about such a guide for consumers (a book that would also have utility for PMPs to provide customers and potential customers), it was Bennie and his enthusiasm that "made it happen."

I must also thank my wife and family for tolerating my long absences behind closed doors as I wrote this book.

— *Gary Bennett*

TABLE OF CONTENTS

Page

HOW TO USE THIS GUIDE

This book provides how-to-do-it information about pest control in homes and other buildings in an environmentally sound manner. Although designed for the general public to use when making decisions about managing pests, entomologists and professional pest managers will also find the book useful. Pest identification, biology, and control are brought together in one single, comprehensive guide.

Each of the pest group chapters has a beginning summary that is an easy, practical guide for readers to use. It includes an introduction to the pest group and its economic importance. The species of importance (their identification, biology, and behavior) will be reviewed, and their control/management (integrating non-chemical and insecticide-based procedures), as well as when to call a professional pest management company will be discussed. A decision on how to attain control of the pest may be made at this juncture.

For those readers who want to know more, a detailed discussion of the pest group and its control follows the summary.

Thus, this guide provides information about how to resolve everyday pest problems in living and working environments in a green manner and how to prevent pest problems from occurring. *Bugs Be Gone* is designed to help consumers eliminate pests as well as to prevent their return.

1

INTRODUCTION TO PEST PREVENTION AND CONTROL

Most insects – and there are about a million that have been named – are beneficial to mankind or at least neutral to us and our environment. Some people say all insects are beneficial, just as all other forms of life because they're essential parts of the complex food chain that supports life on earth. However, it's often difficult for us to think of mosquitoes as a beneficial food source, as fish food when they're larvae in ponds or other bodies of water. More often, we think about mosquitoes as irritating blood feeders and agents of some of the most dreaded diseases on earth, such as malaria, yellow fever and West Nile virus.

But bugs are beneficial. Many insects pollinate plants (flowers, trees, crops, etc.). Our abundant food supply simply wouldn't be possible without insect pollinators. Some insects produce food and fabric. Honeybees produce honey, and silkworm caterpillars (larvae) produce silk. Honey has been collected by humans for thousands of years for food and use in the production of wine, baked goods, candies and ice cream. The silk industry, which has existed for about 4,000 years, produces soft, lustrous and easily dyed fabric.

Other benefits are:

✳ lac is a crude resinous material produced by scale insects that is used in paints, cements and adhesives

✳ cochineal, also a scale insect product, has been used as a dye

✳ the treatment of human ailments with insects or insect secretions

✳ the high nutritional value of insects such as termites, caterpillars, ants, locusts and beetle larvae serve the dietary needs of many cultures throughout the world

Many insects are considered beneficial as biological control agents. Predators and parasites occur frequently in the insect world, including lady beetles, lacewings, and certain ants, bees and wasps. Predators chew and eat other insects or suck juices from their victims. Spiders, a close relative to insects, are perhaps the greatest of all predators of insects. Parasites lay their eggs on or in other insects, and they hatch into larvae, which feed on the host insect. Some parasitic larvae consume enough of the host to kill it and, as such, are somewhere between parasites and predators; thus, they're called parasitoids (like parasites).

Insects are probably better known as pests because they damage or destroy our food supplies, property, and health and welfare. By welfare, I mean some insects are a nuisance. They annoy us or occupy space we don't want to share with them. They're often called bugs, although close relatives such as spiders, mites, ticks and millipedes also are called bugs. Insects and their relatives can become pests in homes, businesses, industrial plants, municipal buildings and outdoor areas frequented by humans. Most insects don't harm the products of humans or their buildings, nor do they transmit harmful diseases. However, many carry diseases, feed on human food, clothing, housing and manufactured goods, and annoy or injure humans and animals through painful bites and stings.

There are a wide range of pests and pest situations that are concerning:

✻ General pests in or around homes, from cockroaches to houseflies, are mainly an annoyance.

✻ Pests that damage homes, such as termites or wood-boring beetles.

✻ Pests that infest food and other stored products, such as clothes moths on woolens or weevils in food products.

✻ Health pests, from mosquitoes to ticks, which are irritating blood feeders and vectors of disease.

PEST THRESHOLDS : WHAT'S AN ACCEPTABLE PEST LEVEL?

The aesthetic injury level is the point beyond which people won't tolerate a pest's presence. Thresholds are determined by the relationship of the pest to people's health, comfort, shelter or aesthetics. They're influenced by:

✳ Pest species involved and its appearance. Ants are beneficial as predators but might be intolerable in and around dwellings.

✳ Individual. One person might be happy to have a nonpoisonous spider in the garden, but another person might be repulsed by it.

✳ Environment. An oriental cockroach infestation might be tolerable in a harbor area, but it won't be tolerated in an upscale neighborhood.

✳ Type of business or structure. A few drain flies in a storage room might be acceptable but not in a hospital operating room.

✳ Specific areas within a structure. The threshold for crickets in the boiler room of a high-rise apartment building will be higher than in the individual apartments.

✳ Insecticide tolerance. Some people might be willing to accept small numbers of pests instead of allowing the application of insecticides in their living environment.

PRINCIPLES OF PEST CONTROL/MANAGEMENT

Pest control – also called pest management or integrated pest management (IPM) – can be defined as a system integrating preventive and corrective measures to keep pests from causing significant problems. In any type of pest management program, the objectives should be achieved at the lowest possible cost with minimum risk or hazard to a family and pets and the desirable components of the environment (indoors and outdoors).

Limiting the reproductive and survival potential of each pest is the key to effective control. This might involve the use of insecticides, but sanitation, exclusion, harborage elimination, and other nonchemical controls are useful, too. Removing their food, water and shelter through sanitation and eliminating clutter where pests can hide; sealing cracks where pests can get into hiding areas; keeping pests out by having tight fitting doors and screens; and using sticky traps or vacuum cleaners to remove pests are examples of ways to control pests. Then, as needed, insecticides can be incorporated into the control program.

Insecticides are used commonly for pest control because they're easy to apply, fast acting and effective against various insect pests. Surveys have shown most people keep one or more household insecticide products. Few people will tolerate insects indoors, while outdoors insects are less disliked. Many outdoor bugs – such as ants, spiders, millipedes, sowbugs and crickets – are allowed to coexist with us, but if they enter our homes through cracks or openings in foundations or through windows or doors that aren't tightly sealed, they become pests. Some of these occasional (accidental) invaders don't survive indoors, and others adapt and do well inside. Many, such as spiders and crickets, move inside to escape unfavorable outside environmental conditions, such as winter weather, and will remain inside until spring arrives.

We apply insecticides to control pests because we dislike their presence, prefer to maintain a pest-free property, and want to eliminate pests that cause disease (ticks, mosquitoes, flies). With the increasing public concern about the effects of insecticides on humans, animals and the environment, we see a greater use of low-toxicity insecticides, naturally occurring insecticides, nonchemical methods and biological pest control methods. (See table).

Every bug problem is solved best by five basic steps:

1. Inspection
2. Identification
3. Selection of treatment methods
4. Treatment
5. Evaluation

Inspection involves examining the premises thoroughly to learn as much as possible about the problem. Look for the harborage areas of the pest – conditions such as moisture, heat or darkness that favor infestations; food and water that can be used by the pest; probable means of entry, such as incoming food and open sewers; and evidence of infestation, such as damage, droppings, tracks, and actual specimens or their cast skins. Inspection will enable you to estimate the severity of the pest problem.

Inspections also will enable you to determine the presence of sensitive individuals (young, old, and pets), pilot lights, exposed food and other items that might influence your pest control methods. Thoroughness during the inspection is important to provide many of these answers, as well as maximum information about the nature of the pest problem. Thus, inspection information plays a key role in the development of the plan of action for limiting the pest problem and preventing its recurrence.

Nonchemical, biorational and biological control methods

Nonchemical	Biorational chemicals (Low toxicity)	Biocontrol
Exclusion screens, caulking, sealing, repairing, inspecting materials before bringing in	**Diatomaceous earth** silicon-containing dust causes water loss and death	**Parasitic and predatory insects** (such as lady bugs and parasitic wasps)
Sanitation disposing of garbage and rotting materials, removing clutter, vacuuming	**Repellents** personal protection from biting pests	**Bacillus bacteria** some pest species are killed by toxins produced by the bacteria
Habitat modification mow lawns, remove debris and wood or rock piles, dry out wet areas, trim vegetation around buildings	**Botanicals** pyrethrum, neem, rotenone, etc. are derived from plants	
Hot or cold temperatures freeze infested food items, heat infested clothes and other fabrics	**Insect growth regulators** chemicals that disrupt the growth, development and reproduction of pests	
Mechanical fly swatter, traps and sticky surfaces, light traps, pheromone (attractant) traps	**Baits** formulation of food materials with a selective insecticide that is fed to pests	

Pest identification is the second key step. It helps make a thorough evaluation of the problem and an appropriate recommendation for control. Once the pest has been identified, it's much easier to inspect for additional evidence of infestation, harborage areas, and the means by which the pest gained entry.

The third step is selection of treatment methods, which might include harborage elimination, building repairs and sanitation to make the control program a more successful and lasting one. Then a decision can be made about other nonchemical methods (vacuuming, trapping, etc.) along with properly applied insecticides (baits, sprays, dusts, etc.). Always select the chemicals that require the least toxic insecticides possible and will do an effective job of controlling the pest when combined with the nonchemical methods.

Treatment (implementation of pest control tools and techniques) is the next step in the pest control process. Use any and all of the aforementioned tools that will eliminate the pest and its recurrence. When treatment involves insecticides, choose legal and appropriate ones for the situation. Modern insecticides offer a wide range of least-toxic, environmentally sensitive, biorational synthetic and natural toxicants, attractants, repellents, insect growth regulators (IGRs), biologicals, and other materials to control pests successfully.

The final step, and one many people forget, is to evaluate the program. Keep an eye out for any pests still alive or the recurrence of the pest problem, so any additional problem can be remedied immediately. Additionally, continue to implement the nonchemical measures (sanitation, exclusion) to maintain conditions that aren't conducive to pests.

At this point, the goal of establishing a program that's environmentally, socially and economically acceptable will have been met.

2

COCKROACHES

SUMMARY: *COCKROACHES AND THEIR CONTROL*

There are five kinds of cockroaches commonly found throughout the U.S. and world. They vary in appearance and habits but, in general, are rather large (1 to 1.5 inches as adults, much smaller as immature nymphs), flattened insects that are brownish or dark and fast moving. Cockroaches seek concealment in the daytime and when disturbed at night. They might be carried into homes and apartments in boxes, grocery bags, drink cartons and produce such as potatoes. In apartments and other dwellings, they move readily from one place to another along water pipes and through cracks and crevices in walls.

IMPORTANT COCKROACHES IN U.S.

The **German roach** is a common species and the one usually found in kitchens. The adults are comparatively small (about 0.5 inch long), tan and often occur in large numbers. The immatures (nymphs) have dark markings that make them appear dark brown to black.

The **American roach,** which is reddish-brown, is the largest of the common roaches – about 1.5 inches long when mature. It's found more often in food establishments, although houses and apartments near such establishments become infested frequently.

The **Oriental roach** is also large (about one inch long) and shiny black or dark brown. It's often called a water bug or black beetle. The species is found frequently in dampness and might enter homes through sewer openings. It might live outdoors during the summer months and move from home to home.

The **Brownbanded** roach is a Southern species but is often found in Northern states. It resembles the German roach in size but differs in habits. It can infest the entire home, rather than confining itself to the kitchen or where there's food. Infestations usually start from luggage, furniture or other materials shipped from one place to another.

The **Woods roach** normally lives under the loose bark of dead trees, logs or stumps. It sometimes invades homes built in or near wooded areas, but it doesn't thrive indoors. Males are almost 1 inch long and are brown with a pale stripe on the outer margins of the wings. They're fairly good fliers and often enter homes this way. They also can be carried in on firewood. The females are short-winged and resemble the Oriental roach, but they're seldom found indoors.

CONTROLLING COCKROACHES

The chances of effective, lasting cockroach control are increased greatly if thorough sanitation precedes proper chemical application. Destroying breeding places (by clearing out garbage and clutter, sealing cracks and openings, etc.) and removing food and water sources might reduce the necessity for chemical applications.

There are a number of insecticides, and usually numerous formulations and ways of applying each insecticide, that might be used for cockroach control. Baits and sprays – labeled as crawling insect control materials – are most effective. Dusts or powders also are available but are more difficult to use. Traps – with a sticky substance inside – can be purchased and used for pinpointing areas where cockroaches are located but usually have to be combined with baits or sprays to obtain satisfactory cockroach control. Baits are easy to use and are best for areas where contamination with sprays or dusts might be a problem, such as near food or dishes.

Cockroach control materials are available in low-pressure spray containers (aerosol cans) that apply a residual deposit of the insecticide. Apply them in about 2-inch wide bands where cockroaches hide, such as in crevices near the kitchen sink and stove, underneath and inside cupboards, around pipes and conduits where they pass along or through walls, in and around water heaters, inside the motor compartment of refrigerators, and behind skirting boards, mirrors and pictures. Also,

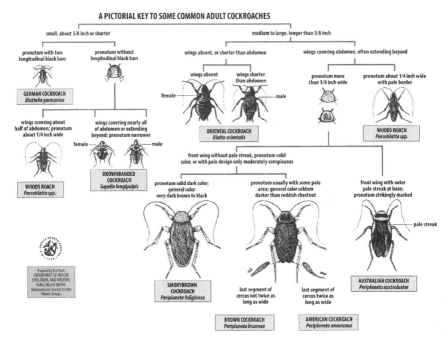

A PICTORIAL KEY TO SOME COMMON ADULT COCKROACHES

treat garbage cans and other refuse containers. Pressurized sprays of this type are quite satisfactory. However, they shouldn't be confused with the high-pressure aerosol bombs designed for applying space sprays. The latter are of limited use in cockroach control, with the additional disadvantage that occupants must evacuate the premises while treatment is under way.

A number of electronic/ultrasonic devices that are supposed to kill or repel cockroaches are available. Most of these devices haven't been tested thoroughly enough to determine if they're effective. A number of these units have been removed from the marketplace by government agencies after they were found to have no effect on insect pests.

Cockroach infestations often require the services of a professional pest control company. A quality professional company is one that is in good standing with the local Better Business Bureau and one that gets good references within the community. A knowledgeable and experienced company will always "do the job right," and will always be ready to return if the problem is not solved within a reasonable time frame.

COCKROACHES

Cockroaches are among the most common insects and are found in human dwellings all throughout the world. They've also been around for a long time – 350 million years. Some scientists consider cockroaches to be one of the most successful animals to inhabit the planet, adapting to many changing environments throughout millions of years. Their presence in almost every part of the world and in a wide range of habitats demonstrates that cockroaches (referred to as roaches by many people) are an outstanding success story in nature. Many of the outstanding biological characteristics also make them some of the most difficult pests to control.

Fortunately, only a few of the cockroach species found in the U.S. infest dwellings. The most common are the German, American, oriental, brownbanded, smokybrown (southeast U.S. mainly) and woods cockroaches. These species represent at least 95 percent of the cockroach control concerns in and around buildings. Other species might infest homes and other buildings but generally will be found in localized situations or under unusual circumstances.

IMPORTANCE OF COCKROACHES
Cockroach excrement, cast skins, body parts and dead bodies contain allergens to which many people exhibit allergic responses, such as skin rashes, watery eyes and sneezing. For some allergic people, and particularly asthmatic children and those who have chronic lung disease, allergic attacks to cockroach allergens can be serious and even life threatening. All forms of contact should be kept to a minimum.

Disease-producing microorganisms, such as bacteria, have been found on cockroach bodies and in their feces. Organisms causing food poisoning, nausea, vomiting, diarrhea and dysentery are deposited on food and utensils as cockroaches feed. Thus, the contamination of food and food preparation surfaces with pathogens is of considerable importance.

Cockroaches also hide in wet filthy areas such as sewers, garbage disposals, and other damp and unsanitary areas. Filth and germs from these sources are spread by cockroaches onto food supplies, dishes, utensils and other surfaces. Cockroaches contaminate far more food than they eat.

Cockroaches produce odorous secretions that leave an unpleasant odor on surfaces they've touched. Food fouled by this characteristic odor is unfit for human consumption. Odors often remain even after food is cooked. These habits and odors are why people are so disgusted and repulsed by the presence of cockroaches. For many, personal disgust and the social stigma attached to cockroaches result in a complete lack of tolerance for them.

IDENTIFICATION
The correct identification of a cockroach infestation is important because pest species have different biologies and behaviors, and it's helpful to know which species you're dealing with. There also are other insects that look similar, such as ground beetles, crickets and long-horned beetles. Cockroaches have flattened, oval bodies, and their heads are concealed from above by a shield-like structure. They have six long, spiny running legs and thread-like antennae. Their color ranges from dark-brown to reddish brown and from tan to black.

Many adult cockroaches have fully developed wings, although few fly. Others have short wings or a lack of wings. In general females have shorter wings than males. Young, immature cockroaches resemble adults but are smaller and wingless. If there's any doubt whether an insect is a cockroach, submit a sample to a pest control expert.

COCKROACH BIOLOGY AND BEHAVIOR
Most cockroaches are tropical and subtropical in origin, generally living outdoors. They're active mostly at night, during which time they forage for food, water and mates. They might be seen in the daytime, particularly when a heavy population is present or when some other form of stress is placed on the population. Such stresses include lack of food or water, exposure to pesticides (particularly pyrethrins or pyrethroids) and exposure to predators, such as ants. Ordinarily, cockroaches prefer a moist environment, and most species prefer a relatively high degree of warmth for areas where they're active.

Some tropical cockroaches feed only on vegetation. However, chewing mouthparts enable cockroaches to feed on various materials humans produce, consume, shed or excrete. They're especially fond of starches, sweets, grease and meat products, but they'll also eat various other materials, such as:

* cheese
* beer
* leather
* bakery products
* starch in book bindings
* glue
* hair
* flakes of dried skin
* dead animals
* plant materials

Generally, they can be considered to scavenge on the fallout of human activity in structures and in unsanitary areas, such as garbage cans or piles, sewage systems and septic tanks. This understanding can be helpful to you when undertaking sanitation procedures to place stress on infesting populations.

Cockroaches usually orient to protected cracks and crevices that provide a warm, humid environment. Some species, such as the American and oriental cockroaches, gather in large groups on open walls in protected places or in open areas outside. While they're often found in groups in their daytime hiding or resting areas (called harborages) and can be found feeding in groups at night, cockroaches aren't social insects like ants, some bees and wasps or termites. Cockroaches generally forage individually for food and otherwise behave in a largely individualistic or nonsocial manner. Thus, although cockroaches aren't social insects, they often form groups.

Besides their ability to move around inside and outside, and some species are good fliers, cockroaches are well known for moving to new areas via hitchhiking. Because they prefer to hide in cracks and crevices in the daytime, they're frequently moved about by people or in products shipped around cities or throughout the country. Careful inspection of grocery bags or boxes, drink cartons, shopping bags, furniture, clothing or other goods coming into a home might reveal cockroaches hiding in these items.

Cockroaches develop by a gradual metamorphosis consisting of three stages – egg, nymph and adult. The female produces an egg capsule, called an ootheca, which contains two rows of eggs. Nymphs hatch out of the egg capsule by working together to break a seam along the top of the egg case. When the seam splits open, the tiny nymphs emerge to begin their life. The nymphs generally resemble adults in appearance and behavior but are smaller, don't have wings or wing pads, and frequently have a different color. Newly molted nymphs are white but will darken to the normal color within a few hours. Some people mistakenly think these recently molted individuals are albino cockroaches. Nymphs undergo a series of molts. With the last molt, the wings (if they exist in that species) are formed completely. The length of time required for the eggs to hatch, for the nymphs to develop and for the life span of the adults varies (within each species) because of temperature, humidity, the quality of their diet and other environmental conditions.

Habitat preference, or where cockroaches choose to live, varies from one species to another. Although most all cockroaches prefer to spend most of their time in narrow, tight cracks and crevices, and spaces where surfaces touch them on their top side and bottom side, the general areas they inhabit differ. German cockroaches prefer dark, warm, humid areas near sources of food and water (such as kitchens and bathrooms). Brownbanded cockroaches prefer drier areas, such as pantries, closets, office and desk areas, and behind items on walls such as pictures. Woods cockroaches prefer trees, shrubs, mulched or wooded areas, but are attracted to lights at night, and thus get indoors accidentally. By identifying a cockroach problem properly and knowing where the problem prefers to reside, you can do a much better job eliminating the problem.

SIGNIFICANT PEST SPECIES
German cockroach
Because they're so common and can develop such large numbers in a short period of time, German cockroaches are the most important cockroach infesting houses, apartments, restaurants, hotels, and other buildings. In some situations or locations, other cockroaches, such as the oriental cockroach in basements and crawl spaces or the smokybrown cockroach

along the Gulf Coast region, are more important. However, the German cockroach is the most common and important species in buildings.

Adults are pale to medium brown and about one-half to five-eighths of an inch long. German cockroaches can be distinguished from other roaches by the two dark stripes on the anterior, dorsal portion (pronotum) of the thorax. Adults of both sexes have well-developed wings, but they never fly. Males are distinguished from females by the slender, tapering shape of the abdomen. German cockroach nymphs resemble the adults except they're smaller, wingless and darker, often nearly black. A single light stripe running down the middle of the back is the most prominent marking on the younger German cockroach nymphs.

Adult females carry the egg capsule protruding from the rear of the abdomen until the eggs are ready to hatch. Females carrying egg capsules are known as being gravid. The egg capsule is light colored, about one-third of an inch long, more than twice as long as wide, and shows about 16 external divisions or segments on either side. The nymphs may break open the capsule while it's still attached to the female, or she may deposit the capsule in crevices and other protected locations where the young will be able to find food and harborage when they emerge. The German cockroach is the only common house-infesting species that carries the egg capsule for such an extended period. Capsules removed from the female more than a couple of days before the normal hatching time will be less likely to hatch unless they remain under conditions of high humidity. This also might be true for gravid females that are killed by an insecticide within several hours to one day or more before the time the egg capsule normally would have hatched. The embryos in the newly formed egg capsule require a reasonably steady flow of water, usually from the adult female, to prevent death from desiccation or drying out. If the humidity is greater than 70 percent, desiccation might not occur, and the egg capsule can survive for as long as a few days after premature dropping or death of the female.

Adult females can produce from four to eight egg capsules in their lifetime. Each capsule contains 30 to 48 eggs. It usually takes 20 to 30 days from the time of initial formation of the first egg capsule until it hatches, with this time generally being shorter under warmer

German cockroach — male on the left, egg capsule–carrying female on the right.

temperature conditions (greater than 25 C). Formation of the next egg capsule usually begins within a couple of weeks.

There are six or seven nymphal stages, called instars, before the molt into the adult stage. The number of nymphal instars might increase under certain environmental conditions, such as poor diet or low temperatures, or if appendages, such as legs or antennae, are lost during the earlier nymphal instars. In the latter case, extra instars will occur to allow regeneration of these missing body parts. Completion of the nymphal stage under room conditions requires 40 to 125 days, depending on environmental conditions such as diet quality, crowding and temperatures. Adult German cockroaches can live as long as one year, but most will die from various causes long before then.

Nymphs have habits similar to those of adults. They're active mostly at night but hide in dark crevices during the day. If German cockroaches are seen during the day, the population is probably so large the available cracks are full already, or food and moisture are in such short supply daytime foraging is necessary. Such behavior indicates the population is under considerable stress. This species usually hides in areas close to moisture and food, which means the cockroaches generally are found in kitchens and other food areas. They prefer to rest on wood rather than on metal or other smooth surfaces. Large infestations occur on metal surfaces when there are few other surfaces available. Examples are on submarines or in large modern food-processing plants and kitchens with stainless steel equipment and wall panels.

The German cockroach is a general feeder but is attracted to fermented foods and beverage residues such as beer spills. If water is present, adults can live about a month without food, but young nymphs will die of starvation within 10 days. Without food or water, the adults die in less than two weeks. Most stages become stressed if deprived of food or water for more than a couple of days. Stressed cockroaches tend to wander or forage for resources aggressively, even during abnormal periods, such as the daytime.

Infestations are sometimes found in areas not generally suspected of harboring German cockroaches, such as dresser drawers in bedrooms. German cockroaches found scattered through nonfood areas of a home or building is usually a sign of a heavy infestation or the repellent effects of insecticide applications elsewhere in the facility. Cockroaches in these areas will find food scarce but can feed on scattered crumbs, soiled clothing, exposed glue used in furniture or cosmetic products. German cockroaches also can be found outdoors during warm months, often around garbage receptacles. This, too, is usually a result of a heavy infestation indoors.

Some of these uncommon patterns of infestation are more understandable in light of recent research about the normal movement patterns of German cockroaches within and between urban apartments. While most German cockroaches, especially the younger nymphal stages, probably don't forage more than a couple of feet from their preferred harborage under field conditions, detailed field research has shown some individuals can be quite mobile within structures. As much as 10 percent (or more) of the adult German cockroaches in a moderately to heavily infested apartment can move into or out of the kitchen area within a week's time. Adult males appear to be the most mobile stage, followed by nongravid adult females and large nymphs. Gravid females rarely leave the harborage.

Similar rates of movement also have been measured between adjacent apartments. Movement between apartments usually doesn't occur unless the two adjacent apartments share common plumbing. Thus, exclusion of German cockroach movement into the wall voids that house plumbing connections, or careful treatment of dry wall voids with insecticides (e.g., dust formulations), will aid greatly in maintaining adequate control in apartment buildings and other large, complex structures, such as hospitals and motels. This understanding of life-stage-specific levels of movement and foraging suggests the youngest nymphs in the population might not be readily controllable except by the most thorough crack and crevice applications, and they might be susceptible to secondary poisoning – following bait application – because of their coprophagy (eating of frass, or excrement, of others) within harborages. Similarly, because gravid females don't appear to forage or feed much at all, they could be the most important and difficult portion of the population to control.

The German cockroach is a relatively active species. Many individuals in the population move around readily within structures. They travel from one location to another and can pass through small openings. They're also regularly carried from place to place in things such as bagged potatoes and onions, beverage cartons, grocery bags, food carts, other food packages, handbags and the folds of clothing. Look closely to find all the places in which cockroaches might be living and determine how cockroaches might be transported into the premises. It might not be possible to eliminate all the German cockroaches in a structure at any one time if a steady flow of cockroaches is being carried into the premises via people, food shipments or other routes. Furthermore, some repellent insecticides use, such a pyrethrins and pyrethroids, might scatter cockroaches widely throughout a building. If all the scattered or satellite populations aren't found and treated, reinfestation of treated areas will occur.

American cockroach

The American cockroach also is known as the waterbug, flying waterbug and, in some areas of the southern U.S., the palmetto bug. It's the largest of the common species, growing to 1.5 inches or more in length. It's reddish brown with a pale brown or yellow border on the upper

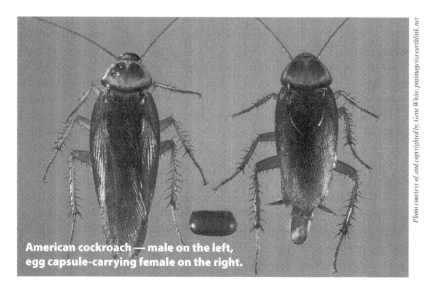

Photo courtesy of, and copyrighted by, Gene White, pmimages@earthlink.net

American cockroach — male on the left, egg capsule-carrying female on the right.

surface of the pronotum. Both sexes have well-developed wings, but the male's extend beyond the abdomen.

The female drops her egg capsule within a day after it's formed. Sometimes it's dropped into a suitable location, such as near a food source, or in a protected area. In the southern U.S., this frequently will be outdoors on moist and decaying wood or other substrates. At other times the capsule might be glued to a relatively hidden surface with secretions from the female's mouth. The egg capsule is dark brown, symmetrically shaped and about five-sixteenths of an inch long (length usually less than width). Egg capsules are formed about one per week until 15 to 90 capsules have been produced. Each capsule contains 14 to 16 eggs. At room temperature, nymphs will hatch in 50 to 55 days. In the process of hatching, nymphs will molt and leave their first cast skins in the egg case.

Young nymphs are grayish brown, and each will molt nine to 13 times before reaching maturity. After the first few molts, nymphs become more reddish brown. The time required to complete the nymphal stage varies from 160 to 971 days. Under ideal conditions, an adult female can live as long as 14 to 15 months, but males live for a shorter period. However, in natural populations, many factors reduce the average life span of American cockroaches.

When indoors, the nymphs and adults usually are found in dark, moist areas of basements and crawlspaces, as well as in and around bathtubs, clothes hampers, floor drains, pipe chases and sewers. In basements, they're usually found in corner areas high on the walls or in floor drains. In the North, the cockroach commonly is associated with steam heat tunnels. In Northern areas, where steam heat tunnels aren't found, the American cockroach is restricted primarily to large institutional buildings, greenhouses and facilities like zoos. The American cockroach also is common around the accesses to sewers, near garbage and on the underside of the metal covers of large sump pumps in boiler rooms. American cockroaches also have been observed migrating from one building to another during warm months in the Northern U.S.

In the South, this cockroach is abundant in alleyways, yards, hollow trees and palm trees. Recent studies in Florida have shown American cockroaches, along with other related species and outdoor cockroaches, generally are associated with trees, shrubs and woodpiles in landscapes. They especially prefer moist, shady areas. Sometimes they're found under roof shingles and flashing or in the attic. Similar studies in Texas have shown American and smokybrown cockroaches often prefer moist, shady areas of ground cover, which are often found around foundations and near swimming pools. The automatic sprinkler systems for irrigating these areas of turf and ground cover provide particularly attractive and favorable living conditions for cockroach populations. When conditions are unfavorable, American cockroaches and other outdoor species might move indoors.

American cockroaches feed on various foods, but decaying organic matter seems to be preferred. They also feed on book bindings, manuscripts, clothing, or glossy paper, if they contain starch. Syrup and other sweets also are attractive. The adults can survive two or three months without food, but only about a month without water.

The adults have well-developed wings but seldom fly, unless temperature conditions are above 85 F, at which point they can be active flyers. They're capable of gliding long distances if they take off from a tree or rooftop. In the South and as far north as Kentucky, American cockroaches have been reported to fly short distances.

Oriental cockroach

The oriental cockroach also is referred to as the waterbug, black beetle, or shad roach. It's found in all parts of the U.S. Total length of the cockroach is about 1.25 inches for the female and 1 inch for the male. The female has small, functionless, rudimentary wings called wing pads. The male's wings cover about three-quarters of the abdomen. Neither the male nor the female can fly. Adults are dark brown or nearly black and usually have a somewhat greasy sheen to their body. Females are broader and heavier looking than males. The female carries an egg capsule for about 30 hours, after which it's dropped or attached to a protected surface near a food supply. They're not glued to surfaces. Females will produce an average of eight capsules, each containing 16 eggs, which will hatch in about 60 days under room conditions.

Nymphs molt from seven to 10 times, and the nymphal stages usually take several months to a year to complete development. Unlike the other house-infesting species, the oriental cockroach generally has a seasonal development cycle. The peak number of adults usually appears in late spring or early summer. The number of adults in the population generally is low by late summer and early fall because of natural mortality and the hatching of nymphs. Few live adults usually are found

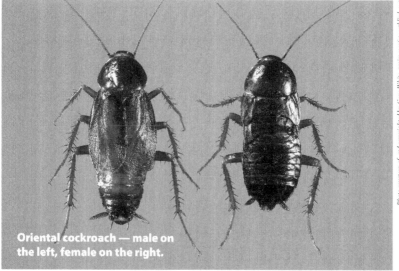

Oriental cockroach — male on the left, female on the right.

in the population throughout the year, but if nymphs haven't reached maturity by late fall or early winter, their development seems to slow considerably, and maturity isn't reached until spring. The nymphs and adults have similar habits and are found associated with decaying organic matter indoors and out. They can be found in yards, beneath leaves, in dumps, in crawlspaces, in the mulch of flowerbeds or in landscape retaining walls. They're also common in high moisture areas such as sewers; water meter enclosures; drains; and dark, damp basements. Nymphs and adults are sluggish and usually are located at or below ground level indoors. They're seldom found on walls, in high cupboards, or in the upper floors of buildings. They're commonly found in bathtubs (by way of the drain) because they have difficulty walking on or up smooth surfaces because of their small tarsal pads, especially between the hooks of their pretarsal claws.

Oriental cockroaches feed on all kinds of filth, rubbish and other decaying organic matter. If water is available, they can live for a month without food, but they die within two weeks without water. In many areas oriental cockroaches generally are found outdoors during warm weather. In periods of drought, there might be considerable movement into structures, apparently in relation to humidity gradients. As cold weather approaches or sometimes during unseasonably cool periods, a similar migration indoors might occur. There might be considerable group movement within heated structures during cold weather, particularly if some areas of a building are maintained at warmer temperatures than others.

Brownbanded cockroach

This is one of the smaller cockroaches, rarely being more than a half inch long. It's light brown and can be distinguished readily from the German cockroach by the presence of two lighter, transverse bands running from one side to the other across the base of the wings and abdomen in adults, and in the same position on the nymphs. Thus, the name brownbanded. These bands might be irregular or broken and are more apparent on the young and females than males. The female has a broader body than the male. Males and females are active, and the adult males fly readily when disturbed. All stages might jump when

Brownbanded cockroach — male on the left, female on the right, and the purse-shaped egg capsule on the bottom.

Photo courtesy of, and copyrighted by, Gene White, pmimages@earthlink.net

attempting to escape. They frequently occur in the same buildings as the German cockroach. Be careful to identify this species correctly because control techniques are different for the two species because of their different distribution and behaviors within structures.

A female brownbanded cockroach carries her egg capsule for a day or two and then attaches it to a protected surface. The egg case is purse-shaped, light brown and cemented in place, usually to the side or under surfaces of infested objects. The egg capsule is about three-sixteenths of an inch long with length less than twice the width, and about eight external divisions or segments along either side. Females will produce about 14 egg capsules during their adult life, each containing about 18 eggs. These hatch in 50 to 75 days, depending on temperature. Under room conditions, nymphs mature in about 160 days. Adults can live as long as 10 months.

Nymphs and adults generally are found on ceilings, high on walls, behind picture frames and light fixtures, or near motors of refrigerators and other appliances. They also are found in light switches, closets and furniture. They don't require as close an association with moisture sources as the German cockroach. This helps explain why they're commonly found in rooms other than the kitchen or bathroom. These cockroaches strongly avoid light and aren't normally seen during the day.

The brownbanded cockroach prefers feeding on starchy materials.

However, it can be found feeding on almost anything and has been known to chew on such nonfood materials as nylon stockings, presumably for the residues of body oils and skin flakes.

When making an inspection for brownbanded cockroaches, look beneath tables and chairs, dressers and chests. Look also behind pictures, along picture moldings, on rough plaster walls and ceilings, and especially on the ceilings and upper walls of cabinets, pantries and closets. No room should be left uninspected, nor should any piece of furniture (wood, metal, or upholstered) if its construction provides shelter. Look for tiny black droppings, attached egg capsules, or cast skins where they've fallen from above onto shelves or ledges.

These cockroaches are more often found in homes, apartments, hotels and hospital rooms than in stores, restaurants and kitchens. They're common in institutional buildings. They're frequently transported in furniture and will spread rapidly throughout an entire building. They've long been abundant in the Southern states, but are found as far north as Canada. In the cooler Northern states they're generally found in the warmer parts of buildings.

Smokybrown cockroach

Smokybrown cockroaches are closely related to the American cockroach but are distinguished by their slightly smaller size. They're slightly more than 1-inch long, and uniform mahogany color. They don't have any lighter coloration around the edge of their pronotum as do adult American cockroaches. Males and females have wings longer than their bodies. Young nymphs have long antennae, which are white at the tip.

Females lay a dark brown to black egg capsule, which contains 24 eggs. Each female produces about 17 capsules, and they're usually glued to a surface, although they might be found lying loosely on the ground or floor occasionally. Their life cycle is similar to other closely related species, except the average adult life span is less than the American cockroach. In a protected area, smokybrown cockroaches will live for about 200 to 300 days at room temperature.

The smokybrown cockroach is restricted in its distribution within the U.S. It's common throughout Central Texas and eastward along the Gulf Coast throughout Florida and up the Eastern seaboard.

It's the most common species of cockroach encountered in some parts of the South, and it's known to be present in some areas of Southern California. It's not generally found in the Northern U.S. except when it's accidentally brought in.

Normally, the cockroach feeds on plant material (especially in greenhouses), but it can feed on almost anything other cockroach species feed on once inside a dwelling. It's commonly found living in wood shingle roofs and in gutters, where it feeds on decaying organic matter. In attics, it's typically found living at the roofline.

Nymphs and adults enter buildings in different ways. They can be brought into the house with firewood or anything else that's stored outside, in garages or in other storage areas. They can enter around doors and windows, through ventilation ports under the eaves of a house, or through any other small cracks or crevices that lead inside. Many homes with brick facades are built with regularly spaced weep holes in the brickwork; cockroaches and many other insects can enter wall voids via these weep hole accesses. They also enter structures via roofs and gutters. Smokybrown cockroaches move in and out of buildings to forage more than American cockroaches and most other outdoor species.

Woods cockroach

Woods cockroach covers a number of cockroach species, usually of the same genus and having similar habits. The species described most generally is the Pennsylvania woods cockroach. Woods cockroaches are small, usually not more than two-thirds of an inch long. Adults are dark brown, and the sides of the thorax and the front half of the wings are margined with yellow. The wings are longer than the body in the male, and those of the female cover only one-third to two-thirds of the abdomen.

The males generally are strong fliers, whereas the females don't fly. The Pennsylvania woods cockroach is distributed widely in the Eastern, Southern and Midwestern U.S. up to Canada.

Egg capsules are produced during the warmer months and are deposited behind the loose bark of dead trees, fallen logs or stumps. Woods cockroaches rarely breed indoors. Nymphs and adults usually are found outdoors beneath loose bark in woodpiles, stumps and hollow trees.

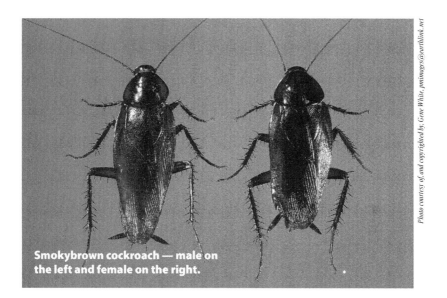

Smokybrown cockroach — male on the left and female on the right.

These cockroaches often become a problem when infested firewood is brought indoors. They'll wander about the house without congregating in any particular room. They can be troublesome especially during mating season, which often is May and June. Male woods cockroaches are strong fliers and will come from considerable distances, often in large numbers. They're readily attracted to lights at night and can gain entry indoors accidentally. Large numbers might also be found in the rain gutters of homes. Woods cockroaches feed primarily on decaying organic matter.

COCKROACH MANAGEMENT

Effective cockroach management requires planning and organization. Prevention of cockroach problems is an easier approach, if that alternative is still available. Eliminate sources of food, water and harborage. Cockroaches are carried into homes in bags, boxes and other items. Examine containers brought into your home carefully for the presence of cockroaches or their egg capsules, especially if they're brought in from locations known to be infested with cockroaches.

Through proper sanitation practices, access to food and water can be limited, thus limiting their ability to survive and reproduce. Don't leave food, pet food or water, dirty dishes, or drinks out overnight. Remove all food and spills from counter tops, sinks, tables, and floors after eating (or at least at the end of the day). Vacuum all crack and crevices to remove food and debris, and sweep or vacuum any food or debris from the floor. Take garbage out daily in closed plastic bags, and keep waste containers clean with lids sealed at all times. Repair leaky pipes and faucets, and increase ventilation to avoid condensation.

A good sanitation program has to include removing cockroach harborage, including boxes (especially those made from corrugated cardboard), newspapers, bags and other items that can clutter rooms. Use caulk to seal spaces and cracks were cockroaches can hide. Seal spaces (with steel wool, expanding foam or other barriers) where plumbing or electrical wiring goes through walls, so cockroaches can't enter the living space and hiding places inside the walls. These exclusion methods are useful as part of a cockroach prevention program.

When a cockroach infestation occurs, plan and organize to eliminate the problem. Before taking steps to control the pest, conduct an inspection to identify any problem areas and which cockroach species is involved. German cockroaches usually reside indoors, mainly kitchens and bathrooms. Check under sinks and in cupboards, closets, and cracks and crevices that provide dark hiding places near food or water. Also inspect for tiny black or brown specks (fecal stains or droppings) that indicate cockroach hiding spots.

For outdoor species like American, smokybrown and oriental cockroaches, look in dark, moist areas close to decaying organic food sources, such as in overgrown ground cover or flower beds and around trees, wood piles or compost piles. Also check for leaking roofs, inspect water-meter boxes, and look at sewer lines near your home, especially those with manhole covers, all of which are favored harborage sites for these cockroaches.

Cockroach sticky traps are useful inspection tools. Traps typically consist of a piece of cardboard covered with sticky adhesive. Cockroaches enter traps and get stuck on the adhesive. Traps help identify areas with cockroach infestations and monitor the effectiveness of control efforts.

Place traps along paths cockroaches might use to travel to and from feeding and hiding areas. Traps should be placed touching walls and in corners with both ends unobstructed. For active infestations, relocate traps if no cockroaches are caught after two or three nights.

Sanitation is extremely important for successful cockroach control. The same sanitation procedures described above under preventing cockroaches are applicable here. Harborage elimination, also mentioned above under prevention, is also key to cockroach elimination. The same methods mentioned above apply here. For outdoor species, keep garbage areas clean and cans well sealed, gutters clean and free flowing, faucets from leaking, and debris (bricks, lumber or firewood) properly stored and away from the foundation of homes, garages, and other buildings.

Other nonchemical control methods include the use of heat greater than 120 F for several hours, or cold at 0 F for 60 minutes or at 32 F for several hours. The latter might be more practical when cockroaches are found in portable items, such as clocks, telephones, etc., that can't be treated with insecticides. The items can be placed inside plastic garbage bags and stored in a freezer overnight.

Traps have been mentioned for inspection and monitoring purposes, they also can be used as part of the control program. When only a couple cockroaches are causing a problem, use several traps in the area where they've been seen, and you might be able to catch the one or two cockroaches. For heavy infestations, traps aren't capable of removing a significant portion of the population when used alone.

Portable vacuum cleaners that have strong suction can be used to physically remove cockroaches from their hiding areas (especially the smaller species such as German and brownbanded cockroaches). Using a flushing agent such as synergized pyrethrins to chase cockroaches out of hiding will assist in making vacuuming more effective. Vacuum cleaners can't eliminate all the cockroaches in a significant infestation, so the technique has to be used in combination with all other control methods.

Many types of mechanical or electrical devices are sold for cockroach control, but no valid studies have shown electromagnetic, ultrasonic, sonic, microwave or electromechanical devices to be effective at killing, repelling, sterilizing or affecting cockroaches. Therefore, none of the devices in the marketplace are recommended.

One last area of nonchemical control that has had limited utility in cockroach management programs is biological control – the use of predators, parasites and disease organisms to limit the size of cockroach populations naturally. Some types of wasps lay their eggs in cockroach egg capsules, and the wasp larvae eat the contents of the cockroach egg capsule. Microorganisms, such as yeasts and other bacteria, can provide population reduction or suppression under limited circumstances. The slow speed of action, low levels of control, and inconsistent results experienced with biological controls renders these approaches of little use in most cockroach management programs. However, some biological control agents might prove useful in the future, especially for outdoor cockroaches, where modest levels of population reduction might be acceptable.

INSECTICIDE METHODS

Many effective insecticides are available, but careful selection and chemical use in conjunction with, and complementary to, other appropriate sanitation and nonchemical methods should be implemented. This integrated pest management (IPM) approach ensures maximum control is obtained with the greatest safety and efficiency. When incorporating an insecticide into your control, remember an insecticide placed into or near cockroach harborage will produce better control than an insecticide placed where cockroaches will only walk over or encounter it occasionally. Thus, search for, locate and treat harborages.

There are a number of insecticide formulations available for use indoors or outdoors, but they vary in how they're formulated, how long they last and how they kill. However, most of them that can be bought in stores have low toxicity to humans and pets when used as directed. Information about toxicity can be obtained from the product label, a Material Safety Data Sheet (MSDS) or county cooperative extension office. Use insecticides after implementing the sanitation and other preventive measures discussed above.

Baits. There are a number of effective cockroach bait formulations available for indoor and outdoor use. Indoors, the most common bait comes in ready-to-use plastic bait stations or tubes containing gel bait, which can be squeezed from the tube into cracks, crevices and other places where cockroaches are found.

Baits consist of food mixed with an insecticide. They give best results in homes where good sanitation has been practiced (no alternative food sources available to cockroaches). Always use the number of bait containers needed to treat the areas where cockroaches are located (label directions will provide guidance); baits next to suspected hiding areas is recommended. Check the bait stations often to make sure the baits haven't been depleted and baits are fresh still.

Dusts. Some insecticides are sold in dust form. Making dust applications is an art form because you need the right equipment and lots of practice to apply dusts properly. However, dusts are useful when correctly applied because they can be distributed into inaccessible void areas that are difficult to treat with other forms of insecticides. Apply dusts lightly, so they're barely visible. Cockroaches will avoid heavy dust deposits, which can become caked, allowing the cockroaches to crawl on them unharmed.

Sprays. Insecticide sprays for cockroaches typically are sold in aerosol cans, but such sprays are available in pump dispensers or as concentrates to mix with water. Sprays generally are easy to apply and can provide fast control. Direct sprays into cracks and crevices where cockroaches hide. Exposed surfaces, especially those used to prepare foods, usually shouldn't be treated with sprays.

Aerosol bombs or foggers generally aren't effective against cockroaches hiding in cracks or crevices. Use sprays rather than bomb applications for better results. Using more foggers than recommended near open flames – such as pilot lights, gas stoves and furnaces – creates fire or explosion hazards.

Equipment. There are many types of bait guns, bait stations or other bait application devices, sprayers, dusters and other equipment available for use when applying insecticides for cockroach management. Compressed-air sprayers, aerosol insecticide systems, and hand dusters are used most commonly.

Insecticide safety. It's the duty of every pesticide user to read product label instructions and follow them carefully. Failure to follow insecticide label directions is illegal. Such failure includes using too much product, using it in a manner not specifically described on the label, and failing to wear proper protective clothing specified in label directions.

FOLLOW-UP

Important aspects of a cockroach management program include continued inspections and necessary insecticide applications to maintain the highest possible degree of cockroach management. Don't fall into a routine of using only certain types of insecticide applications without doing the inspections and whatever else is necessary to find any and all remaining cockroach harborages. The success of your cockroach management program lies in your ability to be organized, thorough and consistent with your program execution. The other key to long-term success is to remain vigilant and do all the follow-up necessary to keep the cockroach problem from recurring. If any aspect of your program is ignored for long, cockroaches – especially German cockroaches – are so prolific that infestations will develop rapidly and undo all the work it took to achieve control.

Cockroach control can be complicated, as you have discovered reading this chapter. This is especially the case if you have an entrenched or large infestation. Professional pest control companies have the knowledge, experience and equipment to handle cockroach problems. Contact a reputable company in your area for fast, efficient and effective cockroach control.

3

ANTS

SUMMARY: *ANTS AND THEIR CONTROL*

Ants are one of the most common pests in and around homes, usually a nuisance when they invade a home or contaminate food. The only pest ant that stings is the fire ant, found mainly in the southern U.S. The best way to avoid ant problems is to seal them out of a house by filling in cracks in the foundation and caulking cracks around doors, windows, plumbing and electrical conduits, and any other avenue of access they can use to gain entry.

Other helpful methods of preventing ant invasion include:
* trimming trees and shrubs so they don't touch the building;
* keeping flowers and grass away from the foundation;
* not leaving food out overnight and storing it in sealed containers;
* repairing dripping pipes and water from faucets; and
* locate and destroy their nests.

Ants generally are considered to be beneficial insects because their tunneling helps aerate soils and many species feed on insects that can become pests. However, ants also can become a problem in homes. Most ants build nests in soil. Those that invade buildings usually nest near foundation walls or under concrete slabs. One species, the carpenter ant, builds its nest in hollow trees, stumps and in the timbers of buildings. It's important to know which ant species you're dealing with and how to know its habits (behavior) and biology (growth, development, environmental influences, etc.) to take the appropriate steps to manage an infestation. Ant control can be difficult.

IDENTIFICATION

Ants generally range in size from one-twentieth of an inch long to 0.5 inch long. They vary in color from yellow to red to brown and black. Like all insects, ants have three distinctive body parts – head, thorax and abdomen. The petiole, a constricted (waist-like) area between the thorax and abdomen called, has either one or two nodes (bumps) that are useful for identification.

Ants are social insects divided into three castes – workers, males and queens. Workers are sterile, wingless females; and in some species, workers may vary in size. The reproductive members of the colony are the males and queens. Males are about the same size as workers, are winged and have a small head with proportionally large eyes. They're produced in older, large colonies, and their sole purpose is to mate with the new queens. They die shortly afterwards. Queens are the largest members of the colony, often two to three times larger than workers. They have wings, but they break off shortly after the mating flight (called a swarm), and have large abdomens. Winged ants that swarm are often mistaken for winged termites. It's important to distinguish them from termites because control methods are quite different (see the chart below).

A generalized ant reproductive.

IMPORTANT ASPECTS OF ANT BIOLOGY

Ants might enter a building to start a new colony. Some species produce winged ants that swarm from the nest during certain times of year,

Winged ants	*Winged termites*
Two pairs of wings, with the hind wings shorter	Two pairs of wings of equal size and shape
Antennae usually are elbowed	Hair-like antennae (straight)
Narrow waist between abdomen and thorax	No narrow waist

mate, then form new colonies. Newly mated females become queen ants in new colonies. They might choose indoor nesting sites if suitable ones aren't available outdoors. When she finds a nesting site, the queen loses her wings and begins to lay eggs, which hatch into legless, grub-like larvae. The queen feeds the larvae as they develop through several stages, molting and growing between each stage. Larvae then form pupae and soon emerge as adult ants. Once worker ants develop, the queen no longer needs to care for the brood.

Some ant colonies can have more than one queen, and mating might occur within the nest without swarming. The ants form new colonies when one or more of the queen ants, along with some workers and brood, leave the nest and move to a new location. Entire colonies often will move from one nesting site to another almost overnight.

Ants also might enter a building to find food and water for their nest. Foraging workers of some species secrete chemical (pheromone) trails to lead other ants to food and water. The ants take food back to the colony and share it with the other ants. They also might move indoors if the weather is hot and dry or wet.

Ants have various nesting habits and food preferences. Some ants build nests in soil, producing characteristic mounds, while others nest in homes behind moldings, baseboards, countertops and similar places. Still other ants nest in decaying or moisture-damaged wood. Ants feed on different types of food, including starches, meats, fats and sweets. Many ants also feed on honeydew, a sweet liquid produced by aphids and scale insects. Knowledge of ant food and nesting preferences is important to control ant colonies.

COMMON INDOOR ANT SPECIES
Carpenter ants
There are numerous species of carpenter ants in the U.S. Some species are found only in certain regions. The most common carpenter ant is the black carpenter ant, a species common to wooded areas with worker ants that are quite large (0.25 to 0.5 inch long). Key identifying characteristics are a petiole (thin waist area) with one node (bump on top) and a thorax (area to which the legs are attached) with an evenly rounded upper surface that has no spines.

Foraging worker ants will leave the nest to gather food and moisture for the rest of the nest mates. Most of the worker ants forage during nighttime, making it more difficult to locate the nest. They seek food such as other insects, honeydew, and other meats and sweets. Carpenter ants differ from termites in that they don't consume wood; they hollow it out to form nests. They prefer to nest in wood that's been softened by moisture or wood rot fungi, which makes it easier to hollow out galleries. While the damage to wood usually isn't as serious as termites, they can weaken building structures.

Carpenter ants construct their nests in:
* hollow trees
* hollow log
* hollow tree stumps
* firewood piles
* fence posts
* other dead and decaying wood
* indoors in porch pillars
* under roofing or flooring
* around tubs, sinks, showers, and dishwashers
* in soft polystyrene and other forms of insulation
* hollow spaces such as doors and wall voids

Carpenter ant tunnels are clean and smooth, making the wood appear that it's been sandpapered. The sawdust-like wood the ants chew from the nest galleries sometimes can be found beneath the nest as a sign of their infestation.

A mature colony contains winged males and females (kings and queens about 0.75 inch long) that usually swarm in the spring. If these swarmers are found in a building, it's likely a colony is nesting indoors.

Pharaoh ant

The Pharaoh ant is an imported species that's found its way to the U.S. and most parts of the world through commerce routes. The ants are small, about one-twelfth to one-sixteenth of an inch long, and can be found in any building. They're found most commonly in hospitals, apartment buildings, schools and nursing homes. They're occasionally found outdoors in some southern states.

The Pharaoh ant is orangish-brown or yellow and has a petiole with two nodes. It usually needs to be identified by an expert because its small size and close appearance to others pest ants. Pharaoh ants don't sting and usually don't bite. They feed on sweets (particularly mint, apple jelly, honey, etc.), and greasy or fatty foods (pies, butter, liver and bacon). They can nest in light sockets, potted plants, wall and cabinet voids, attics, cracks and crevices. They especially like warm places close to sources of water. Their nests usually are difficult to find. Their trails can reach 150 feet.

Colonies consist of one to several hundred queen ants, sterile female worker ants, winged male and female reproductive ants (sexuals), and immature ants. Pharaohs don't swarm. Colonies multiply by budding, a process in which a large part of a colony migrates with some immatures to a new nesting site. This often occurs when a colony becomes too large or is under stress.

Fire ants

Fire ants are the most notorious of the pest ants because of their aggressive stinging. They're the only pest ant that stings. A couple species in this group have been imported from South America and are found in the southern U.S. The red imported fire ant is the most aggressive and widespread. Red imported fire worker ants are one-sixteenth to three-sixteenths of an inch long and are usually reddish or dark brown. Queen ants are larger (three-eighths inch) and lose their wings after mating. This ant prefers to nest outdoors in soil. The ants construct characteristic hills or mounds in open areas and nest under rocks and landscape timbers, at the bases of tree trunks, in decaying wood and in clogged rain gutters. Occasionally, they're found indoors nesting in wall voids, decaying wood or utility housings.

When a mound or nest is disturbed, the sterile female worker ants respond quickly and will run up vertical surfaces to attack the intruder. They bite and hold on to the victim with their jaws while injecting venom with stingers at the ends of their abdomens. Fire ant stings produce a burning sensation and often cause whitish blisters. Most people can tolerate the stings, but some people are sensitive to fire ant venom and must seek medical attention.

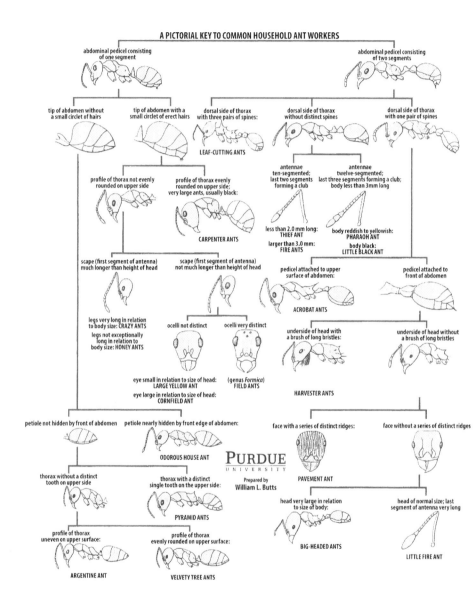

Foraging workers might enter a house in search of food, moisture or nesting sites, particularly during hot, dry periods or during floods. Fire ants are omnivorous but eat mostly insects and other invertebrates such as ticks and chiggers. They often feed on the sugary honeydew produced by aphids, mealybugs and other insects.

Each colony contains one or more queen ants, which can produce about 800 eggs per day. A mature colony can contain more than 200,000 adult and immature ants. Fire ant reproductives swarm to establish new colonies.

Odorous house ant

Worker ants of this species are small, about one-tenth of an inch long, brown, and have a pungent rotten coconut smell when crushed. They have a single node on the petiole that's hidden by the abdomen, and the top of the thorax has an uneven profile.

The odorous house ant has expanded its range to most parts of the U.S. recently. Although it's mainly an outdoor nesting ant in soil under stones, boards, patio blocks, mulching plastic and most any other object laying on the ground, it has become a more serious indoor pest as it has expanded to most areas of the country. It nests in buildings in wall voids, under and around foundations and slab flooring, as well as wood floors.

The ant forms large colonies (each one has multiple egg-laying queens) that can result in large numbers of foraging workers appearing rather suddenly searching for food. Indoors, they'll feed on sweets and other foods, including meats. Outdoors, they prefer aphid honeydew, but also will eat other sweets and insects.

The odorous house ant expands its territory principally by budding, as described for Pharaoh ants. However, it's also known to have mating swarms in the spring. Thus, it's not uncommon to have multiple nests in and under a home, which adds to the difficulty of controlling this ant.

Argentine ant

The Argentine ant is another ant that's found its way to the U.S. from South America. It's found mainly in the southern U.S. and some Western states. It's not as common in areas infested by the red imported fire ant. Where it does occur, colonies can be quite large, with workers foraging 200 feet or more from the nest. The colony has tremendous capacity for growth and expansion because of multiple queens and splintering of new colonies. Mating swarms also occur in spring.

The worker ants are one-tenth of an inch long and light to dark brown and can be found indoors and outdoors. Outside nests are found beneath boards, stones, concrete, and within decaying plant matter and mulch. Nests are often found at the base of plants and trees that are infested with honeydew producing insects. Indoors, nests are found in wall voids, bath traps and insulation.

Honeydew is a staple of Argentine ants, but it will feed on other insects, as well as a wide range of sweets and proteins, such as meats, indoors.

Pavement ant

The pavement ant is about one-sixteenth of an inch long, reddish brown to black, with pale legs and antennae. It can be identified by the parallel lines or ridges that are readily visible on top of the head and thorax.

The pavement ant is found throughout the U.S., but tends to be more of a pest problem in Northern states. Nests usually are found outdoors under stones, next to buildings, and under cracks in concrete; although they become more of a pest in walls, under floors and in insulation. They can be a particular nuisance around homes with slab-on-grade construction. Foragers enter buildings through cracks in the slab and similar openings. Mating swarms occur in spring and early summer, although they occur indoors during the winter when the nest is under a heated slab foundation.

Pavement ants feed on honeydew and live and dead insects in the outdoor environment. As a household pest, they're attracted to pet food, meats, other greasy foods and sweets.

Other pest ants

There are numerous other pest ants that are more regional or not as serious as the aforementioned species. Regarding ant management, the same principles will apply to these minor pest ants as those that have been discussed in detail.

MANAGEMENT
Prevention

Ants enter homes and other buildings in search of food, water or a place to build a nest. There are numerous steps that can be taken to eliminate or limit these resources, not only indoors, but outside the structure as well. Food resources available to ants can be limited by keeping the home clean. Remove spilled food and drink, and store food in tightly sealed containers. Make sure cooking utensils and dirty dishes are cleaned after preparing and eating food. Water sources such as leaking faucets and plumbing should be repaired, sink and dishwashing areas kept dry, and wet or rotten wood dried out and repaired. Outdoors, keep moist areas associated with flowerbeds and mulch away from the foundation, and keep shrubs and other plants trimmed away from the side of the house and free of honeydew-producing insects that attract ants. Foraging ant trails can be disrupted temporarily using a mild solution of vinegar and water.

Removing nesting sites and keeping ants from entering the home can be accomplished in a number of ways. Caulk cracks, crevices, and any other openings that might allow ants entry. Replace worn weather-stripping around doors and windows. Manage plant materials around the home. Trim grass and shrubs close to the foundation, remove ivy growing on walls, and cut tree limbs away from the roof. Remove decomposing leaves and debris from rain gutters; store firewood away from the house; and check potted plants, firewood, and other materials for ants before bringing them indoors.

Ant IPM

Being observant and inspecting as thoroughly as possible will provide many clues to solving ant problems. When ants are found, take time during the day and at night to observe their habits, such as their food preferences and where they're active. Because the goal is to locate the nest and destroy it, it's important to find out as much as possible about their behavior. Follow ant trails to assess where they're coming from. Fill a bottle cap or pieces of foil with jelly, peanut butter, or some other greasy or sweet food; follow their trails to these baits; and, hopefully, locate the nest or get close to the nest. If nests are outdoors, look for worker ants traveling along edges of buildings, around door and window frames, plumbing, electrical or telephone conduits into a home, fences and railings up to the home, and the borders around landscape beds, sidewalks, and driveways. These observations will be most helpful in focusing in on the ant nest, or in general knowing where the ants are coming from, and whether they're coming from outdoors or inside the home. Indiscriminately spraying insecticide on trailing ants or around your home has little effect on solving the problem. For carpenter ants, conducting these inspections at night work best because the species is nocturnal.

Treat ant nests if possible. Insecticides are available as sprays, dusts, aerosols and baits. Many are labeled generally to control ants, while some are labeled to control specific ant species. Select a formulation and an insecticide that will control the pest ant causing the problem, and in the location – indoors or outdoors – where the problem is located.

If the nest can't be found, or inaccessible for another reason, it might be necessary to drill holes into wood or wall voids to reach the ant colony. Ants may have multiple nests, and some might have satellite colonies in addition to the main nest. Other ants might move their nest quickly when disturbed.

Ant baits are formulated as liquids, gels, pastes, granules or solids. Over-the-counter baits available in grocery stores, discount stores, lawn and garden centers, etc., contain ingredients such as hydramethylnon, sodium tetraborate (borax), abamectin, fipronil and orthoboric acid. These are slow-acting insecticides, and must be combined with a food substance attractive to the pest ant so workers will collect the bait, return to the colony and feed it to all nest mates. Sweet baits (sugar or sucrose) are preferred sometimes, while oil or protein baits work better other times. Bait preference varies, so persistence in trying various baits might be necessary. Baits shouldn't be confused with bait traps, which only kill foraging workers, not the ants in the nests.

Boric acid products are considered least toxic and are formulated in sugar water commonly or as a gel or solid bait. Follow directions carefully because a bait with too much boric acid will be repellent to ants. Never place any baits in areas accessible to small children or pets. Boric acid is slow acting, so using the proper food material for the bait. Keeping it fresh and moist is most important. After three to four weeks of a careful, thorough baiting program, the ants should be controlled. Be careful when using boric acid outdoors because it's toxic to plants.

Granular baits usually are best for outdoor nesting ants. Some can be used as a broadcast for lawn treatment or for spot treatments such as directly to nests or ant mounds. Some granular baits are labeled for indoor locations such as wall voids.

Label directions should always be followed carefully when using baits. Use fresh bait and the correct number of bait stations and amount of material. Make baits more effective by removing other food sources such as spilled food, pet foods and greasy surfaces. Don't use residual long-lasting sprays in areas where baits are located. This often will prevent foraging workers from eating the bait. And be patient – baits often are used when the ant nest can't be found; thus, it takes three to four weeks sometimes to eliminate some colonies. If the colony is large, not all the ants in the colony will be killed.

The most effective insecticide formulations for direct application to nests are sprays or dusts. Dusts often are preferred because they don't stain and will last longer than sprays. However, dusts are more difficult to apply. The technique of applying dusts in light, even layers in the ant nest area using dusting equipment is quite difficult, and requires extensive experience. Additionally, dust can't be used in wet or humid situations.

Insecticide sprays also can be used to treat ant nests. They can be used to treat cracks, plumbing or telephone lines coming into the home, and any other places ants might gain entry. Residual spray barriers also can be used around and up foundation walls to prevent or eliminate ant movement to indoor areas. Many over-the-counter sprays – ready to use or in concentrate form for mixing with water to spray – are available in stores and lawn-and-garden shops. Homeowners should follow label directions closely when using insecticides. Because perimeter sprays are used to kill foraging workers to prevent their entry indoors, retreatment might be needed once the protective residual barrier dissipates.

Entire landscapes shouldn't be treated unless ant infestation, such as fire ants, is widespread. Always read and follow the instructions on the label. Most ants are beneficial in the landscape, and control is warranted only when they become pests.

Ant control can be quite complicated and difficult to achieve. Contact a professional pest control company for best results.

ANTS

Ants are a diverse and worldwide group of insects containing about 10,000 different species. They're among the most successful insects and are considered to be the most serious pest group in homes and other buildings by pest management professionals in the U.S. They're social insects that live in colonies that include a collection of workers, one or more reproductives (queens), eggs, larvae and pupae.

Ant colonies build nests. The worker ants construct and maintain the nest, as well as gathering food and moisture for their nestmates. Many species prefer to nest in the ground. Others are found in wood, such as dead logs, fence posts, hollow trees or even wood within structures. When ants nest in wood, their damage usually will be much less compared to termites because ants will hollow out only a nest gallery. Unlike termites, ants don't eat wood and can't digest cellulose. Nests afford the ants considerable protection from their enemies; protection against extremes of weather; and proximity to their food, water and other resources. There's practically no food item (besides cellulose) that won't be eaten by an ant species, and most species will eat various foods.

About 25 species commonly infest homes because they're looking for a place to nest or food to take back to their nest. Pest ants typically are wall nesting or ground nesting. Common wall-nesting ants include carpenter, odorous house, Pharaoh, thief and acrobat ants. Fire, the Argentine, pavement, and little black ants are some of the common ground-nesting pest ants. Many ants, including some of the aforementioned, will nest in outdoor and soil environments, as well as buildings.

PROBLEMS THAT ANTS CAUSE
Ants might affect people adversely by:
* stinging or biting
* invading and contaminating food
* nesting in lawns, golf courses or within premises
* stealing seeds from seed beds or feeding on germinating seeds
* defoliating or gnawing into plants and plant products
* fostering other injurious insects (e.g., aphids or scale insects on ornamental plants)

✳ gnawing holes in various types of fabrics
✳ removing rubber insulation from telephone wires or other equipment
✳ killing young poultry, birds, livestock or game
✳ annoying humans and animals with their presence
✳ possibly transmitting certain human diseases after crawling over sputum, feces or carrion

Some carpenter ants can cause considerable structural damage to wooden structures. However, only a small number of all the ant species are damaging or medically significant. Most species are neutral or nondamaging, and some are beneficial predators on other pests (e.g., red imported fire ants depress tick populations in many areas). Thus, control programs usually are necessary because ants are a nuisance homeowners or others don't want to accept. Apart from their economic importance, ants are considered to be the most important group of living organisms in terrestrial habitats, from an ecological perspective, according to some experts.

ANT IDENTIFICATION

Ants usually have elbowed antennae (bent in the middle). The first segment closest to the head is called the scape. It's followed by a series of much smaller segments, and in some species, the last two or three segments are enlarged into a more or less recognizable shape referred to as a club.

The first one or two segments of the abdomen, where it attaches to the thorax, are much smaller than those that make up the rest of the body region, which is called the gaster. This typically gives ants a rather thin-waisted appearance. This thin waist is properly known as the abdominal pedicel, which might consist of one or two segments. Each segment is enlarged on the upper surface. This enlargement can vary in shape from a slight hump to rather high, flattened, plate-like structure. When identifying ants, it's important to know the shape and segmentation of the pedicel, which is sometimes called the node. It's an important characteristic used to separate ant species and identify ants from other types of insects.

Adult male and female ants of many species are winged just like adult termites. In ants, the front pair of wings always are longer and wider than the hind pair. When at rest, they extend just slightly beyond the tip of the abdomen.

Because winged ants can be confused with winged termites, it's important to remember all four wings on termites are the same size and shape. Other termite features that distinguish them from ants are a broad waist – no pedicel – and straight antennae – no elbow.

The mandibles are the most conspicuous of an ant's mouthparts. They're supplied with well-developed musculature, and, in the workers, are used to carry and break up food, to excavate nests in wood or the ground, and to attack or defend the nest from enemies.

ANT BIOLOGY

Ants have four stages in their growth and development – egg, larva, pupa and adult. Adults normally are workers, reproductive females (queens) or reproductive males.

Eggs are almost microscopic in size and vary in shape according to species. Larvae that hatch from the eggs are soft, pear or gourd shaped, legless, and off-white in color. The head and mouthparts are at the narrow end of the body. Adult workers that tend the nest will move the eggs, larvae and pupae around within the nest and feed and groom the larvae. After several days to some weeks of feeding, during which time several molts are completed, the larvae will enter the pupal stage. Pupae resemble an adult ant but are soft, white and don't move about or feed. In some species, all the pupae are naked, while in others, they're enclosed in silk cocoons. In still others, some pupae might be naked while others will be in cocoons. Pupae, especially those in cocoons, are often called ant eggs. When an ant colony nesting in the soil or under a stone or board is disturbed, worker ants can be seen scurrying about carrying these pupae, but close inspection will reveal the smaller larvae and the tiny eggs also are being carried out of sight, away from the intruding source of danger. Early and small larvae are often stuck together and moved as a single clump.

Adults require several days to reach complete maturity after emergence from pupae. During this period, the body of the adult hardens and attains mature color. Four to eight weeks, or sometimes more, are required for development from the egg to the adult stage. This development time varies according to environmental factors, such as temperature, food abundance and disturbances.

Ants live in colonies and have a well-developed caste system for the division of labor between adult forms. In many common species, the colony is established by a newly mated queen, who sheds her wings and digs a small gallery or seeks a small cavity under a stone, a piece of bark or a recess within a structure to start the nest. The queen seals herself in this cell and remains nearly dormant while the first group of eggs develop in her body. When mature, the eggs are laid and hatch in the sealed nest cell.

The queen's flight muscles are reabsorbed inside her body to provide energy for this long period before workers will be available to forage for food. When workers become available to forage, they feed the queen along with the rest of the colony. The queen nurses and feeds the first group of larvae until they pupate. Workers developing from these first eggs are always undersized because of the relatively small food supply available to them. Workers of the first brood dig an opening out of the nest gallery and begin to forage for food for themselves and the queen. With an additional supply of food available, the queen is able to lay more eggs. Workers, all sterile females, care for the new eggs, larvae and pupae in each succeeding generation.

The success rate for colony founding is low because of environmental extremes, competition within species, predation and other factors. Successful colonies of many species often take more than one season to develop populations large enough to even be noticed. It will often take a year or two for colonies to develop to the point where substantial numbers of new males and queens are formed. These are usually winged forms called alates, or swarmers, which are capable of reproducing. As the colony develops, these alates leave the nest at suitable times to mate. Queens then establish new colonies. Mature colonies will continue to produce groups of swarmers as well as sufficient numbers of workers to keep the colony healthy and well protected, sometimes for many seasons. In some species there might be multiple queens in a mature colony, while others will have only one queen laying eggs. If the queen should die at some time after the colony has become well established, a worker or one of the other female reproductives can sometimes begin to produce eggs and take over this function in the colony. Mating with a male reproductive is required for viable eggs to be produced by this new queen.

Ant colonies normally have three distinct adult castes: workers, reproductive females (queens) and reproductive males. When all the workers in a colony are basically the same size, the colony is monomorphic. When different sizes are present, the colony is termed polymorphic. Sometimes the division of labor, such as nest tending, defending or foraging, will be assumed by workers of these different sizes. Some workers will have specific tasks suited to their specially adapted features. In other species or situations, younger workers tend the nest or do other tasks closer to the colony, while the older workers serve as foragers.

Queens generally are the largest individuals in the colony. Unmated queens usually retain their wings; the mated queens don't. After development of the first group of eggs, the queen is cleaned, fed, and otherwise cared for by the workers, so her primary function becomes egg laying. However, for colonies with only one producing queen, she also produces pheromones that serve to maintain her dominance over the colony and coordinate colony development and function. Where there are multiple queens contributing to reproduction within a colony, patterns of pheromone production and effect will be more complex.

Males perform no function other than to inseminate potential queens. In those species that have winged queens, males also will have wings. The male dies within a few days of mating. Mating may take place in the nest, on the ground, or in the air. Adult males don't remain in the nest long, and many are killed by predators and the elements without mating.

FOOD PREFERENCES

Ants are found in almost every habitat; thus they can be found eating various food items. Some ant species feed on various materials, while other species feed on a narrow range of foods. Food preferences also can change over time, depending on the needs of the colony. Periods of high egg production typically require foraging workers to bring protein to the queen(s), while at other times foragers might prefer to gather sugars or greases to promote larval growth or to meet their own energy needs.

Liquids, or small particles in suspension, which are sucked from food material are ingested by adult ants and most of the larvae. The youngest larvae must be fed on liquids, and liquid food is used for all the larvae in some species.

Foraging ants bring food or water back to the colony and pass it to other nest-tending workers by a mouth-to-mouth process called trophallaxis. Nest-tending workers pass the food to larvae or the queens. Workers might stimulate larvae to regurgitate liquid food for use within the colony. Thus, there's often a complex pattern of food transfer, or flow, within the colony. The direction of the flow is toward the larvae and reproductives. Because of this flow, ant baits that include a nonrepellent and slow-acting toxicant in a suitable food bait formulation are useful and effective. Foraging workers will feed on the bait and not be killed before they pass it along to other colony members, allowing complete colony kill.

In nature, many ants obtain energy-rich sugar by feeding on the sugary honeydew excreted by aphids or other sucking insects on plants. Some ants tend, and even defend, these other insects as a food resource. Thus, controlling honeydew-producing insects on plants inside the home or around the foundation might be an important factor in decreasing the presence of such ants inside.

Dead insects, earthworms, and other organisms are scavenged frequently. Live insects might be preyed on. Indoors, dead flies and gnats can be found on windowsills and in light fixtures, so these are good areas to place ant bait or apply a residual insecticide spray or dust. Some ants, such as leaf-cutting ants, cut, strip and carry away plant leaf tissue into the nest mound that is used as a substrate to grow fungi, on which the ants feed. Other ants typically gather seeds as food.

To date, no universally effective ant bait has been developed. This is because there are so many pest species, with variable food preferences and highly discriminating feeding behaviors. The feeding preferences of any particular colony infesting a premise also will vary depending on the season, the nature of the other food resources available and many other factors. Development of a universal ant bait is unlikely, but advances in bait formulation technology for ants have been made, and this is an active area of research for bait manufacturers and urban entomology researchers.

IMPORTANT PEST SPECIES

Because ants are small, and there are more than 25 species that can become pests, pest species identification can be difficult. And because of the wide variations of feeding and other habits of different ant species, resolving an ant problem often requires exact identification of the species involved. A pictorial key (for worker ants) is included in this chapter, but even with a hand lens or magnifying glass, it might be difficult to identify the ant species that's causing your problem.

Carpenter ants

Carpenter ants are among the most conspicuous of ants found in and around homes, being large and typically blackish or dark bodied. Foraging workers have large mandibles with which they can bite or give a strong pinch. Workers vary greatly in size from one-quarter of an inch to three-quarters of an inch long. Many species are black, perhaps with faintly grayish bands on the abdomen. Others might have brown or reddish coloration along with the black, so they appear distinctly two toned. Two dozen species are known in the U.S., and various species occur throughout the U.S., with one or two primary pest species in the Midwest and Northeast, and one or two primary species along the West Coast. In the Western states, the same species found in the East and Midwest typically occur at higher altitudes, while other species are found nearer to sea level. About 13 other species that infest buildings

Carpenter ant.

Photo courtesy of, and copyrighted by, Gene White, pmimages@earthlink.net

might be encountered. Depending on the species, some might be common, but most aren't often seen inside homes.

Carpenter ants will establish nests in a number of different locations. Outdoor sites include stumps, hollow logs, telephone poles, fence posts or other similar large pieces of wood. Wood that's moist or partially decayed is preferred by many species, especially in the northeastern U.S.; however, cracks, crevices and other cavities might be used to start a nest in sound wood. Ants can be carried into homes in firewood or enter and establish colonies via other routes. Often ants move into a building solely to feed. Among the other methods, foragers often simply enter homes via tree limbs or wires that touch the house. Therefore, the nest, which is the source of infestation, might or might not be in the home. Most often, the primary nest, where the queen is located, will be away from the home or other infested structure, while nests located within the structure will be secondary, or satellite nests, where no egg-laying queen is present. Indoor nests can be found in hollow doors, windowsills, porch substructures, roofs, baseboards, fireplaces, shingles or naturally hollow areas. The nest also might be just a hollow pipe with several hundred ants in it. In wooded areas where many carpenter ant colonies could be present around an infested home, more than one satellite nest, associated with different primary nests (and thus separate colonies), might be encountered. These biological factors can complicate and frustrate control programs.

Carpenter ants excavate nest galleries in wood. These galleries resemble the work of termites but can be distinguished by their entirely clean and almost sandpapered appearance. They're frequently hollowed in moist or unsound wood, although carpenter ants can burrow in sound wood. Carpenter ants, which don't use wood for food, cut galleries with the wood grain and prefer to follow softer areas of the wood. The galleries generally are smooth and clean, hence the name carpenter ant. Some of the harder wood layers often remain as walls separating the many tunnels. Openings are cut in these walls at frequent intervals to provide passageways for movement from section to section of the nest gallery. Access to the outside can be through natural cracks or openings in the wood. Sometimes, however, the ants cut special openings, which are called windows.

Winged reproductive forms swarm primarily in the spring, but they might also do so at other times of the year. Under some conditions, winged males might appear indoors as early as warm spells during February or March, but the females tend to emerge later. Once new colonies begin to mature, several sizes and forms of adult ants will be found in the nest. There's usually only one egg-laying queen per colony, which is said to be mature when winged reproductives, or alates, are formed. This takes three to six years for most colonies, at which time 2,000 to 3,000 (or more) individuals will be present. There's seldom any further increase in numbers because of the constant drain of the many swarmers produced each year. Alates might be produced at any time but usually develop in the late summer. They swarm after spending the winter in the nest. From 200 to 400 winged individuals might be produced each year in a mature colony.

The carpenter ant diet includes various animal and plant foods. The ants will feed on other insects, living or dead, and almost anything people eat. Aphid honeydew is particularly attractive. They feed on many sweets and meats – including syrup, honey, jelly, sugar, meat, grease and fat – found in kitchens and storage areas.

Foraging ants will travel 100 yards or more from the nest for food, and they may wander throughout the house. Workers can lay down trail pheromones, at least on major foraging trails, but they're often seen scattered about and foraging without any noticeable effect of a trail pheromone. Food can be carried back to the nest, but it's taken into the crop near to where it is found more often. Later, it's regurgitated in the nest for use by the queen, developing larvae or the nonforaging workers.

Carpenter ants are of economic importance because of the damage they do to structures, the food they contaminate, and their unsightly and unwanted movement inside and outside of buildings. Their nesting activities can weaken building structures, although not usually as seriously as termites. This damage can often be considered primarily a symptom of water damage and wood decay, as they usually will not extend galleries far beyond this softened wood and into the sound wood of structures. This is particularly true for species found in the Eastern and Midwestern U.S., but Camponotus modoc has been observed to do substantial structural damage in the Pacific northwest.

PHARAOH ANT

The Pharaoh ant is light yellowish to reddish-brown. Workers measuring one-fifteenth to one-twelfth of an inch long. They're found in localized regions throughout most of the U.S. and parts of Southern Canada. They've become a common pest in many areas and an important source of business for pest management firms. Pharaoh ants can be distinguished easily from thief ants by the presence of three segments in the antennal club. They're an important ant pest in homes, apartments, hotels, grocery stores, restaurants, hospitals, nursing homes and other facilities throughout much of their range. Their small size, which enables them to get into almost anything, and their wide food preferences make Pharaoh ants difficult to eliminate from structures in many cases.

Nests rarely are found but occur between walls, under floors, above ceilings, behind baseboards and switch plates, in old trash, in folded bathroom linens, or outside in gardens and along walks. Pharaoh ants nest on porous substrates in warm places near furnaces, heat ducts and hot water pipes that are near moist conditions or open sources of water. Ants range widely from their nests, usually over established trails marked by trail pheromones. Workers frequently are seen trailing along windowsills, countertops and baseboards.

Pharaoh ants.

Photo courtesy of, and copyrighted by, Gene White, pmimages@earthlink.net

In the warmer climates of the Southern U.S., Pharaoh ants frequently are found foraging and nesting on the outside of buildings or in adjacent landscape areas. This is especially true in humid regions or where other sources of constant moisture, such as sprinkler systems and evaporative cooling units (e.g., on rooftops), are present. Under such circumstances, inspections and control programs must be extended beyond the interior portions of the building. In areas where severe winters and cool or cold nights during the summer prevail, Pharaoh ants are unlikely to be found foraging and nesting outdoors.

Pharaoh ants will feed on such an array of materials. Substances such as syrups, fruit juice, honey, jelly, cakes, pies, greases, dead insects, or meats and blood are fed on frequently. In hospitals, they'll often feed on blood and other bodily fluids, medical waste or intravenous feeding fluids.

Even though several effective bait formulations are available for Pharaoh ant control, the ant can be persistent and difficult to control. It has a tendency to appear suddenly in various places within a structure. Its tendency to forage over wide areas and to nest in well-protected or well-hidden areas contributes to control difficulties. Additionally, attempts to control this species with spray or dust applications indoors, or the occurrence of other forms of stress on the colony or colonies, frequently will cause the colonies to split into subcolonies that scatter to other locations within the structure. This behavioral process is called budding and commonly is observed of this species, which makes it an especially difficult pest to control.

Pharaoh ant colonies might be large – tens or hundreds of thousands of workers and many queens. Moderate to large colonies frequently will bud to form numerous subcolonies, as a queen or queens and a group of workers carrying brood will move away from the larger colony and begin a new colony unit. The colony might or might not become a distinct unit because workers might switch between different colonies or subcolonies.

The mature sexual forms are winged but don't fly, so swarms are never seen. Mating occurs in the nest and throughout the year. Occasionally, when a particularly good food resource is found, especially close to the nest, some queens can be seen traveling to and from the food locations. But typically, the queens remain in the nest and aren't seen or can't be controlled without the use of an effective bait that the foragers must bring back to the nest and feed to the queens.

Fire ants

Fire ants are discussed in the Stinging Pests chapter.

Odorous house ant

Odorous house ants emit an unpleasant smell when crushed. The pungent odor is compared to rotten coconuts by some people. It's a common household pest distributed almost throughout the U.S. It's a particularly common problem along the West Coast and Atlantic Coast and in New England and Midsouthern region of the U.S. Workers are one-twelfth to one-eighth of an inch long and brownish-black. This ant is confused frequently with the Argentine ant but can be distinguished easily by its darker color and the fact the front of its abdomen overhangs and hides its flattened petiole.

Nests are located in various situations indoors and outdoors. Outside, nests usually are shallow and found underneath a board or stone. Indoors, the ants frequently nest in walls and underneath floors. Colonies are large and usually contain many active queens. Workers forage along regular trails, and the food habits of odorous house ants and Argentine ants are similar. Odorous house ants tend to move indoors late in the year when honeydew, one of their primary foods, becomes less abundant. Honeydew availability might also be reduced at

Odorous house ants.

Photo courtesy of, and copyrighted by, Gene White, pmimages@earthlink.net

other times, such as during and just after periods of excessive rainfall. These ants might then range more widely for food, often causing them to enter homes, where they'll feed on sweets, meat and other proteins.

Argentine ant

The Argentine ant is a severe pest in the Southern U.S. and in California (and in many other parts of the world), although isolated occurrences have been reported in more northern areas of the U.S. In areas of heavy infestation, it might be found in practically every home.

Workers are one-twelfth to one-eighth of an inch long and are light to dark brown. Queens are much larger, as long as one-sixth to one-quarter of an inch long. Many fertile queens are present in each nest. Mating usually takes place inside the nest, so winged forms aren't usually found. In addition to laying eggs, queens also clean and feed themselves and are active in feeding and grooming immatures.

Nests typically are located in moist soils next to or under buildings, along sidewalks or beneath boards and plants. They're usually near sources of water and food. Occasionally, the ants might nest within a structure or other locations not typically considered soil related, such as under a bathtub set above a slab-on-grade foundation, under the cracks or expansion joints of slabs, under insulation in an exterior wall void, and in potted plants or flower boxes. Argentine ants prefer sweet foods, principally sugars, syrup, fruit juices, secretions of plants and honeydew. Workers forage for food along regular paths extending out from the nest and branching out to explore every portion of an area. Foragers might enter houses in large numbers, particularly when conditions outside the building become too wet or dry. Their foraging range often is sufficient that the nests might be located on properties adjacent to clients' yards and homes, thus complicating effective control efforts that typically rely on eradication of colonies at the nests.

This ant is well adapted to urban and suburban environments and will persist where other species don't thrive. It might be the only ant species present in many locations. Workers are aggressive and often eliminate other ants in an area. However, different Argentine ant colonies can coexist in the same area, so the number of colonies per unit area might be quite high. Other research about the genetic relatedness (or variation) between Argentine ants in certain regions has suggested colonies of this species might be extremely large and cover large areas – even referred to as supercolonies. Effective control or suppression of argentine ants in such regions can be difficult.

Pavement ant

This is a small (one-eighth to one-sixteenth of an inch long) reddish-brown to black ant with paler legs and antennae. The abdomen is all black. Readily visible on the head and thorax are parallel lines or ridges that don't differ in color from the cuticle but give the cuticle a grooved texture. There's a pair of small spines at the back of the thorax, and the body has a sparse array of small hairs all over it.

The pavement ant is common throughout the Atlantic Coast region and Midwestern U.S. and along the West Coast. It's an occasional pest in the Southern U.S. Nests usually are found outdoors under stones, next to buildings, and under cracks of pavement, although they're occasionally found in walls, under floors and in insulation. Pavement ants can be a particular nuisance around homes with slab-on-grade construction. Foragers enter buildings through cracks in the slab and similar openings. This slow-moving ant enters buildings in search of food, preferring greasy and sweet materials. This includes various foods, including meats, pet food, sweets, bread, nuts and insects.

Pavement ants.

Photo courtesy of, and copyrighted by, Gene White, pmimages@earthlink.net

Thief ant

This is one of the smallest household ants. It's one-twenty-fifths to one-fifteenths of an inch long. Workers vary from yellow to dirty brown and have a two-segmented antennal club. Thief ants are found throughout most of the U.S. They often live in nests of larger ants, where they might feed on the larvae of their hosts, thereby earning their common name. Their chief foods in homes are greasy materials, such as cheese and meats, although they feed on sweets occasionally. Bacon, ham and other prepared meats are attractive to thief ants. They might feed on stored seeds and dead animals.

This ant is so small it might often escape notice around kitchen sink and cabinet areas. Unobservant people might complain about the flavor of food without realizing it's infested with thief ants. The ant usually comes in from outdoors, but it might nest in cracks and crevices of walls or cabinets and commonly beneath tile countertops in kitchens. They can be persistent and difficult to control.

Acrobat ants.

Photo courtesy of, and copyrighted by, Gene White, pmimages@earthlink.net

Acrobat ants

Ants of this genus hold their abdomen over their head and thorax when excited, hence the common name acrobat ants. They range from yellowish-brown to red and black to black and have a characteristic heart-shaped abdomen that's flattened on the upper side and curved below. The workers range in size from one-tenth to one-sixth of an inch. They're not normally found in households but might wander inside from time to time searching for food. Some species in this genus might be found in decayed or partially decayed wood and in such wood inside homes. They're seldom found in sound wood.

Little black ant

This is a small (one-fifteenth of an inch long), slow moving and jet-black ant found in all states. Nests normally are located outdoors in relatively open areas. The ants also will nest in rotten wood, woodwork and masonry of buildings. Colonies have multiple queens and might become large. Most of their feeding is on plant secretions, but they'll invade houses in search of food occasionally. Once inside, they feed on sweets, meats, breads, grease, vegetables and fruit.

Crazy ant

The crazy ant is found in scattered locations in most states. Workers are about one-tenth of an inch long and dark brown. Their legs and antennae are much longer in proportion to the other parts of their body compared to what's normal for other house-infesting ants.

The crazy ant has become an important household pest in Florida and along much of the Gulf Coast region of the U.S. and in Arizona. In the Northern U.S., it's more common indoors than outdoors because it can't survive outdoors during cold winters. It's habit of seeming to run aimlessly about the room accounts for its name. Crazy ants nest in small cracks, crevices and voids inside, and they wander throughout the building searching for food. They prefer to feed on animal matter, grease and other insects, but will readily eat sweets of all kinds.

Ghost ant

This is a small to tiny ant (one-twelfth of an inch long) that has a characteristic pale, whitish abdomen, legs and antennae, but a dark-colored head and thorax. This species has become an important household pest throughout much of Florida and Hawaii and is present in California and the Pacific Northwest. The ants can develop large colonies with many queens. Colonies can divide or split through a budding process similar to the Pharaoh ant and white-footed ant. Generally, they nest outdoors under mulch, rocks, boards or other items, or under loose bark of trees and in lumber and firewood piles. Removing these nesting areas will aid control programs. Finding all the nest areas and treating them directly with insecticide spray or soil drench can achieve satisfactory control. The ants also might respond to some baits.

White-footed ant

This pest species was introduced to Florida before the mid-1980s but has become a significant pest in the Central and Southern parts of the state. It's also known from Oahu in Hawaii, and its spread from these areas is likely, perhaps aided by association of colonies with root balls of nursery plants. Workers are medium to small ants (one-eighth to one-sixth of an inch long), black to dark brown but with distinct yellowish-white tibia and tarsi on each leg, thus appearing white footed. The ant doesn't bite or sting or cause any structural damage, but many homeowners consider it a nuisance because they frequently forage in kitchens, bathrooms and around exteriors of homes or buildings. The ant primarily is a honeydew feeder, so it will nest in soil, mulched areas or aboveground locations around landscapes and then tend aphids, scales or mealybugs on plants. However, they're also known to nest in homes occasionally.

White-footed ants appear successful and a difficult nuisance to control around homes because colonies of this species frequently become large, upwards of two to three million individuals. Interestingly, research has shown about one-half of the colony is fertile, reproductive females, called intercastes, that are inseminated by wingless males. Winged reproductives swarm and leave the colony typically in July or August in South Florida. After colony formation, the wingless queen is replaced by the reproductively capable workers (intercastes). As colonies grow larger, they can occupy many nest sites interconnected by foraging trails or divide to form new colonies by budding.

The large colony size, multiple nesting sites, and aggressive foraging around and into homes make this ant difficult to control. Research shows thorough baiting programs – guided by careful inspections and observations of foraging trails and likely nesting areas – will provide the best possible suppression. Because the ants respond best to sweet, liquid baits, these must be replenished regularly to remain attractive to foragers. Control of honeydew-producing pests on landscape plants also can aid suppression. The ants also feed on dead insects, so they also might respond to protein-based baits. If the ants are foraging or nesting in wall voids or attics, the use of residual dusts might be necessary.

Large yellow ant

This ant, which is common from New England to the Midwest, also is known as the citronella ant because of the citronellalike odor given off when the ant is crushed. This is the most dependable characteristic for field identification of this species. Workers are reddish yellow to reddish-brown and about one-fifth of an inch long. Winged reproductives swarm in basements and around house foundations in early spring and are often mistaken for termites. Outdoor nests are found in old logs and stumps and under stones. The ant might bring large piles of dirt to the surface of the ground at the entrance to its nest outdoors or indoors, which frequently cause homeowners alarm. Aside from the debris created, the ant does no harm. Workers feed on the honeydew produced by subterranean aphids and mealybugs, and they won't be encountered foraging indoors.

Big-headed ants

The soldiers of these ants, which are workers that serve strictly a defensive function, have exceptionally large heads in relation to their body size, hence the common name for the ants. The minor workers don't have enlarged heads but can be recognized by the shape of their heads, which narrows abruptly behind the eyes. Big-headed ant workers are one-eighth to one-quarter

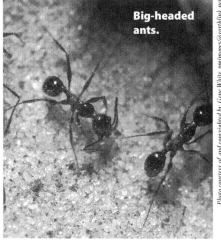

Big-headed ants.

Photo courtesy of, and copyrighted by, Gene White, pmimages@earthlink.net

of an inch long. The ants are found in warmer and dryer regions of the U.S. and have habits similar to fire ants. Nests are found in exposed soil or under cover and in rotting wood. They rarely nest indoors but might invade homes to forage for food. They prefer meats, grease and breads. They superficially resemble fire ants but can be distinguished from them by the presence of 12 segments in the antenna with a three-segmented antennal club.

Cornfield ant

This abundant ant is an important pest in homes in the Northern
U.S. and especially in the Pacific Northwest. It's light to dark brown.
Workers are about one-tenth of an inch long. As its name indicates,
it's a common ant in cornfields. In homes, it prefers sweet substances.
Outside, it feeds on dead and live insects, plant sap and honeydew.
Common nesting sites include rotting logs and stumps, under stones
and in exposed soil. It often builds small craters in lawns. The ant is
the most common nuisance ant pest of picnics in its range.

Field ant.

Photo courtesy of, and copyrighted by, Gene White, pmimages@earthlink.net

Field ants

The many species
and varieties of
these ants infest
fields, lawns and
gardens throughout
the U.S. Their
length varies from
one-eighth to one-
quarter of an inch,
and they might
be brown, black
or reddish or have combinations of these colors. Foragers prefer sweet
foods but also will feed on other insects as predators or scavengers.
Nests commonly are built as earthen mounds along fences, sidewalks,
flowerbeds and in lawns.

Field ants are most likely to be pests of recreational areas. When
infestations are heavy, individuals might wander into homes searching for
food. The Allegheny mound builder builds large mounds of earth during
its nesting activities. The species is seldom found in homes but has caused
fire ant scares in the Northeast. Other common species of field ants are
relatively large and black, resembling the carpenter ant. Pest management
professionals must be careful when identifying field and carpenter ants.

Some field ants capture the larvae and pupae of other ants and raise
them in their own nests. The emerging adults become slaves for the field
ants, so they're sometimes called slave ants.

Harvester ants

Harvester ants are comparatively large, red to dark brown or blackish ants that range from one-quarter to one-half of an inch long. They can be recognized by the long hairs that form a brush under their heads. The hairs clean their legs and antennae, carry water and remove sand during nest excavation. Harvester ants are found in warmer and drier regions of the West and South most often, but one Eastern species, found in Florida, might be encountered. They're normally found in fields or lawns where they clear large areas of vegetation around their nest openings and gather seeds they store in their burrows. They'll invade homes rarely. Their severe stings make them pests when they occur in lawns, parks or athletic fields.

Leaf-cutter ants

Leaf-cutter ants remove foliage from vegetation and carry it back to the nest. Leaf fragments are chewed and added to large underground fungus gardens that provide the colony's food. It's possible for them to remove all the leaves or needles from a tree in one night. In the U.S., leaf-cutter ants occur in Texas (where they're called cut ants), Louisiana and Arizona. The reddish or rust-colored workers range from one-twelfth to one-half of an inch in length, but the winged reproductives can be 1.25 inches or longer. The dorsal part of the thorax has at least three pairs of spines.

Leaf-cutter ants nest in well-drained sand or loam soils. Mounds are formed in the shape of a large funnel. The nest is often 10- to 12-feet deep and may cover one-quarter acre. The nesting behavior also results in the ants being called town ants. They never nest indoors but might enter houses while foraging, often to carry away seeds. Workers travel well-defined trails that might extend some distance from the nesting area. Since the colony remains in one spot for several years, the foragers might be found traveling some distance from the nest.

False honey ant

This ant is widely distributed throughout the U.S. The shiney workers vary from light to dark brown and are about one-eighth to one-sixth of an inch long. They're usually not troublesome in homes and spend most of their time close to the ground. They typically nest in clay soils in well-shaded areas. Coarse, earthen pellets usually surround the nest entrance. Within the nest, certain workers are fed large quantities of sugary liquids by other workers who forage. These liquids are stored in the greatly distended abdomens of the "honey-pot" ants and regurgitated to other colony members as required.

Pyramid ants

These ants are common in the Southern U.S. and in California. They vary from uniformly dark brown to brown with a reddish tint. Workers have a distinct single tooth on their thorax, which causes the thorax to form a pyramid shape that gives the ants their common name. Workers are one-fifteenths to one-twelfths of an inch long and are found commonly in gardens and flowerbeds. They often tend aphids on ornamental plants, feeding on honeydew, but also frequently enter homes along distinct foraging trails.

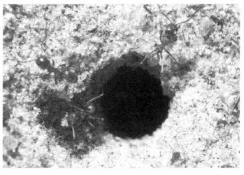

Pyramid ants.

Photo courtesy of, and copyrighted by, Gene White, pmimages@earthlink.net

Velvety tree ants

Velvety tree ants are pests principally in California. They're easily identified by their glistening, velvety-black abdomen, red thorax and brownish-black head. Their nests are located in old tree stumps, in cavities in trees, under tree bark, beneath stones on the ground, and, occasionally, within the walls or attics of homes. Foragers commonly enter homes, where they contaminate food in the kitchen and seek other insects for food.

The California velvety tree ant is distributed widely throughout the state. It occurs in the foothills and the mountains of Southern California and at lower levels in the Northern area of the state. Foragers travel along trails and constantly ascend and descend trees, such as oaks and poplars, often at a considerable distance from the nest.

The ants tend honeydew-producing insects, such as aphids or scale insects and kill and eat other insects. They often invade picnic or outdoor barbecue areas, contaminating food, stinging people, and, when crushed, producing a foul odor similar to the odorous house ant. Their sting is painful, and the pain might persist for some time.

Little fire ant

This small tropical ant is established in Florida and in California. It's about one-fifteenths of an inch long and reddish. Characteristically, it moves slowly. The ants are sensitive to cold, appearing only in the warmest weather. Their sting is painful.

In the U.S., little fire ants are rarely a serious household pest. They're usually encountered by homeowners outside, most often in citrus trees and landscaped areas. They usually nest in exposed or covered soil, rotten wood, plant cavities and trash, and inside houses occasionally. When foraging indoors, they prefer foods such as fats, peanut butter and other oily materials.

Asian needle ant

Native to China and adjacent East Asian areas, this species was first identified and recorded in the U.S. in the 1930s. More recently, it has become a significant urban pest along the Mid-Atlantic coastal areas from Georgia to Virginia. There's no doubt it'll spread throughout the Southeastern U.S. Workers are small – about one-tenth to one-eighth of an inch long – and have a black body and lighter brown mouthparts and legs. The female reproductives or swarmers are larger – one-quarter of an inch long – though the winged males are about the size of the workers. Colony size for this species appears to be small – several hundred individuals – and there can be multiple reproducing queens. They prefer to nest in moist and dark areas beneath stones, logs and similar landscape items or other debris around homes. Nests usually are shallow at not more than several inches into the soil. Several colonies can be living near each other, so the total population present (infestation) can be many thousands. The species appears to feed mostly on other small insects and arthropods. It can inflict a painful sting if pressed against the body and is capable of producing an anaphylactic shock reaction. Unlike fire ants, the species doesn't readily attack to defend itself or its nest.

Rover ant

This species is native to Argentina but has been introduced into the U.S., where it's present in the Gulf Coast region, Mid-Atlantic states and in certain urban areas of the southwestern U.S. Workers are tiny to small – one-sixteenth to one-twelfth of an inch. They're reddish-brown with pale tarsi and mandibles and have brownish-yellow antennae with nine segments. They don't sting, but they've become a nuisance in homes and other facilities because of their presence in large numbers. Alates also are produced in large numbers and are attracted to lights at night. In some Southern areas of the U.S., they've been collected almost throughout the year. The ant nests in rotting wood and soil and has been observed feeding on honeydew. Not much is known about their biology and feeding preferences, except they generally respond well to sugar-based liquid baits.

MANAGEMENT

Prevention

Ants enter homes and other buildings in search of food, water or a place to build a nest. There are a number of steps that can be taken to eliminate or limit these resources indoors and outdoors.

Food resources available to ants can be limited by keeping the home clean. Remove spilled food and drink and store food in tightly sealed containers. Make sure cooking utensils and dirty dishes are cleaned after preparing and eating food. Water sources such as leaking faucets and plumbing should be repaired, sink and dish washing areas kept dry, and wet or rotten wood dried out and repaired. Outdoors, keep moist areas associated with flowerbeds and mulch away from the foundation, and keep shrubs and other plants trimmed away from the side of the house and free of honeydew-producing insects that attract ants. Foraging ant trails can be disrupted temporarily using a mild solution of vinegar and water.

Removing nesting sites and keeping ants from entering the home can be accomplished in a number of ways. Caulk cracks, crevices and any other openings that might allow ants entry. Replace worn weather-stripping around doors and windows. Manage plant materials around the home – trim grass and shrubs close to the foundation, remove ivy growing on walls and cut tree limbs away from the roof. Clean rain gutters of decomposing leaves and debris; store firewood away from the home; and check potted plants, firewood and other material for ants before bringing them indoors.

Green pest management options for ants

❋ Additional emphasis on prevention, inspection and monitoring.

❋ To the extent possible, find all ant nests and treat them directly with natural pyrethrin sprays or drenches (outdoors in soil, or with one of the plant-derived essential oil sprays "minimum risk" – green or organic – insecticides).

❋ Determine what the ants are feeding on, and remove those food sources.

❋ Use thorough caulking, screening or other exclusion methods to minimize ant movement into the home.

❋ If nests can't be found or directly treated indoors, boric acid or one of the inorganic desiccating dusts can be applied for residual control.

❋ Use boric acid or one of the inorganic desiccating dusts to treat in dry areas around doors, windows, and cracks and openings in the foundation perimeter.

❋ Boric acid baits are available, formulated with sweet, grease or protein food bases.

❋ Boric acid bait formulations can be used as granules to scatter in the landscape, or as liquids, gels or pastes in plastic stations designed for use in landscape areas.

❋ Some of the conventional nonrepellent insecticides available as baits and sprays are considered reduced risk and can be used in green ant management programs.

Ant IPM

Being observant and inspecting as thoroughly as possible will provide many clues to solving ant problems. When ants are found, take time during the day and at night to observe their habits, such as their food preferences and where they're active. Because the goal is to locate the nest and destroy it, it's important to find out as much as possible about their behavior. Follow ant trails to assess where the ants are coming from. Fill a bottle cap or pieces of foil with jelly, peanut butter, or some other greasy or sweet food. Then follow their trails to these baits and locate the nest or get close to the nest. If nests are outdoors, look for worker ants traveling along edges of buildings; around door and window frames; plumbing, electrical, or telephone conduits into the home; fences and railings up to the home; and the borders around landscape beds, sidewalks and driveways. These observations will be most helpful in focusing in on the ant nest, or in general, knowing where the ants are coming from, and whether they're coming from outdoors or inside the home. Indiscriminately spraying insecticide on trailing ants or around your home has little effect on solving the problem. For carpenter ants, conducting these inspections at night work best because the species is nocturnal.

Treat ant nests if possible. Insecticides are available as sprays, dusts, aerosols and baits. Many are labeled in a general way to control ants, while some are labeled to control specific ant species. Select a formulation and an insecticide that will control the pest ant causing the problem, and in the location – indoors or outdoors – where the problem is located.

If the nest can't be found, or for some other reason is inaccessible, it might be necessary to drill holes into wood or wall voids to reach the ant colony. Ants might have multiple nests, and some might have satellite colonies in addition to the main nest. Other ants might move their nest quickly when disturbed.

Ant baits are formulated as liquids, gels, pastes, granules or solids. Over-the-counter baits available to grocery stores, discount stores, lawn and garden centers, etc., contain ingredients such as hydramethylnon, sodium tetraborate (borax), abamectin, fipronil and orthoboric acid. These are slow-acting insecticides and must be combined with a food substance attractive to the pest ant so workers will collect the bait, return to the colony and feed it to nestmates. Sweet baits (sugar or sucrose) are preferred sometimes, while oil or protein baits work better other times. Bait preference varies, so persistence in trying various baits might be necessary. Baits shouldn't be confused with bait traps, which only kill foraging workers and not ants in the nests.

Boric acid products are considered least toxic and are commonly formulated in sugar water or as a gel or solid bait. Follow directions carefully because a bait with too much boric acid will be repellent to ants. Never place any baits in areas accessible to small children or pets. Boric acid is slow acting, so using the proper food for the bait. Keeping it fresh and moist is most important. After three to four weeks of a careful, thorough baiting program, the ants should be controlled. Be careful using boric acid outdoors because it's toxic to plants.

Granular baits usually are best for outdoor nesting ants. Some can be used as a broadcast for lawn treatment or for spot treatments such as directly to nests or ant mounds. Some granular baits are labeled for indoor locations such as wall voids.

Label directions always should be carefully followed when using baits. Use fresh bait, the correct number of bait stations and the correct amount of bait material. Make bait more effective by removing other food sources such as spilled food, pet foods and greasy surfaces. Don't use residual, long-lasting sprays in areas where baits are located; this often will prevent foraging workers from eating the bait. And be patient – baits often are used when the ant nest can't be found; thus, it takes three to four weeks sometimes to eliminate some colonies, and if the colony is large, not all of the ants in the colony will be killed.

The most effective insecticide formulations for direct application to nests are sprays or dusts. Dusts often are preferred because they don't stain and will last longer than sprays. However, dusts are difficult to apply. The technique of applying dusts in light, even layers in the ant nest area requires a lot of experience. Additionally, dust can't be used in wet or humid situations.

Insecticide sprays also can be used to treat ant nests. They also can be used to treat cracks, plumbing or telephone lines coming into the home, and any other places ants might use to gain entry. Residual spray barriers also can be used around and up foundation walls to prevent or eliminate ant movement to indoor areas. Many over-the-counter sprays (ready to use or in concentrate form for mixing with water to spray) are available in stores and lawn and garden shops. Homeowners should follow label directions closely when using insecticides.

Because perimeter sprays are used to kill foraging workers to prevent their entry indoors, retreatment might be needed once the protective residual barriers dissipates.

Entire landscapes shouldn't be treated unless the ant infestation, such as fire ants, is widespread. Always read and follow the instructions on the label. Most ants are beneficial in the landscape.

4

TERMITES

SUMMARY: *TERMITES AND THEIR CONTROL*

Property owners and renters become concerned about the thought of a hidden pest destroying their dwelling. Termites can damage wooden parts of a structure extensively over long time periods, such as one to several years.

Termites are social insects. They have different castes or groups of individuals that perform different functions in the colony. Winged reproductive forms swarm from mature colonies to disperse and establish new colonies. Worker termites, the ones that damage wood by eating the springwood layers, are white and soft-bodied. They feed the other forms in the colony and expand the nest size. Soldier termites with enlarged mandibles (teeth) are responsible for protecting the colony from intruders.

Termites need wood for food and soil for moisture, so wood in contact with soil is ideal for termite development. But if this doesn't occur, the insects might build shelter tubes from mud to bridge or span foundation walls and other masonry that separate wood from soil. They construct the tubes on walls or inside them in voids and cracks. Occasionally, when a leaky roof or pipe provides moisture, termite infestations are established without soil contact.

Infestations generally develop from colonies in soil, and termites enter a building through structural wood or foundation walls adjacent to the soil. In cases of houses built partly or completely on slabs, infestation is through expansion joints, cracks, and utility and sewer pipe openings.

Whether pretreating at the time of construction or treating an existing structure, the basic principle of termite control is to break the connection between wood and soil. This is done by laying down a chemical barrier to eliminate all possible points of entry.

Property owners need to be aware of termites and the destruction they can cause, as well as when and where termite control or prevention is needed and how prevention or control might be accomplished. However, when any of these services are needed, it's a good idea to call a professional pest control company (see tips for selecting a Termite Control Service at the conclusion of this chapter).

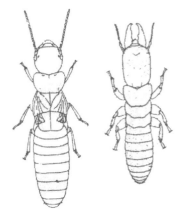

A supplementary reproductive termite (left) and a solider termite.

PRETREATMENT (TREATMENT DURING CONSTRUCTION)

Homes and other buildings can be pretreated at the time of construction to protect them against termite attack. Few people would consider building a new house and not insure it against damage caused by fire and other calamities; but many more houses are damaged each year by termites than fire. For effective pretreatment termite proofing, much of the chemical barrier might need to be under concrete slabs. Obviously, it's much easier to put down a chemical barrier before the concrete is poured than it is afterward.

AREAS NEEDING PRETREATMENT

For effective termite prevention, pretreatment is needed in three areas during construction:

✳ Treatment of the entire soil surface to be covered with concrete, including garage floors, entrance platforms and filled porches.

✳ Additional chemical applications to the soil beneath those areas that lie adjacent to foundation walls, beneath interior walls, around sewer and utility openings, and at other possible points of entry.

✳ Treatment of footings and backfill outside foundation walls and inside walled areas where there's a crawl space. Accessible areas like these could be treated later, but it's easier to do at construction time.

APPROVED PRETREATMENT INSECTICIDES

Chemical pretreatment (termiticides) is accepted by federal and state agencies as a method of termite proofing. Most professional pest control companies are equipped to pretreat according to specifications, and they can guarantee effectiveness. Building contractors and others don't provide this guarantee. There are many chemical termiticides that can be used for pretreating. They're all restricted to use by professional applicators only and should be used according to label directions, which vary from product to product on pretreating. Ask to see a copy of the label if there are questions about how the job is to be done.

TERMITE IDENTIFICATION

It's not difficult to identify termites and termite damage in facilities. The only problem is identifying swarmer termites – which are the first sign a termite infestation exists – from winged ants, which are relatively harmless. A swarmer termite is black generally, and its four equally-sized cloudy white wings are twice as long as its rather straight body. The winged ant, although similar in color, has a wasp-like waist and four clear wings unequal in length – all much shorter than its body. Although they're seldom seen, the white, soft-bodied worker termites can seriously damage a structure. They eat the soft grain of wood, leaving a thin shell outside and only splinters inside.

WHEN AND HOW TO CHECK FOR DAMAGE

A termite's natural habitat includes stumps, posts and other wood that comes in contact with the ground. However, because termites might be found in these materials near the home, it doesn't mean the home is or will be infested.

To check for termites, any wood near the foundation or soil should be probed with an ice pick or screwdriver, especially the plates, header joists, ends of floor joists and any hardwood flooring. Presence of earthen shelter tubes on foundation walls and wood is evidence of infestation. Termites build these tubes from bits of soil to close up breaks in infested wood. The tubes resemble long streams of mud running up basement walls or along foundations. The tubes indicate an even more serious infestation problem.

If damage is found, there's no need to hurry to apply control measures. Termites work slowly, so a few weeks or even months delay is of little consequence. There's plenty of time to select the pest control company and termite control program with which you feel most comfortable. Cost estimates for the work may vary, so obtain and evaluate bids, descriptions of work to be done, and details of any guarantees from at least two companies. Study this information, then make your decision.

WHERE AND HOW TO TREAT

Soil on both sides of exposed foundation walls and soil surrounding supports should be soaked down to the foundation footing at the labeled rate. One technique involves digging a V-shaped trench against the wall. It should be at least 1 foot deep or deeper if necessary to ensure penetration to the footing. Soil at the bottom of the trench can be loosened with a spade or iron bar to allow further penetration.

For outside basement walls (were the footing is deep), most pest control professionals apply the chemical by injecting it along the foundation through a hollow rod attached at the end of the hose in place of a spray nozzle. This is called rodding. The result is a continuous chemical barrier from footing to surface.

Treating slab-constructed buildings. Treatment includes saturating much of the soil beneath the slab. The chemical is injected (1) through holes drilled in the slab at prescribed intervals next to all foundation walls, interior partitions and utility openings, or (2) by rodding from outside the building. Modifications of heat ducts, radiant heat pipes or other special situations that exist beneath slabs might be necessary.

Treating concrete slabs against foundations. If concrete for garage floors, patios, walks, etc., was poured against the foundation of the house, soil under the slabs that lies next to the foundation also must be treated. This is done by drilling the slab at prescribed intervals next to the foundation walls and injecting the chemical under pressure at the labeled rate.

Treating dirt-filled porches. Filled porches are treated one of two ways: (1) The slab can be drilled as described above or the porch foundation drilled at each end next to the building and the chemical injected by rodding; or (2) the porch can be excavated from each end next to the building foundation. Then the area should be treated with a chemical at the labeled rate.

TERMITE BAITS

Termite baits are an alternative control methodology to soil-applied termiticides. Some of the termite baits are available through pest control companies. Other baits are available to homeowners through retail stores, but their effectiveness isn't known.

The principle of termite baiting is simple. Termite bait stations are installed underground around the perimeter of the house every 10 to 20 feet and 2 feet out from the house. Collectively, a station is a piece of wood impregnated with a slow-acting toxicant contained in a childproof plastic housing. Stations are installed and then rechecked monthly

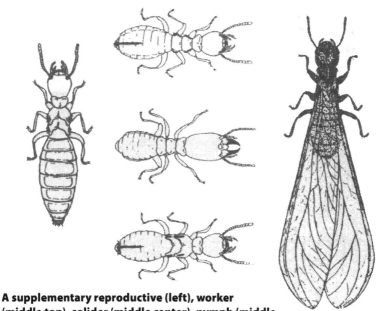

A supplementary reproductive (left), worker (middle top), solider (middle center), nymph (middle bottom), and winged primary reproductive (right).

thereafter for termite activity. Baits take advantage of the social nature of termites. Foraging termites consume the bait, then share it with their nestmates, resulting in a slow colony decline and eventual elimination of the termite colony

From the homeowners perspective, there are advantages and disadvantages to the use of termite baits compared to the use of liquid termiticides.

Advantages. One advantage is a professional rarely has to enter the structure to install bait stations. Another advantage is that the toxicant is distributed from a point source compared to soil-drenching with liquid termiticides, so baiting is a more environmentally friendly method of termite control. Also, bait use doesn't require drilling of structural concrete, which is required for the application of soil termiticides.

Disadvantages. The major disadvantage using termite baits is the length of time it takes to eliminate a colony. With liquid termiticides, control is immediate. With baits, control might take several months to a year depending on several to many environmental factors that limit termite foraging.

SPECIAL NOTE

There are other types of termites—drywood termites—that don't nest in the soil that can damage wood. These will be discussed at the end of this chapter.

Termite control is complicated. Professional pest control companies have the knowledge, experience and equipment to do this kind of work correctly and effectively. Contact a reputable company in your area to do the work.

TERMITES

Termites are social insects with several types (castes) of individuals in a colony. Each type serves the colony differently. They're referred to as social insects because there's a division of labor among the different types of individuals in the colony, similar to honeybees, many other bees, and most ants. Winged reproductive forms in a termite colony (called swarmers) emerge from mature colonies to disperse and establish new colonies. Worker termites – the ones that damage wood by eating the springwood (soft) layers – are white and soft-bodied. They feed the other forms in the colony and expand the nest size. Soldier termites with enlarged mandibles (teeth) are responsible for protecting the colony from intruders. This social structure is essential to their survival.

There's nothing quite so disconcerting to a property owner as the thought that a hidden pest is secretly destroying the wooden parts of the structure. Termites are the most important of the wood-destroying pests. They're found throughout the world, and one group, the subterranean termites, are found in every state of the U.S. These insects are common in soil, dead trees, and in wooden structures; but most people know little about them and have tremendous anxiety when the insects are found in their homes.

In the natural environment, termites are beneficial, serving as scavengers of fallen logs and dying roots. These insects become destructive only because the wood of buildings has been placed in situations accessible to termites. The "man-made" environment generally is excellent for termite development. Scarcely a building in the Southern U.S. has escaped the attack of subterranean termites, and damaged structures are numerous throughout the Northern U.S. According to the latest professional pest control industry calculations, subterranean termites cause more than $5 billion worth of damage annually in this country.

Subterranean termites need wood for food and soil for moisture. Wood in contact with soil is ideal for termite development. Termites also might construct mud tubes to cross over or through foundation walls that separate wood from soil. In cases of houses built on slabs, infestation occurs through expansion joints, cracks and utility plumbing openings. Thus, termite colonies in the soil use these various methods to gain access into buildings.

Termites, other than subterranean termites, of importance to homeowners include drywood termites that generally live (feed and nest) in undecayed structural wood in buildings that has a low moisture content. Unlike subterranean termites, they don't require any contact with the soil to live. Thus, they can damage buildings and movable wooden objects such as furniture significantly. Estimates of treatment costs per year are more than $500 million. In the U.S., drywood termites are found in a narrow strip from Virginia to Florida on the Atlantic Coast, along the Gulf of Mexico, Arizona, New Mexico, from California to Mexico on the Pacific Coast, and Hawaii. More details on drywood termites can be found at the end of this chapter.

SUBTERRANEAN TERMITE BIOLOGY

There are more than 10 species of subterranean termites that damage wooden structures in the U.S. However, they all have a similar life history with essentially the same castes within their life cycles.

Termites develop by way of a gradual growth and development (metamorphosis) from eggs laid by the primary (queen) or supplementary reproductives. Larvae hatch from the eggs and undergo several molts – they shed their skins as they grow larger – through which different larvae develop into one of the four different castes: workers, soldiers, winged (primary) reproductives or swarmers, and supplementary reproductives. In new colonies, larvae from the first small batch of eggs usually all become workers. Nymphs and soldiers aren't produced normally until later egg laying.

In the termite species where a distinct worker caste occurs, workers are the most numerous individuals in a termite colony. They, along with the nymphs, perform all the work of the colony – feeding the other castes, grooming the queen, excavating the nest, and making the tunnels. In the process of making nests and tunnels and ingesting food, they chew and eat wood, causing the destruction that makes termites important economically. Workers usually are light colored and don't have wings or any specialized structures.

Soldier termites serve specifically to protect the colony from its enemies. Their heads are large, hard and have much larger mandibles than the other castes. When openings are made into termite colonies, the soldiers gather with their large heads and strong mandibles facing outward and protect the colony from invaders.

Supplementary reproductives of both sexes are wingless or have only short, nonfunctional wings. These reproductives are developed as needed and quickly replace a primary queen who's injured or dies. They also usually develop in addition to the primary queen and become the most important source of eggs in the colony. Supplementary reproductives, with a group

Worker termite.

of males and workers, might become isolated from the main colony and can establish a new colony, spreading the original infestation without being visible above ground at any time.

Primary reproductives (swarmer termites) are the caste most often seen by homeowners. They have completely developed wings and eyes. The winged adults usually are much darker than the other members of the colony. All four wings are the same length and extend more than the length of the body beyond the tip of the abdomen. Although functional workers develop in a few months, it usually requires 12 months of progressive colony growth for swarmer termites to occur. Male and female reproductives leave the colony in great numbers (swarms), usually in the spring and occasionally in the fall.

These swarms often are the first visible indication termites are present. Environmental conditions must be just right before termites will swarm. The temperature, moisture (within and outside the colony), light conditions and barometric pressure influence swarming activities. As a general rule, swarmers emerge on warm, sunny days when humidity is high (e.g., often on days following rain showers).

After a brief flight, the wings break, and males and females pair and attempt to establish a new colony in the soil. They're particularly defenseless at this time, and most die or are killed by their natural enemies (birds, ants, etc.), or they succumb to desiccation and other environmental factors. Each surviving pair makes a small cell in which they mate and lay eggs.

After a colony becomes established, the supplementary reproductives are responsible for the production of most of the eggs. In a colony of one million individuals, the queen might have laid as few as 10,000 of the eggs. The supplementary reproductives are responsible for the remainder.

Swarmer termites are often confused with flying or swarmer ants. Because ants often are seen swarming in and around buildings, it's important to distinguish between the two so appropriate control measures can be made. There are three ways to separate termites from ants. First, ants have a thin waist between the thorax (body region to which the legs are attached) and the abdomen (body region behind the legs), while termites are broad waisted. Second, termite wings are all the same size and shape, whereas the forewings of the ant are larger, longer

Photo courtesy of, and copyrighted by, Gene White, pmimages@earthlink.net

Winged reproductive termites swarming from a colony.

and of a different shape than the hind wings. Third, termite antennae are straight, and ant antennae are elbowed.

THE TERMITE AND ITS ENVIRONMENT

Termites require specific environmental conditions to survive. Most times moist soil or other moist environments provide these conditions. Moisture is critical to termite survival because all castes, except the swarmers, are soft-bodied insects that lose water rapidly upon exposure to dry air. Thus, an available moisture supply is critical to termites. Because of this, termites construct tubes (called mud tubes) that pass over exposed areas. The mud is also "plastered" throughout the termite galleries inside the wood. Termite tubes serve to conceal the termites, provide the termites a moist environment and protect them from their enemies (ants). Termites maintain contact with the soil unless there's a constant above-ground source of moisture. The negative response to light that termites exhibit is intimately involved with keeping the termite in a concealed environment and might have come about as a response to the need to conserve water.

On occasion, freestanding mud tubes will be built straight down from the infested wood toward the ground if they're in a protected area, such as a crawlspace under a house. This usually occurs after a colony has become well established and feeding has progressed a distance from the initial shelter tunnel. In this way, the colony can obtain the necessary moisture without having to travel great distances.

The retention of moisture isn't the only important factor associated with water in the life of the termite. The warm, moist conditions that prevail within the closed system of the nest provide an ideal site for the growth of microorganisms, particularly fungi, which provide a source of protein and vitamins essential to the termite. The accumulation of termite fecal material in the nest helps promote fungi growth.

The most striking facet of this intricately interdependent system is the delicacy with which it's balanced. It's not uncommon to discover the remains of a termite colony slowly being crowded out by the fungi growth that has progressed at such a rate the termites couldn't keep up with it. If sudden temperature shifts or other factors result in the accumulation of water within the galleries, the termites might drown.

Each autumn, the termites in the temperate zone (most states in the U.S.) normally respond to the gradual decreases in temperature by moving further down in the soil, where the necessary conditions of temperature and humidity can be maintained. In the spring, the colony responds to increased temperatures and moisture in the soil above and again moves upward. In structures where warmth and moisture are present during the winter, termites might be present above ground the year round.

The type of soil has a great effect on the ability of subterranean termites to flourish. Subterranean termites generally prefer a sandy soil over a clay soil. However, they'll survive in many types of soil.

FEEDING

Subterranean termites have preferences in the type of wood (sugar maple, slash and loblolly pine) they'll eat, although no wood is completely immune to attack. Termites harbor one-celled organisms in their digestive tracts that convert the cellulose in wood into substances the termites can digest. Decayed wood is eaten faster than sound wood. Termites facilitate decay by increasing the moisture content in wood being attacked. An average, mature colony of Eastern subterranean termites contains about 60,000 workers and can consume about one-fifth of an ounce of wood each day, while an average Formosan termite colony (350,000 workers) would consume about one ounce. Although the quantity of wood eaten is relatively small, the mud and moisture brought into a structure compounds the damage done, so detection and control of an infestation at an early stage is highly desirable.

Concrete and steel – and other noncellulose based building materials – will continue to be a secondary choice as building materials because of cost and aesthetic factors. Thus, the good practices mentioned in the control and prevention section will be central to keeping termites out of homes and buildings.

COMMUNICATION IN THE COLONY

For social insects, communication is needed to maintain efficient social integration and division of labor. The most basic means of communication among termites is via chemical (pheromone) communication. Each colony develops its own characteristic odor. Any intruder, be it a termite from

Subterranean termite feeding galleries in a piece of wood, including mud and fecal spots.

another colony, an ant or any other natural enemy, is recognized instantly as foreign when it enters the colony. An alarm pheromone is secreted by the colony, and this triggers the soldier termites to attack and kill the intruder, which is then walled off from the colony with fecal matter. If a hole in the termite workings occurs, it's immediately patched by the workers.

Sound is another means of termite communication. Termite soldiers and workers bang their heads rapidly on the surface of their mud tunnels or wood galleries when the colony is disturbed. The vibration of the surrounding surface is perceived by others in the colony, and they, too, take up the banging activity. This activity serves to mobilize the colony defenses just as the aforementioned alarm pheromones do.

One of the primary means of communication is via trophallaxis, which is the mutual exchange of nutrients and the transfer of food between colony members. Trophallaxis permits the efficient movement of nutrients within the colony, enhances recognition of colony members, distributes chemicals involved in caste regulation, and transfers cellulose-digesting protozans. Termites exchange food from the mouth and hind gut (anus). When termites shed their skin during moltings, they also lose their hind gut contents, including the protozoa they need

Termite worker feeding a member of the colony using a process called trophallaxis.

Photo courtesy of, and copyrighted by, Gene White, pmimages@earthlink.net

for digesting wood. To get a new supply of protozoa, they must feed from the hind gut of other colony members. The feeding of the queens and soldiers by the workers is also a form of trophallaxis. In addition to serving as an exchange of food and nutrients, trophallaxis helps in recognition of nestmates and the distribution of chemicals involved in caste regulation.

Worker termites forage continuously for new sources of food. They also forage randomly in many locations throughout their foraging territory, looking for food. When a foraging termite worker finds a source of food, it recruits others to the food source by laying a chemical (pheromone) trail. The more foragers that find the food and return with it to the colony, the more intense the pheromone trail becomes. As the food source is depleted and the foragers no longer deposit the pheromone, the trail deteriorates and is eventually abandoned.

The proportion of the castes in the colony also is regulated chemically. For example, soldiers and reproductives produce chemicals that are distributed to other colony members by trophallaxis. These chemicals inhibit the production of additional soldiers and reproductives. Termites might react to a high level of soldier-produced chemical by killing some of the soldiers. Thus, the needs of the colony are met, and the proper balance of the different castes is maintained.

In most subterranean termite colonies, nymphs can molt into alates or supplementary reproductives; workers can change into soldiers, nymphs, or supplementary reproductives; and nymphs that have begun developing wing buds might lose them with additional molts and return to the worker stage. All these changes are regulated chemically within the colony, depending on its needs. For example, high levels of juvenile hormone – chemicals that keep termites in an immature stage – in the colony will result in the production of soldiers. Low levels result in nymphs.

INSPECTING FOR TERMITES

Homeowners can keep an eye out for signs of a termite infestation; however, it's a good idea to call a professional pest control company (see Tips for Selecting A Termite Control Service) for an inspection every five to 10 years or follow up when termites or evidence of termites is found. Sometimes an active infestation is obvious, such as when the colony swarms. Other times, the problem might be more difficult to see and requires a great deal of effort, situation awareness, and the use of specialized techniques and information to diagnose correctly.

Swarming termite colonies are easy for property owners to see, but ants and other insects also swarm about the same time of year. The workings of subterranean termites differ from all other wood-destroying organisms and can be used to make the determination if termites are involved. Termites remove only the soft layers (spring wood) within the annual rings of the wood grain, penetrating the hard layers only to get from one soft layer to another. This frequently leaves a damaged piece of wood looking like the pages of a book. However, the most distinctive feature of subterranean termite damage is the presence of a brown, mud-like material that lines the galleries in an irregular pattern.

Subterranean termites travel constantly from their nests in the ground to the wood. They make these trips only inside wood or in the mud tubes they construct. Single tubes, when they're built in the open, are about the diameter of an ordinary lead pencil and often can be seen easily by the homeowner.

Termites might excavate the wood so only a thin layer of wood is left on the surface between their cavities and the outside. When this layer is broken, they'll cover the hole with the same material used to make their tubes. This mixture of soil, feces and saliva also is used frequently to cover the crack between two boards so they can move about in a protected environment.

As a general rule, subterranean termites are found at or near ground level. Occasionally, they are found above the level of first-floor windows, especially in warmer regions of the country. An inspector must thoroughly examine all areas of a house below ground level, including the basement and crawlspace walls, supporting piers and beams, sill plates, floor joists and subfloors. Particular attention must be paid to all places where concrete steps, porches or concrete slabs adjoin the structure.

Cavities in the wood can be detected by probing the wood with a tool, such as a screwdriver, awl, geologist's pick or pocketknife. A thorough inspection can be made using the small blade of a penknife to probe the wood, leaving scarcely visible marks in the wood. The sharp blade will penetrate deeply and detect cavities as easily as larger tools.

Live termites in mud tubes or within wood is evidence of their presence. Failure to find live termites doesn't necessarily mean they're not present in the structure.

THE INSPECTION REPORT

A pest control company can present results of a termite inspection and have a work plan for the treatment. It's important to obtain an adequate diagram of the building together with a sufficient description of the structure and the problems to be solved.

A well-designed inspection form offers many advantages because it allows the inspector to include all pertinent information. Such a form should include cross-ruled paper on which a diagram of the structure can be drawn to scale. The drawing should include the type of construction, all cross-walls, stairways, doorways, porches, stoops and other parts of the structure that will affect the treatment methods. It's most important it be drawn accurately and to scale because this might reveal blind areas, which are often sites of severe infestation and damage. Each place where live termites are found should be indicated clearly on the diagram.

If a termite bait program is considered, bait placement in the soil around the perimeter of the house will be indicated on the diagram. Bait placements inside the structure also will be shown. When a soil treatment method is used, other information will be shown on the graph. All damage, inaccessible areas and other unusual situations should be indicated. Additionally, details of construction should be shown, including:

✳ the materials of which the outside walls and foundations are made (e.g., concrete block, stone, etc.) and whether the foundation extends below grade;

✳ the places where it will be necessary to drill through the concrete floor, such as in doorways, stairways, supporting walls, porches, sidewalks and driveways;

✳ whether the building has a basement or a crawlspace or is a concrete slab on grade;

✳ the location where ventilators should be installed; and

✳ the conditions that might be conducive to termite attack (such as improper grade).

Pest control companies might prefer to include additional items or find local conditions are such that additional information is necessary.

Pest control company inspections also will ascertain any risk of contamination should a termiticide need to be used. Wells, springs and cisterns can be contaminated by termiticide applications. If any of these are present in or near the structure, termite management must be conducted with special care. Alternative methods of successful management – using limited amounts of insecticides, baits, or no insecticide at all (e.g., mechanical alteration) – generally require more labor and are more expensive. However, it might be necessary to employ these methods to avoid a contamination problem.

PREVENTING TERMITES

The most effective and economical time to implement termite prevention techniques is during the planning and construction process. Whether preconstruction or postconstruction, limiting favorable food (wood), moisture and shelter conditions to termites can prevent or help eliminate infestations.

A majority of structural termite infestations are associated with the contact of wood to the ground. Structural wood in contact with the soil provides termites with food, shelter, moisture and entry into a structure that's difficult to detect. Exterior wood should be at least 6 inches above ground level, and may require regrading or pulling soil or mulch back from the foundation to eliminate wood-to-ground contact. Timbers in crawlspaces should be at least 18 inches from the ground. Wood in doorframes, stair carriages, wood posts, etc., should be cut off at the bottom and be supported by a concrete base. If wood-to-soil contact is unavoidable, wood can be treated with a preservative. However, termites can enter through cut ends and cracks in treated wood and are able to build tunnels over the wood surface.

Wood, cardboard, paper or other cellulose materials in the soil can attract termites to a structure. These materials shouldn't be buried in fills during the construction process. Mulch and wood chips also can attract termites by providing a food source and favorable moisture conditions. Pea gravel or crushed stone can serve as a substitute for mulch, but if mulch is used, it shouldn't be allowed to contact wood siding or framing of doors or windows. Firewood, landscape timbers, compost piles and other cellulose material stacked close to a structure attract termites and provide a hidden point of entry. To prevent

A swarmer termite, dispersing from a colony to look for a mate.

infestations, these materials should be stacked as far from the structure as is practical. Dense vegetation shouldn't be allowed to grow against the siding and foundation of a building. Shrubs, vines and trellises make inspection difficult and can trap moisture, increasing conditions favorable for wood decay and termites.

High moisture conditions around a structure can contribute to a termite infestation. In addition to reducing vegetation in contact with the building, soil around a structure should be sloped so surface water drains away from the structure. Proper installation and maintenance of gutters, downspouts, and splash blocks and proper positioning of lawn sprinklers or irrigation systems to avoid pooling water will reduce soil saturation.

High humidity in crawlspaces also can lead to termite problems. Plumbing or appliance leaks can lead to damp wood and soil conditions in this type of area. Areas of crawlspaces beneath potential trouble spots should be inspected and any leaks or problems repaired. In some climates or areas, soil conditions might contribute to crawlspace humidity. Polyethylene sheeting can be placed over soil in a crawlspace to reduce evaporation from the soil and condensation on structural timbers. Adequate ventilation can further reduce moisture problems. A vent area of one square foot per 150 square feet of crawlspace area is required for most building codes. Total vent area can be reduced in crawlspaces with a vapor barrier.

Plumbing leaks can lead to favorable termite conditions inside a structure and can allow a colony to survive above ground with no soil contact. Roof leaks or inadequate drainage also can cause this problem. Water leaking into wood areas below the roof or standing water on the roof surface potentially lead to wood decay or other moisture problems that can be conducive to termite infestation. Special attention should be given to flat or low-pitched roofs where drainage problems might be more frequent.

Certain types of construction are conducive to termite attack. Dirt-filled porches are susceptible to termite attack because such construction joins the exterior wall of the building above the top of the foundation and in close proximity to structural timbers. Attached planter boxes also bring soil in close proximity to structural timbers and should be separated from the foundation by at least three inches.

Foam insulation and stucco used near the foundation can serve as a route of entry into a structure as termites can tunnel behind or though such materials to reach wooden structural members.

Use of termite-resistant woods might be another nonchemical alternative for subterranean termite prevention. California redwood, red cypress, and red and yellow cedar have been shown to have some level of termite resistance. Certain extractive chemicals in the wood can be distasteful or hazardous to termites. However, these chemicals lose their potency or are lost from the wood with time, making these woods susceptible to termites.

TERMITE CONTROL

Whether pretreating at the same time of construction or treating an existing structure, the basic principle of termite control is to break the connection between wood and soil with a chemical barrier, or use a bait termites will feed on and carry back to the colony causing the colony's demise. Applying a chemical barrier will eliminate all possible points of entry, while a baiting system will be fed on by any termites in the area, killing the termite colony. Again, as mentioned in the section on inspecting for termites, select a knowledgeable, experienced and reliable professional pest control company for your termite control needs.

Property owners need to be aware of termites and the destruction they can cause. Consumers also need to be generally knowledgeable about when and where termite control or prevention is needed and how prevention or control can be accomplished. When buying property, building a home or adding on to an existing structure, or making a decision to treat an infestation in a building, the following information should be useful.

Homes and other buildings can be pretreated at the time of construction to protect them against termite attack. Few people would consider building a new house and not insure it against damage caused by fire or other calamities. But each year more houses are damaged by termites than fire.

For effective pretreatment termite proofing, much of the chemical barrier might need to be under concrete slabs. Obviously, it's easier to apply a chemical barrier before the concrete is poured than it is afterward. For effective termite prevention, pretreatment is needed in three areas during construction:

1. Treatment of the entire soil surface to be covered with concrete, including garage floors, entrance platforms and filled porches.

2. Additional chemical to the soil beneath those areas that lie adjacent to foundation walls, beneath interior walls, around sewer and utility openings, and at other possible points of entry.

3. Treatment of footings and backfill outside foundation walls and inside walled areas where there's a crawl space. Accessible areas like these could be treated later, but it's easier to do at construction time.

Another helpful measure is to make sure no wood comes in contact with soil and all wooden foundation forms, stakes, stumps and scraps of wood are removed from any area before it's covered with dirt or concrete. Also, the soil surface in unexcavated areas should be cleared of wood scraps.

Capping concrete block foundations with a 4-inch solid block gives added protection, provided the cap blocks are joined tightly and there are no openings in the mortar.

Chemical pretreatment is accepted by the FHA as a method of termite proofing. Most pest control professionals are equipped to pretreat according to specifications, and they can guarantee effectiveness. Contractors and others don't provide this guarantee.

When treating existing homes and buildings where termites have been found, there's no great hurry to apply control measures. Termites work slowly, and a few weeks or even months of delay is of little consequence. Thus, there's plenty of time to select the pest control company and the termite control program with which you feel most comfortable. Cost estimates for the work might vary, so obtain and evaluate the bids, descriptions of work to be done, and details of any guarantees from at least two companies. Study this information and then make your decision.

Label directions for treating termite-infested buildings vary from one insecticide to another. Thus, insecticide labels should be referred to for more specific treatment directions. Labels can be obtained from a pest control company.

Soil on both sides of exposed foundation walls and soil surrounding supports should be soaked down to the foundation footing at the labeled rate. One technique involves digging a V-shaped trench against the wall. It should be at least 6 inches deep or deeper if the label directions so indicate.

For outside basement walls (where the footing is deep), most pest control professionals apply a chemical by injecting it along the foundation through a hollow rod attached at the end of the hose in place of a spray nozzle, which is called rodding. The result is a continuous chemical barrier from footing to surface.

Treating slab-constructed buildings. Treatment involves saturating much of the soil beneath the slab. The chemical is injected (1) through holes drilled in the slab at prescribed intervals next to all foundation walls, interior partitions and utility openings, or (2) by rodding from outside the building. Where heat ducts, radiant heat pipes or other special situations exist beneath slabs, modifications of these general treatment procedures might be necessary.

Treating concrete slabs against foundations. If concrete for garage floors, patios, walks, etc., was poured against the foundation of the house, the soil under the slabs that lies next to the foundation must be treated, too. This is done by drilling the slab at prescribed intervals next to the foundation wall and injecting the chemical under pressure at the labeled rate.

Treating dirt-filled porches. Filled porches are treated one of two ways: (1) The slab can be drilled as described above, or the porch foundation drilled at each end next to the building and the chemical injected by rodding; or (2) the porch can be excavated from each end next to the building foundation. The area then should be treated with a chemical at the labeled rate.

Baiting for termites isn't new, but it's a technology that has been commercialized only recently. The principle of termite baiting is simple. Termite bait stations are installed underground around the perimeter of the house every 10 to 20 feet and 2 feet out from the house. Collectively, a station is (1) a piece of wood impregnated with a slow-acting toxicant contained in (2) a childproof plastic housing. Stations are installed and rechecked monthly by a pest control professional for termite activity. Baits take advantage of the social nature of termites. Foraging termites consume the bait, then share it with their nestmates, resulting in a slow colony decline and eventual elimination of the termite colony.

From the homeowner's perspective, there are advantages and disadvantages to the use of termite baits compared to the use of liquid termiticides.

Advantages – One advantage lies in the fact that the professional rarely has to enter the structure to install bait stations. Another advantage is that the toxicant is distributed from a point source, compared to soil-drenching with liquid termiticides; baiting is thus a more environmentally-friendly method of termite control. Also, the use of baits does not require drilling of structural concrete, as is required for the application of soil termiticides.

Disadvantages – The significant disadvantage when using termiticide baits is the length of time it takes to eliminate a colony. With liquid termiticides, control is immediate. With baits, control might take several weeks to a year depending on several to many environmental factors that limit termite foraging.

DRYWOOD TERMITES

Drywood termites usually live in undecayed structural wood that has a low moisture content, and they're typically found in the warmer states along the coastlines. Their biology and behavior is different than subterranean termites and is generally described in the following paragraphs.

A male and female pair (king and queen) work their way into the wood chosen for the nest. The opening through which they enter the wood is sealed with a plug of brown cement-like material about one-eighth of inch in diameter. Behind the plug, they excavate a chamber where the queen lays the first eggs. The nymphs (referred to as larvae by some termite specialists) that hatch from the eggs go through a more complex metamorphosis (several larval/nymphal stages) than subterranean termites before becoming soldiers and reproductives. The nymphs perform the work of the colony. There's no distinct worker caste, as with subterranean termites.

During the swarming season, nymphs make round holes one-sixteenths to one-eighths of an inch in diameter through which the reproductive forms leave the wood. When swarming is completed, the holes are plugged the same way as the original entrance holes.

Damage done by drywood termites is different from that caused by subterranean termites. These termites cut across the grain of the wood, excavating large chambers connected by small tunnels. The chambers and tunnels used by the colony are kept clean. Excreta and debris are stored in unused chambers or cast out through small openings in the wood surface. These small openings sometimes are called kick-out holes.

Entrance into wood is made usually from a crack or crevice the termites can enter before boring into the wood. This might be a crack in the wood, the joint between two pieces of wood, or even the space underneath roofing or sheathing paper.

Because of their ability to live in wood without soil contact, nonsubterranean termites are frequently carried in infested furniture and other wooden objects into geographical areas where they're not normally found. For this reason, pest management professionals should be aware of their habits to recognize them when they appear.

Drywood termites can attack wood products of all kinds. Structural timbers and woodwork in buildings as well as furniture and other wooden objects might be damaged. Although serious damage is done to buildings and other wood products in some areas of the U.S., these termites are usually less injurious than subterranean termites because they're less widespread.

INSPECTING FOR DRYWOOD TERMITES

Drywood termites are found in wood within almost any part of a structure and in wooden furnishings of all kinds. When performing an inspection, systematically inspect all exposed and accessible wood, especially on perimeter walls, on the exterior and interior of the building. It's important to inspect all accessible parts of the attic and crawlspace, if present. Drywood termites typically are found in dry wood. Infestations are found around the perimeter of buildings often and where wood is joined together. Large, well-established infestations commonly extend over central areas of structures.

When inspecting for drywood termites, it's necessary to look for visible damage and the plugs (kick-out holes) in entrance and exit holes.

The inspector should look particularly for the characteristic fecal pellets (about one-sixteenth of an inch long, hard texture and have six distinct concave surfaces) pushed out from the termite galleries. Soundings of the wood should be made, the same as for subterranean termites. Tapping the wood will cause a hollow sound where there are internal galleries. Or sound-detection devices (stethoscopes or sound amplification devices) can be used by professional inspectors to determine if termites are present. Wood can be probed with tools such as an ice pick, screwdriver or the blade of a penknife to discover termite damage and live termites in their galleries.

Other evidence of infestation includes visible flights of adults, shed wings and surface blisters, which result from galleries close to the surface of the wood. Shelter tubes made of pellets and chewed wood cemented together occasionally serve as a bridge or passageway from one piece of wood to another. Cementlike walls can partition off large chambers or close large openings to conserve humidity.

Sometimes live swarmers, or shed wings from swarmers, are the first evidence of an infestation. Therefore, it's important to keep in mind the following wing characteristic that separate subterranean from nonsubterranean termites: Nonsubterranean termite wings have crossveins between the costal vein, which forms the anterior margin of the wing, and the radius vein, the second-most-anterior vein originating from the wing base. These crossveins are lacking in the wings of subterranean termites.

This inspection tip can assist you in situations in which you have swarmers or happen upon an infestation in your home, furniture or other structure. Most importantly, it's provided as background for working with a professional inspector.

DRYWOOD TERMITE TREATMENT
Treatment for drywood termites consists principally of structural fumigation or wood treatment. The direct wood treatment method – used for local treatment, such as wood injection – should be used only in the case of limited infestations. Extensive infestations should be controlled by fumigation or heat. Whole-structure treatment usually involves fumigation, while partial (compartmental) treatments can be

accomplished with heat. As with subterranean termite control, drywood termite control is complex.

Fumigation is done with sulfuryl fluoride (Vikane), as an example. The entire building is covered tightly with a gastight cover, and the gas is introduced. Vikane has the advantage of rapid and uniform dispersion within the temperature range for climates where drywood termites are found. Such fumigations should be done only by professionals thoroughly trained in the use of fumigants.

To prepare for the use of a liquid, aerosol or dust formulation, holes are drilled into the infested timbers through the termite galleries, using a half-inch drill in larger timbers and smaller drills elsewhere. Insecticide is then forced through the holes to be dispersed through the galleries. The use of liquid insecticides such as borates (disodium octaborate tetrahydrate), controls drywood termites when active galleries and access points in infested wood are pressure injected. Drione is an example of a dust, which should be injected into the termite galleries in small amounts. Too much dust will plug the galleries, and the termite will wall off and thus isolate these areas.

When treating limited infestations, aerosol and liquid formulations are used most often. After an insecticide has been injected into wood, the openings should be plugged with wooden dowels.

Other methods of drywood termite control used on a more limited basis, and still in need of further research and development, include heat, fumigation, extreme cold, electrocution and microwaves. For heat treatments, structures are tarped as they would be for conventional fumigation. Hot air is generated by specialized heaters and blown into the covered structure, or a section of the structure, until temperatures reach a constant 140 to 150 F. Fans are used to circulate the heated air and to achieve uniform temperatures within the area being treated. Theoretically, timbers within the treated area will reach 120 F. After 35 minutes at this temperature, termites will be dead. Thermocouples, or temperature probes, are used to monitor heated timbers selectively. This can be quite an expensive process when treating an entire building because of the prolonged time needed to achieve the needed temperature. Heat fumigation is more practical and economical for manageable-size areas with exposed timbers and where items that could be damaged by heat can be removed easily.

Liquid nitrogen has been used to create -20 F temperatures for at least five minutes for localized treatment of termites. Only limited areas can be cooled to this temperature at one time. Covering the surfaces surrounding the treatment area with insulating mats increases the efficiency of the treatment and reduces condensation. Many variables influence the efficacy of cold treatments, so additional research is needed.

Electrocution by delivering high-voltage and high-frequency electrical energy to targeted sites in timbers using a handheld unit is another option. Spot treatments for drywood termites are made by delivering the electric charge to the infested wood. Theoretically, the termites will be shocked and killed by the passing current. Drilling holes into wood and/or inserting copper wire into drill holes improves the passage of current into infested areas. The devices are designed to avoid structural damage and electrocution of the management specialist. As with other localized treatments, identifying all infested areas within a structure is essential to eliminate all of the termites.

Units producing electromagnetic energy at microwave frequencies also have been used on a spot treatment basis to eliminate drywood termites from structural timbers. The high-energy zone is limited, so heat-vulnerable items usually don't need to be removed from the structure. However, this distance limitation on microwave transmission means treatment areas are localized, so infestations and their boundaries must be identified precisely to achieve control.

TIPS FOR SELECTING A TERMITE CONTROL SERVICE

There's no need to become frightened or unduly alarmed if you learn termites are, or might be, attacking your home. The insects work slowly, and your house won't be ruined or collapse overnight.

Don't permit anyone to rush you into purchasing termite control service. A few-week-or-month delay won't make any difference. There's always time to purchase the service wisely and at your convenience.

Purchase termite control service with the same care and discrimination you'd use in the purchase of any other service for your property. Here are some ways you can investigate before you invest:

1. Ask companies for references for past work and take time to check the references carefully.

2. If the company is located in your town or city, make sure it's a responsible company that has an established place of business. This can be done through a chamber of commerce or the Better Business Bureau.
3. If the company is out-of-town, it's even more important you make sure it's reliable. Check to see it has an established place of business in the town where it's said to be located. Most fraudulent companies work in communities where they're not known. Ask for references and check them carefully. Reliable firms welcome this approach.
4. Purchase value, not price. If the price quoted seems too high or too low, secure other estimates.
5. Ask a termite control specialist to provide you with a written statement of the work proposed and the cost. Take time to consider the estimate. It's customary to guarantee termite control work on a year-to-year basis or for a multiyear period. Make sure you know exactly what guarantee is offered by the firm. Guarantees vaguely referring to termite control are unacceptable. Determine if a yearly charge will be levied during the guarantee period or whether the charges are included in the initial price of the job. A guarantee is no better than the person or company who gives it to you and isn't evidence a company is reliable. Most fraudulent operators use a showy contract and guarantee as part of their sales promotion. You'll probably be asked to sign a work order when you hire a company. Understand clearly what obligations you're assuming and what you're getting in return.

5

OTHER
WOOD-DESTROYING INSECTS

SUMMARY: *POWDERPOST AND OTHER WOOD-DESTROYING BEETLES*[1]

Powderpost beetles are second only to termites as destroyers of seasoned wood, such as the type used in buildings and furniture. There are several kinds of powderpost beetles, but they all damage wood about the same way and require the same control measures. Some species attack the sapwood portion of hardwoods, such as oak, hickory, ash and walnut. Other species feed on heartwood and sapwood and will attack pines and softer woods.

DAMAGE TYPE AND WHERE IT OCCURS

The surface of powderpost beetle-infested wood is perforated with numerous small shot holes each about the size of pencil tip. Any slight jarring of the wood causes a fine, flour-like powder to sift from these holes. When cut or broken, the interior of infested wood can reveal masses of the finely packed powder.

Subflooring, hardwood flooring, joists, sills, plates and interior trim are the parts of buildings most frequently attacked. Other wood products such as hickory furniture, implement handles and ladders also can be damaged. If infestations in wood aren't treated, the structural strength of the wood can be seriously depleted.

---

[1] Some insects other than beetles will attack wood, with carpenter ants and carpenter bees being the most common. They are discussed in the ant chapter and stinging insects chapter, respectively.

LIFE HISTORY

Powderpost beetles are small (about one-twelfth to one-fifth of an inch long) and usually reddish-brown to almost black. They emerge from infested wood from late winter through early summer. During this time, the females lay eggs in the wood pores. These eggs hatch into tiny curved grubs that eat into the wood, packing their burrows with the finely pulverized wood. When completely grown, the grubs go through a pupal state and emerge as beetles. Powderpost beetles require a few months to several years to complete one generation, depending on the species and starch content of the wood.

Other beetles might infest structural wood, such as the old house borer. Most long-horned beetles – larvae in the wood are called round-headed borers – and metallic wood borers – larvae are called flat-headed borers – attack wood before it's cut for use in construction. Thus adult beetles might emerge from the wood used in a building, but they don't reinfest the structural timbers and require no control measures.

PREVENTION

Before buying wood, inspecting it for exit holes where adult beetles have emerged. Buy and use only wood that has been kiln-dried or treated with a wood preservative. Most wood-boring beetles won't infest wood that's painted, varnished, waxed or covered with a finished surface. Avoid introducing new sources, such as firewood, of these beetles. Adult beetles can emerge from wood temporarily stored in the home, and then infest wood in the home. Ventilation and moisture control in crawl spaces and attics, as well as other indoor areas, will help prevent beetle problems.

Be sure to carefully inspect antique furniture, picture frames, bamboo products and other wood items before purchasing them. If you see holes or powder-like frass associated with these items, don't purchase them, or treat the items properly before placing them in your home.

CONTROL

Powderpost beetles damage wood slowly, so there's plenty of time to decide on control options. Selecting the best control program depends on the severity and location of the infestation, potential for reinfestation and cost of treatment. Get at least a couple of estimates from reputable pest control companies.

The first step in controlling these beetles is to determine whether the infestation is active. Wipe and vacuum all dust from the wood, and examine the wood several days later. New holes (circle old ones with a pencil to see if new holes appear later) and fresh sawdust will be visible if the infestation is active. Check more than once if it's unclear whether old dust has been dislodged because of vibration or new dust is found. If the infestation isn't active (no new dust or new holes are found), no control is necessary.

The beetles lay eggs only on bare, unfinished wood. They won't infest wood that's painted, varnished or sealed. Thus, by finishing any infested wood, beetles will be prevented from reinfesting the wood after emerging from it. (Finishing wood doesn't kill insects in the wood.)

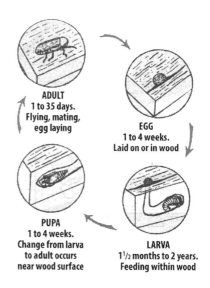

ADULT
1 to 35 days.
Flying, mating, egg laying

EGG
1 to 4 weeks.
Laid on or in wood

PUPA
1 to 4 weeks.
Change from larva to adult occurs near wood surface

LARVA
1½ months to 2 years.
Feeding within wood

The larval, or grub, stage, in which the wood-destroying beetles do their damage, is long in proportion to the rest of the life cycle.

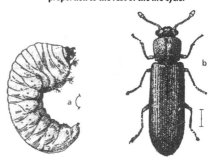

lyctid powderpost beetle: a, larva; b, adult

If the infestation is localized, replacing wood is often a sound choice. As an example, an infested door or window frame can be replaced with uninfested wood. The new wood should be painted, varnished or sealed, in case beetles might still be present in the area.

Infested small wood items such as furniture, wooden artifacts and home furnishings can be treated with heat or cold. Beetles can be killed by freezing the wood at 0 degrees for four to seven days. Powderpost beetles can acclimate to gradually falling temperatures, so the decrease must be sudden for this technique to work. Wood left outdoors for extended periods of time should be placed in plastic wrap to prevent absorption of moisture that can damage wood products. Heating wood products at 120 degrees for two hours should kill these beetles, but be sure the item is heated all the way through. Use caution when freezing or heating because some wood products and their finishes might be damaged.

Insecticides applied to the surface of infested wood can be used to kill adult beetles emerging from infested wood. All surfaces being treated must be sprayed or painted thoroughly with an insecticide labeled for use against powderpost beetles. Insecticide treatment will penetrate only slightly into wood, thus, many larvae inside the wood won't be killed. Because these treatments will last only for a limited time, multiple applications might be necessary. Be sure to read the insecticide label carefully for proper application and reapplication methods and timing. Also use care when treating hardwood floors and other finished surfaces to avoid marring the finish. When in doubt, treat a small, hidden area first.

Inspecting for and controlling wood-boring beetles can be extremely difficult. Contact a pest control company experienced in this area of pest control for best results.

POWDERPOST BEETLES AND OTHER WOOD-DESTROYING INSECTS

A large number of insects other than termites can damage wood and wood products. Powderpost beetles, other wood boring beetles, carpenter ants, and carpenter bees cause millions of dollars in damage to wood products each year. Carpenter ants are discussed in the chapter about ants, and carpenter bees are discussed in the chapter about stinging insects.

Powderpost beetles and other wood-destroying beetles infest and damage wood significantly. Many of these, such as the various bark beetles and round- and flat-headed borers, are found alive as larvae most frequently in unseasoned wood, but they also can be found in seasoned lumber. Concern about these beetle larvae is greatest in seasoned wood because it's the wood used in construction and the beetle larvae excavate burrows in the wood.

The characteristics of the damage to the wood by these insects generally are sufficient evidence to identify the pest causing the problem, but positive identification of the beetle causing the damage always is useful to diagnose the problem and help prescribe a correct treatment. Characteristics of damage caused by common wood-boring insects in buildings are shown in the accompanying table.

CHARACTERISTICS OF DAMAGE CAUSED BY COMMON WOOD-BORING INSECTS
Powderpost beetles
Powderpost beetles include three closely related families (Lyctidae, Bostrichidae, and Anobiidae). The common name is appropriate because the larvae reduce timbers to a mass of fine, powderlike material. The adults do little damage to wood, serving primarily to reproduce.

Among the many difficult kinds of insects that attack wood and wood products, the destructiveness of powderpost beetles is second only to termites. They infest and reinfest dry, seasoned wood, with the interior of such wood (usually the sapwood only) being completely riddled with holes or galleries and packed with wood dust or frass. Pinhole openings, often called shot holes, perforate the surface of infested wood. The size of these holes varies depending on the family and species of the beetles involved. Hardwoods (ash, oak, walnut and pecan) and softwoods (pine, fir and some maple) are attacked, although the family Lyctidae is specific to hardwoods.

POWDERPOST BEETLES INFEST:
* flooring
* studs
* girders
* other parts of buildings
* crating
* paneling
* furniture
* tool handles
* gunstocks
* other wood articles

Infestations often are built into structures as a result of using infested lumber. These beetles are brought into homes in infested firewood frequently. Beetles that attack softwoods often fly into crawlspaces beneath buildings and lay eggs on exposed wood there. The first evidence of infestation is usually piles of fine sawdust on or beneath wood and small holes in the surface. At that point, infestations might have been present from three months to three years or more, depending on the species involved, environmental conditions and wood type. In hidden areas, such as crawlspaces, serious damage might be done before the infestation is discovered.

Lyctidae
Adult lyctids lay their eggs in the surface pores of hardwoods and bamboo (although it's not wood). The eggs are long and cylindrical, rather than round like many other insects. Larvae, which bore into the wood as soon as they hatch, are white with dark brown heads and mandibles. The front end of the body is larger than the back and bears three minute pairs of legs. Lyctids larvae can be identified easily by examining the last pair of spiracles (breathing openings on each abdominal segment), which are much larger than the others.

Characteristics of damage caused by common wood-boring insects

Insect type	Shape & size (inches) of exit/entry hole	Wood type	Age of wood attacked*	Appearance of frass in tunnels	Reinfests structural timber?
Ambrosia beetles	Round 1/50-1/8	Softwood & hardwood	New	None present	No
Lyctid beetles	Round 1/32-1/16	Hardwood	New & old	Fine, flourlike, loosely packed	Yes
Bark beetles	Round 1/32-3/32	Bark/sapwood interface	New	Fine to coarse, bark colored, tightly packed	No
Anobiid beetles	Round 1/16-1/8	Softwood & hardwood	New & old	Fine powder, and pellets loosely packed; pellets may be absent and frass tightly packed in some hardwoods	Yes
Bostrichid beetles	Round 3/32-9/32	Softwood & hardwood (bamboo)	New	Fine to coarse powder, tightly packed	Rarely
Horntail or wood wasp	Round 1/16-1/4	Softwood	New	Coarse, tightly packed	No
Carpenter bee	Round 1/2	Softwood	New & old	None present	Yes
Round-headed borer	Round-oval 1/8-3/8	Softwood & hardwood	New	Coarse to fibrous, mostly absent	No
Flat-headed borer	Oval 1/8-1/2	Softwood & hardwood	New	Sawdustlike, tightly packed	No
Old house borer	Oval 1/4-3/8	Softwood	New & old	Very fine powder and tiny pellets, tightly packed	Yes
Round- or flat-headed borer, wood machined after attack	Flat oval 1/2 or more; or irregular surface groove, 1/8-1/2	Softwood & hardwood	New	Absent or sawdust-like, coarse to fibrous; tightly packed	No

*New wood is defined as standing or freshly felled trees and unseasoned lumber. Old wood is seasoned or dried lumber.
Source: M.P. Levy, A guide to the inspection of existing homes for wood-inhabiting fungi and insects, U.S. Department of Housing and Urban Development, Washington, D.C. 1975.

Larvae live in the wood, creating galleries (tunnels) as they eat. When the larvae are almost full grown and ready to pupate, they bore near to the surface of the wood and pupate. Adults bore through the surface soon after pupation, pushing a fine, powdery wood dust out of the wood as they emerge. Adult activity is greatest in early spring. They're inactive in the day, concealing themselves in cracks and holes in the wood. At night, they become active, are attracted to lights, and might be seen crawling on windowsills, floors and furniture.

Adults are flattened and reddish-brown to black. They're small beetles, varying in size from three-thirtyseconds to seven-thirtyseconds of an inch long. The head is distinctly visible from above, which isn't the case in most species of the other two powderpost beetle families.

Lyctids (and Bostrichids) can't digest cellulose, so this material passes through the larval digestive tract virtually untouched and accounts for the large amount of powdery frass left by the beetles. Because the carbohydrate content of wood is a limiting factor in the development of these beetles, it's advantageous to the females to find wood with a high starch content on which to lay their eggs.

It's been shown females of some lyctid species can select favorable wood by a so-called tasting process. Wood that has a low starch content (less than 3 percent) and less than 6-percent moisture content is seldom attacked. Lyctids almost always are found infesting the sapwood of hardwoods, especially those that have been seasoned inadequately. Common examples are implement handles made of ash and oak and flooring or furniture made from oak, maple, walnut and other hardwoods. Only hardwoods have pores, which are necessary for the female to lay eggs. Some hardwoods, such as ash, elm, oak, pecan and walnut, are attacked more readily because of large pores. Only the sapwood layers of hardwood are eaten because the required starches are present.

Bamboo, which is attacked by some lyctids, is technically classified as grass, but it meets the requirements necessary for lyctid attack. Occasionally, bamboo furniture, baskets, screens, etc. might be infested. Lyctids can complete a life cycle in one spring and summer season if temperature, starch content of the wood and moisture conditions are good. However, they usually require a year to complete development when they're in wood that has been built into a structure. This is primarily because of

Comparative biological information about the three powderpost beetle families

Characteristic	Family		
	Lyctidae	*Bostrichidae*	*Anobiidae*
Size	1/12-1/5"	1/8-1"	1/8-1/3"
Shape	Flattened	Cylindrical, roughened	Oval, compact pronotum
Color	Brown to black	Brown to black	Reddish brown
Head visible from above	Yes	No	No
Antennal club	2 segmented	3-4 segmented	None
Egg placement	Deposited in pores of hardwoods	Female bores into wood to lay eggs	Laid in cracks or old exit holes in wood
Required moisture content of wood*	6-30%	6-30%	13-10%
Average life cycle	1 year	1 year	1-3 years

*Wood found in structures is considered dry with a moisture content less than 20 percent.
Source: M.P. Levy, *A Guide to the Inspection of Existing Homes for Wood-Inhabiting Fungi and Insects*, U.S. Department of Housing and Urban Development, Washington, D.C., 1975.

the dryness of the wood. In an unoccupied or poorly heated building, they often reinfest available hardwood for many generations.

Lyctid damage is characterized by the presence of extremely fine, flourlike powder falling from the surface holes. The frass left by other wood borers usually contains pellets and has a coarse texture and a tendency to stick together. When inspecting damage, old damage must be distinguished from active beetle infestations. Newly formed holes and frass are a light color and clear. Old holes and frass are dark.

There are 66 known species of lyctidae, of which 10 are known to exist in the U.S. In addition to these 10 established species, others are discovered periodically infesting wooden articles shipped into the U.S.

Anobiidae

There are a number of species of Anobiids encountered as wood borers in structures in the U.S. Three species are among the more well known and economically important – the furniture beetle, deathwatch beetle and *Euvrilletta peltata.* The furniture beetle is found primarily in the Eastern half of the U.S.; and although named the furniture beetle, it also infests structural timbers. The deathwatch beetle is found throughout the U.S. It attacks building timbers in poorly ventilated areas where moisture tends to collect. Its common name is derived from the ticking sound the adult makes inside infested wood – a sound that's audible in the hush and stillness of night, a mating call.

Euvrilletta peltata is a significant pest in crawlspace timbers in the Southeastern U.S. Infestations can become so problematic a loss of structural strength to sills, joists and subflooring areas can occur.

The following table summarizes comparative information about the three powderpost beetle families.

Anobiid beetles lay their eggs in cracks and crevices of seasoned wood. As soon as they hatch, young larvae burrow into the wood, where they'll live and tunnel for a year or more. When mature, they burrow toward the surface of the wood where they pupate. After emerging from the pupal skin, the adults bore to the surface of the wood and escape.

Mature larvae of anobids are curved slightly (D-shaped), wrinkled and have tiny hairs on the body. They have three pairs of short legs, and their mandibles usually are toothed on the inner edge. Larvae of the various species vary from one-quarter to almost one-half of an inch long.

Adults are small beetles, usually less than one-third of an inch long. They vary from red to blackish-brown. The dorsal view of the thorax provides a fairly distinctive characteristic for identification of many of the members of this family. The widest point of the thorax is slightly forward of the base, which tapers slightly backward and toward the midline, giving the thorax a rough, diamond-shaped outline. The pronotum forms a hood over the head, and when viewed from above, completely conceals the head. Also the tibia on the leg of an anobiid doesn't have spurs like the Lyctid and Bostrchid beetles.

Unlike termites, some of the anobiids are able to digest wood without the aid of cellulose-digesting protozoa. Although the growth of certain fungi within the burrows can serve as a source of protein and increase the rate of development of the larvae, it's known some species

Timbers attacked by common wood-boring insects

Insect	Timbers attacked					
	Unseasoned	Seasoned	Softwood	Hardwood	Sapwood	Heartwood
Lyctids		+		+	+	
Bostrichids	–	+	–	+	+	
Anobiids		+	+	–	+	–
Round-headed borers	+		+	+	+	–
Old house borers		+	+		+	
Flat-headed borers	+	–	+	+	+	+
Wharf borers		+	+	+	+	+
Scolytids	+		+	+	+	+

Note: + means yes; – means occasionally
Source: M.P. Levy, *A Guide to the Inspection of Existing Homes for Wood-Inhabiting Fungi and Insects,* U.S. Department of Housing and Urban Development, Washington, D.C., 1975.

can complete the life cycle on a steady diet of cellulose alone because of the presence of an enzyme that converts the cellulose to useful nutrients.

Anobiids infest all types of seasoned wood (hardwoods and softwoods), although they usually are more problematic pests of the sapwood of softwoods. As a result, infestations are common in crawlspaces and basements because most framing lumber in buildings is pine. Cabinets, furniture and woodwork also are infested. Infestation is characterized by small, round holes on the surface, with fine to coarse powder sifting from them. The frass is characterized by the bun-shaped pellets within the mass.

The life cycle takes one or more years, depending on the species involved and environmental conditions. The adults emerge in greatest numbers from April through July and will reinfest wood if the moisture content of the wood is high enough. In crawlspaces, reinfestation occurs most frequently where ventilation is poor and humidity is absorbed by the wood members. Attics and wall voids rarely are infested because ventilation and temperature control remove moisture. If a house has no problem with excess moisture in the basement or crawlspace, has central heating and cooling systems, and doesn't remain closed up or unoccupied for long periods, widespread, extensive damage by anobiid beetles is unlikely.

Bostrichidae

The economic importance of the bostrichid beetles in houses is much less than the other two powderpost beetle families. Most of the hardwoods attacked aren't those commonly used for interior floors, woodwork and trim. Most of the species don't reinfest wood after it's seasoned, so the damage is limited to that inflicted by one generation. However, this damage can be considerable because of the speed and completeness of their attack on portions of wood having a high starch content (sapwood portion of the wood).

Adult bostrichid beetles bore into wood to lay their eggs, which is different than other powderpost beetle families. Mature larvae are curved and wrinkled, lack hairs on the body, and possess three pairs of short legs. The mandibles aren't toothed on the inner margins, and the front half of the body is larger than the back half.

Most bostrichids are larger than beetles from the other families of powderpost beetles. Consequently, their entrance and exit holes are larger (more than one-eighth of an inch). These holes don't contain frass, but the galleries do. The frass is packed tightly, tends to stick together and is meallike (contains no pellets).

Upon emerging from their pupal skins (usually in spring), adults bore to the surface of wood. Adults vary from one-eighth to 1 inch long and are dark brown or black. The body is cylindrical (except that of *Polycaon stouti*) with a much-roughened thorax, and the antenna bears a club of three distinct and separate segments. The head usually isn't visible from above.

Bostrichids are unable to digest cellulose and don't have partnerships with organisms that are capable of digesting cellulose. They're dependent on the starch and other nutrients in the wood they infest. There are a considerable number of species in this family, and they attack a wide range of materials. They're most commonly encountered in hardwoods, but certain bostrichids commonly infest softwoods and sometimes become important pests in softwoods. Although primarily a pest of seasoned wood, some species will be found in unseasoned wood occasionally. The bamboo powderpost beetle is encountered in the U.S. commonly. It's a small (about one-eighth of an inch long), cylindrical brown beetle that's a pest primarily of curtains, ornaments and furniture made from bamboo. It's also found in stored grain products and spices.

Polycaon stouti (Le Conte) is a larger black bostrichid (about three-quarters of an inch long) found infesting hardwood lumber, furniture and other wood products in the Western U.S. Occasionally, it's found in other parts of the country in furniture that has been moved from the West Coast. The adults differ from other bostrichids because the head is visible from above.

The lead-cable borer is a cylindrical, reddish-brown beetle about one-quarter of an inch long that attacks the lead sheathing of aerial telephone cables. Where the sheathing is penetrated, moisture enters, and a short circuit can occur. The beetle also attacks solid wood, with larvae feeding on the wood for about nine months before pupating. It's found along the U.S. Pacific Coast.

The red-shouldered bostrichid is a cylindrical black beetle about one-quarter of an inch long that has patches of red at the base of the elytra (hard, outer wings that cover the abdomen). Although it can infest log cabins, rustic furniture and structural timbers, it's more of a nuisance than an economic pest because it emerges from dead or dying trees in large numbers.

Ranging in size from one-quarter to one-half of an inch, the oriental wood borer is brownish-black and has a prothorax with several projections. The elytra have several rows of deep puncture marks, and toward the rear, the wing covers are curved inward creating a concave area. The beetles are found in several areas in Florida and as far north as North Carolina. They also can be found in items imported from India and Southeast Asia. Packing cases, boxes, plywood, furniture and lumber commonly are infested, and it's been found infesting 35 species of trees.

Long-horned beetles (round-headed borers)
Species in this family (more than 1,200 species recorded in the U.S.)

feed as larvae on living trees, recently felled trees and logs, and seasoned lumber. Indoors, the only species of considerable economic importance that can reinfest dry, seasoned wood is the old house borer. Some species that begin their development in dying trees, logs or unseasoned lumber are able to complete their development as the wood seasons. The adults of these borers will emerge from the wood after it's been incorporated into a structure. They won't reinfest the wood because of its dryness, but they're of significant concern to property owners who find them or evidence of their activity.

Another common source for these beetles is firewood brought indoors. Sighting of adult beetles can lead to a false impression of structural attack. Thus, firewood should be brought indoors only when it will be used soon thereafter.

The beetles of this family lay their eggs in cracks or crevices in bark or on the surface of rough-sawn timbers. The larvae are wood borers.

Mature larvae are large, varying from one-half to 3 or 4 inches long. The body is long and narrow and a light cream color. The rear portion of the head is partly drawn into the body, so only the mandibles and other mouthparts are seen easily. Larvae are called round-headed borers.

Adults are large, conspicuous beetles varying in length from one-half to 3 inches long. They can be distinguished from other beetles easily by their long, thin antennae, which might be longer than the body; thus, adult beetles are called long-horned beetles. Many species have conspicuous markings on the wing covers.

The most common structural pest of this family, and the only one that commonly infests houses and other structures, is the old house borer. Larvae hollow out extensive galleries in seasoned softwood (e.g., pine). The old house borer is frequently a pest of newer structures, although it's found in older buildings. It's well established along the U.S. Atlantic Coast, but infestations have been reported as far west as Louisiana and Minnesota.

Adults are about three-fourths of an inch long and grayish-brown to black with two white patches on the elytra. The dorsal surface is covered densely with light-colored hairs. There are two black, shiny bumps on the pronotum (shield-like area over the top of the head). When these bumps are surrounded by long, grey hairs, the result is an owl-like appearance.

The life cycle of the old house borer ranges from three to 12 years, although it can be considerably longer if environmental and nutritional conditions are unfavorable. Because this beetle has a long life cycle and can infest the same piece of wood again and again, it might be many years before serious structural damage is recognized. The exit holes of emerging adults don't occur in large numbers until the infestation has been established for several years. This, along with the fact that larvae will feed extensively without breaking through the surface of the wood, make it necessary to inspect infested wood carefully to detect old house borer damage. Rough wood being examined should be probed or struck to detect weakness or the presence of boring dust. If exit holes are present, they'll be broadly oval and about one-quarter to three-eighths of an inch in diameter.

Like other members of this family, the old house borer is able to digest cellulose. Because carbohydrates are readily available to this insect, the limiting nutritional factor appears to be the supply of protein. Larval development is more rapid in wood infested with wood decay fungi because these fungi are a source of protein for the larvae.

Bark and timber beetles
Bark beetles are small, cylindrical beetles. The larvae don't have legs. The larvae excavate extensive galleries immediately beneath the bark on the surface layers of wood. Timber beetles, on the other hand, excavate tunnels within solid wood. Some timber beetles derive nourishment directly from the wood. Others feed on fungi they cultivate within the galleries, in which the eggs are deposited. These beetles are often (but not always) associated with wood from trees that are dead or dying before the wood is processed.

Bark beetles can create problems in log cabins, park shelters and similar structures made of roughhewn wood in which the bark is left intact or small areas of bark are left in place. Other common sources of bark beetles are rustic lawn and porch furniture and firewood brought indoors during winter.

Timber beetles are troublesome sometimes when they emerge from improperly seasoned wood used in hardwood floors or in decorative paneling. Although the emerged beetles can be a nuisance for a short time, they can't reinfest the dried wood or bark, and they cause no loss of strength to the wood from which they emerge.

Ambrosia beetles are another group of beetles belonging to the scolytid family and family Platypodidae. They're so named because their larvae feed only on ambrosia fungus, which grows in moist, usually green, wood. The adult beetles introduce the fungus spores into their tunnels, and wherever the fungus grows, the wood is stained blue, black or dark brown. These stains around the tunnels and holes are the key to identifying ambrosia beetle damage. This damage is confused with powderpost beetle damage sometimes, even though the stains are evident. It's important to know the difference because powderpost beetles can reinfest wood in structures, and ambrosia beetles can't.

If live ambrosia beetles are found indoors, the most likely source is firewood that has been cut recently. Because their attack ends before or shortly after wood is brought indoors, no control is needed.

Wharf borer

The wharf borer adult, which is about a half inch long, is yellow to light brown, and the tips of the wing covers, the legs, and the underside or the body are black. The body is covered densely with short yellow hair, and the wing covers each have four lengthwise raised lines.

This beetle, as an adult, resembles the long-horned beetles in general appearance but belongs to a different family of beetles. The larva, which is about an inch long, is narrow and cylindrical. It bears wartlike swellings on the upper side of the last two segments of the thorax and the first two segments of the abdomen.

The insect's common name is derived from one of the places it's found commonly. It can be a serious pest in pilings and wharves, where the larvae excavate extensive galleries, weakening the timbers and providing excellent sites for invasion by rot organisms. Wharf borers can be found in buildings in which poor drainage or faulty plumbing accounts for the presence of moist wood, especially pilings. It's also a problem in wood lying on damp ground (especially in crawlspaces) and wood that's been buried beneath the soil. Wharf borers have been found in association with redevelopment activities in which old buildings are torn down and some of the old wood has been buried.

The wharf borer is found commonly along the Atlantic and Pacific Coasts and near the Great Lakes. It's also caused damage and annoyance in the other areas throughout the U.S. Whether the larvae do considerable damage in structures is debatable because the wood on which they feed is moist and usually decayed already. The presence of the borer, however, compounds the problem. In addition, thousands of adults can appear suddenly after emerging from wood and create a nuisance in their attempt to escape from the structure. Swarming occurs primarily in the summer months.

Flat-headed wood borers (metallic wood borers)

Active infestations of flat-headed borers (as the larvae are called) are seen rarely in structures, but wood damaged by the larvae is encountered often. If adults happen to emerge within buildings, they won't reinfest structural timber.

Adults are hard-shelled, boat-shaped beetles with bright colors and a metallic luster giving rise to the common name metallic wood borers. Usually, the elytra are ridged or roughened. They're strong fliers and seek weak or injured trees to infest in the spring and summer months.

The white to yellow larvae are legless grubs that have a conspicuous widening and flattening of the thorax just behind the head (thus the name flat-headed borer). They tunnel in and under the bark and eventually move into the sapwood and heartwood of dead or dying trees. Most flat-headed borers feed until winter, pupate and emerge in the warmer months through an oval exit hole. The larval tunnels are broadly oval and about three times as broad as high, and are tightly packed with fine frass.

Other wood-infesting beetles

Another group of beetles that doesn't contribute to significant structural damage but should be recognized is the family Curculionidae, the weevils. These beetles sometimes are called snout beetles because their heads are prolonged into a distinctive snout. They're small, about one-eighth to one-fifth of an inch long, and black to reddish-brown. The elytra are pitted heavily. Larvae are whitish, grublike, legless and about one-eighth of an inch when grown fully.

The female excavates holes in the wood or uses cracks and crevices to deposit her eggs. The larvae bore primarily with the grain in some species but might take a more random route with other species. Adults and larvae can be found feeding in the galleries. Adults leave exit holes when emerging from the wood, about one-sixteenth of an inch in diameter, irregularly shaped holes one-tenth to one-twelfth of an inch in diameter. Frass is fine and powdery with tiny pellets and is packed in the galleries. The damage appears similar to that of anobiid beetles, but the pellets, frass and tunnels are much smaller.

Wood-boring weevils aren't common and don't cause significant amounts of damage but might cause confusion if detected because of their unusual appearance. There are a few species of weevils that will attack seasoned wood, but they're most often found in damp or slightly decayed wood. They attack hardwoods, softwoods and plywood and are found in all regions of the country. Moisture control is the best solution for these weevils in most cases.

The telephone pole beetle is only about one-sixteenth of an inch long as an adult. Antennae are 11-segmented, the first two segments of which are longer than the final nine segments. The head is wider than the prothorax, which narrows where it meets the elytra. Body color varies from light to dark brown.

Relatively little is known about the telephone pole beetle's biology, but what is known is unusual for the insect world. Until recently, only female specimens of this beetle have been collected. The females are parthenogenetic, or are capable of reproducing without mating. Even more bizarre, these beetles are paedogenic, meaning the larvae are capable of producing larvae or eggs before maturing into adults. Maturation of larvae seems to occur at the same time in a particular infestation, with beetles emerging by the thousands.

The telephone pole beetle commonly infests rotting oak or chestnut logs. High moisture content is a prerequisite for proper development. It's reported to infest wood that's used inside buildings. Some of the more common infestation situations include telephone poles (hence its nickname) and wood paneling in bank vaults. The beetle is native to North America and is transported to other countries occasionally. Infestations are resolved best by vacuuming emerging beetles and eliminating moisture problems in wood.

PREVENTION OF WOOD-BORING BEETLES

Those who use wood must take precautions to reduce the chances of building an infestation into structures, furniture and so forth. Steps that can be taken to prevent beetles from infesting buildings include:

* inspecting wood prior to purchase
* using properly kiln- or air-dried wood
* sealing wood surfaces
* using chemically treated wood
* ensuring good building design

These preventive measures have limitations but are good building practices where no beetle attack has occurred yet.

Although careful visual inspection of wood is essential, some infestations might not have progressed to the point where they can be detected. Using kiln- or air-dried wood in construction is one of the least-expensive and most-practical preventive measures. Still, there are a few beetle species that can survive and reinfest wood that has been dried properly. Sealing wood surfaces with varnish, shellac or paint eliminates the habitat necessary for egg laying, but usually it's not feasible to seal the surfaces of structural timbers. Using chemically treated wood (e.g., treated by fumigation, wood preservatives or insecticides) will provide beetle-free wood, but using such treated wood usually is cost prohibitive. Additionally, fumigation won't protect wood from a future infestation. Using good building design and practices – such as proper ventilation, drainage, and clearance between wood and soil – tends to reduce the moisture content of wood in a structure, creating less-favorable conditions for beetle development. Central heating and cooling systems also speed up the wood-drying process.

INSPECTING FOR WOOD-BORING BEETLES

Periodic inspections are needed to locate any evidence of attack by wood-destroying beetles. All exposed surfaces of painted or unpainted wood must be examined for evidence of damage such as presence of beetles, holes in wood and frass. It might be necessary to call a pest control company because the symptoms and signs of the pests might be difficult to identify. It's essential to determine whether the pest will reinfest the wood or not. If the pest was in the wood when construction occurred and doesn't reinfest the wood, no treatment is needed.

It's important to know if the infestation is still active. Fresh frass, which is the color of newly sawed wood, or live larvae or adults in the wood are signs. Only an active infestation needs to be treated. Beetles don't cause damage rapidly, so it's not necessary to rush into any kind of control program. Get several opinions and estimates before purchasing any treatment.

MANAGEMENT OF WOOD-BORING BEETLES

No wood-destroying beetles in buildings develop rapidly in dry wood. If the use of vapor barriers, ventilation and central heat can dry wood and keep it dry, the use of other management measures might not be necessary. This wouldn't be a rapid means of management and probably wouldn't replace others completely. Regardless of the method, it's wise to recommend every effort be made to reduce the moisture content of the wood to be protected to below 20 percent. Moisture meters can determine the moisture level in the wood.

Where economical and practical, infested wood should be removed and replaced. This is practical only in limited infestations. Wood adjacent to the wood removed must be inspected carefully to be certain it's free of beetles.

Electric current and heat treatment, as discussed for drywood termite management, have uses in some wood-boring beetle infestations. Every situation should be evaluated before deciding on the treatment method or combination of methods.

To obtain the best results, combine knowledge of the beetles and insecticides. The most difficult problem encountered in such treatments is getting the insecticide to the insects, concealed and well shielded in their burrows. Although a material with a long residual life would kill the beetles shortly after they emerge, it's desirable to kill them in their tunnels so they won't mar the surface of the wood with emergence holes. The best penetration into the tunnels is obtained by using a fumigant, but the danger in handling these materials and the fact they have no effective residual life limits their usefulness. Residual sprays provide effective control in most cases. To reduce splashing, sprays should be applied at a low pressure using a flat-fan nozzle to obtain thorough coverage. A compressed-air sprayer can be used to inject insecticide directly into the galleries made by beetles. Penetration into certain finishes (paint, varnish, water-repellent stains, etc.) is limited and repeated injections into exit holes is necessary.

When treating finished wood, such as furniture or flooring, it's best to use an oil solution to avoid spotting or changing the appearance of the finish. Even with the oil solutions, it's best to apply a small amount to an out-of-the-way area and allow it to dry before making a complete treatment. The oil carrier might have a solvent action on some wood finishes. Therefore, keep all objects off treated areas for about 24 hours or until the stickiness has disappeared. Don't allow any surface to be walked on or handled until it's thoroughly dry. Insecticide should be applied to the entire surface of the infested wood using a flat-fan nozzle at low pressure or by using a soft-bristled paint brush. If there are only scattered patches of infestation, treat only the infested boards. Avoid overtreating (if the solution runs off or puddles), particularly on hardwood floors laid over asphalt paper or based mastic. The asphalt will be dissolved by excess oil and might bleed through the finished floor. Any excess solution should be wiped up immediately. Be careful not to mar the surface if the finish has been softened temporarily by the spray.

Insecticide applications take time to work, and multiple applications might be necessary. If additional emergence holes occur, or more sawdust such as frass is produced, additional treatment will be needed. Activity will cease in time as reinfestation ceases.

When it's impossible to control powderpost beetles via insecticidal sprays, it's necessary to resort to fumigation. For example, fumigation is necessary when the beetles have moved into walls and other inaccessible areas. Thus, the entire building is covered with gasproof tarpaulins and fumigated with a gas, such as sulfuryl fluoride (see product labels). Such fumigations should be done only by professionals thoroughly trained in the use of gases. Detailed directions, as well as instruction, can be obtained from the product manufacturers.

If the old house borer is to be managed, programs involve only the treatment of softwoods to which the pest is restricted. Infestations of this beetle often involve extensive excavations, and larvae might be considerable distances from the obvious points of infestation. If the infestation is too widespread for spot treating with residual sprays, fumigation might be necessary. Other long-horned beetles require no management.

The presence of ambrosia, bark, and timber beetles is an incidental occurrence, and the number of beetles emerging is small generally. Such situations seldom require treatment because reinfestation is rare, although the killing of emerging beetles using some type of knockdown insecticide is desirable sometimes.

Buprestid beetles also don't require management because, like the long-horned and bark beetles, they infest dead or dying trees before the wood is processed, and if they emerge after construction, they don't reinfest the seasoned wood.

Wharf borer management, in situations in which replacement of structural members isn't necessary, requires the use of a wood preservative solely or in combination with an insecticide. The fungicidal properties of the materials will combat the rot organisms that are almost always associated with this insect. The toxicant should be injected into the infested wood under pressure. Damaged lumber should be replaced with pressure-treated lumber only. It's also important to remember the correction of excessive moisture in infested wood is a prerequisite to any insecticide use. If emerging adults are creating a nuisance, repeated use of a quick knockdown contact spray, such as synergized pyrethrins, will result in effective management.

When wood-boring beetles infest furniture or other movable articles, one of the most effective and rapid means of management is vault fumigation. If a vault isn't available, infested articles can be wrapped in tarps and then fumigated. Another proven tactic is to subject the infested materials to dry heat, which must be approached with caution because it might result in warping or damage to the finish. Rustic furniture can be dipped in solutions of appropriately labeled insecticides.

WOOD DECAY

Wood decay, often called wood rot, isn't a problem caused by insects; however, because the strength and integrity of wood can be compromised by wood boring insects and decay fungi, they're often discussed together as pest problems. Decay of wood in buildings is a problem in moist, humid parts of the U.S. Moisture is necessary for fungi growth that cause rot. A fungus sends minute threads, called mycelia, through damp wood, taking its food from the wood as it grows. The visible body of the fungus is on the outside surface. This is called the fruiting body, and, when mature, produces millions of tiny spores (seeds) present in the air and soil.

Two significant types of fungi can attack wood – surface molds and rot fungi. Fungi that color the wood green, grey, pink, orange, black or blue are called surface molds, mildews, and sap or blue stain fungi. They don't reduce the strength of the wood they grow on. The decay or rot fungi bleach wood or make it brown and crumbly. They reduce the strength of the wood and can be as destructive as termites and other wood-destroying insects, many of which are attracted to moist wood. White rot gives wood a white bleached appearance. The strength of the wood decreases gradually until it becomes spongy and stringy when broken. Brown rot turns wood brown and breaks it into brown cubical pieces with cracks perpendicular to the wood grain. It's the principal cause of building decay in the U.S., and it causes rapid loss of strength in infested wood. Water-conducting fungi (*Poria spp.*) are recognized by papery white-yellow mycelial fans and dirty white to black rootlike structures, called rhizomorphs, that can conduct water as far as 25 feet from a moisture source to the wood. Thus, the fungus can attack wood other fungi can't, and it can destroy large amounts of wood in a year or two.

The surface molds and stain fungi grow more rapidly than decay fungi and often appear on wood during construction. Fungus growth won't continue after construction if the wood dries out. However, the presence of stain fungi indicates that conditions at one time were suitable for decay, and an inspection with a moisture meter should be conducted to see if the wood is still moist enough to support decay fungi.

It's most important to point out the application of fungicides or insecticides to fungus-infested wood or soil won't stop the wood decay. Only by eliminating the moisture source can wood decay be completely controlled. Therefore, the application of chemicals by pest management professionals is of minor importance in fungus management. The first step in correcting a fungus condition is to determine the source of moisture and eliminate it if possible. All badly rotted wood should be removed and replaced with sound, dry lumber. When it's not possible to eliminate the source of moisture entirely, the replacement lumber should be pressure treated with a wood preservative before installation. Treated wood also should be used where the timber will contact the soil or be driven into the ground.

When wood is used in the construction of a building, it should be well seasoned to prevent it from containing enough natural moisture to support decay fungi. Wood shouldn't be used in those parts of construction where it can be moistened by wet soil. In extremely wet or humid areas, construction lumber is treated frequently with preservative chemicals to prevent fungus damage.

Wood in unventilated crawlspaces under houses is subject to much dampness. Condensation of water after evaporation from soil is the most common source of liquid water and subsequent decay problems in homes. Installing a vapor barrier and treating the wood can provide proper drainage and ventilation.

Measuring wood moisture with a moisture meter is an important method to determine:

✸ whether wood has a moisture content (20 percent or above) that will lead to decay

✸ small changes in the moisture content of wood to demonstrate the success of a moisture management program

✸ the likelihood of infestation or reinfestation by wood-boring insects

✸ whether fungi seen on the wood surface are growing still

The electric resistance of wood decreases as its moisture content increases. This is the basis for the operation of portable moisture meters, which measure the resistance between two needles inserted into wood and give a direct readout of moisture content. The higher the meter reading (decreasing electric resistance), the higher the amount of moisture in the wood. Meter readings can be affected by the wood species involved, moisture distribution, grain direction, chemicals in the wood, weather conditions and temperature. Thus, directions and information supplied with the meter must be understood and followed to ensure accurate readings.

Water should drain away from a properly constructed building. This is accomplished through proper grading, roof overhang, and the use of gutters, downspouts and drain tile. Proper grading should be taken care of before construction and usually is expensive if done later. The other methods should be used to move water away from the foundation walls. It's also important condensation (from air conditioners, for example) be properly drained. Indoors, dehumidifiers should be used where moisture in the air is likely to be a problem.

Proper ventilation in crawlspaces can be achieved by installing one square foot of opening for each 25 linear feet of wall. The openings should be located in areas to provide cross ventilation. The opening should be unobstructed. Where screening, wire mesh or louvers are used, the total opening should be greater than one square foot per 25 feet of wall.

Attic vents are recommended at the rate of one square foot of vent for every 150 to 300 square feet of attic floor space. Vents should be located near the ridge and at the eaves to induce airflow. Where louvered openings can't be used, globe ventilators, fan exhaust ventilators or special flues incorporated in a chimney might be best. Inlet openings under the cornice or roof overhang are required in all cases. Flat roofs where the same framing is used for ceiling and roof require openings between each joist. Any opening provided should be screened and protected from the weather.

Installing a vapor barrier on the soil surface of unexcavated areas will cause soil moisture to condense on the barrier and return to the soil rather than condense on the floor and joists above. Adequate barriers can be made by covering the soil with roofing paper or 4-mil to 6-mil polyethylene sheets. Properly installing the barriers is essential; a small portion of the soil surface should be left uncovered. This will allow wood in the crawlspace to dry slowly, minimizing warping and cracking. Inspection one to three weeks after installation will allow for proper adjustments of the vapor barrier so the wood can recover from the excess moisture.

When moisture problems result from poorly constructed or poorly maintained buildings, these problems have to be corrected before wood decay management can begin. Problems such as faulty roofing, siding and plumbing usually require the services of other specialists. If the source of moisture is removed and the wood dries out, decay will be stopped.

6

PESTS OF FOODS AND STORED PRODUCTS

SUMMARY: *INSECT PESTS OF STORED FOODS AND THEIR CONTROL*

Insects infesting stored foods – such as cereal, rice, spaghetti, crackers, nuts, dried fruits, spices and most any dried food products, as well as nonfood items such as animal foods and seeds, ornamental plant displays, dried flowers, potpourri and rodent baits – are some of the most common household pest problems. Food pests (usually the immature forms of beetles and moths – eggs, larvae and pupae) contaminate more food than they consume. Many infested products are unfit for human consumption and have to be discarded. The insects often are discovered when adult beetles or moths leave an infested food to crawl or fly about the house. They often accumulate on window sills in their attempts to escape the home.

GRAIN AND FLOUR BEETLES

These reddish-brown beetles are usually less than one-eight inch long. Their small, wormlike larvae are yellowish-white with brown heads. Larva of the saw-toothed grain beetle and red and confused flour beetles are elongate and tubular. Larvae of the cigarette and drugstore beetles are somewhat C-shaped and appear hairy. The grain and flour beetles are common in flour, cereal products, dried fruits, nuts, dried pasta products and seeds. The cigarette and drugstore beetles primarily are pests of dried plant products such as spices, macaroni, dried flowers and tobacco products. The larvae usually are found in infested material, whereas adult beetles often crawl around the kitchen and other areas of the home, as well as feeding on the infested material.

DERMESTID BEETLES

Members of this family generally are scavengers and feed on various products of plant and animal origin, including leather, furs, skins, dried meat products, woolen and silk materials, cheese and cereal grain products. Dermestids can be divided into three groups based on the type of food preferred. Larder beetles prefer products of animal origin, such as dried meats, leather products and cheese. Only occasionally are they found in food materials of plant origin. Carpet beetles also prefer products of animal origin – wool, leather, furs and feathers – but might be found throughout the house feeding on carpets, upholstery, clothing and even on accumulations of lint. Their invasion of stored food products is more or less accidental. Cabinet beetles prefer cereal grain products and are the most common pantry pests of the group. Larval stages of these beetles do most of the damage. Adults are thought to feed mainly on flower pollen outdoors but can feed on stored products.

Adult cabinet beetles are elongate oval and one-eighth to three-sixteenths of an inch long. They might be solid black or mottled with yellowish-brown markings. Larvae are long and narrow, yellowish to dark brown and hairy. Most species grow to about to one-third of an inch long.

GRAIN WEEVILS

These beetles – which have long snouts, are dark brown and are less than three-sixteenths of an inch long – feed primarily on stored whole grain but may feed on other plant matter. Their larvae are small, white, legless grubs that feed and develop inside individual kernels. They leave small round exit holes in kernels they infest.

SPIDER BEETLES

Several species of spider beetles are reddish-brown and three-sixteenths of an inch long (long legs and a general spider-like appearance) and might be found infesting all types of stored food products. The C-shaped, grub-like larvae and the adults feed on the infested material.

FLOUR MOTHS

These are small moths with a wingspan of about 0.5 inch. Of the two more common species, the Indianmeal moth's forewings have a copper-like color on the outer two-thirds and whitish-gray at the basal (head) end. The Mediterranean flour moth's forewings are a pale gray with transverse wavy black lines. The larvae of both species are pinkish-white and web together the materials (grain products) in which they develop. The adult moths fly about the house near the site of the infestation but are nonfeeding. The mature larvae might also leave their food and crawl about cupboards, walls and ceilings looking for a place to pupate.

ANGOUMOIS GRAIN MOTH

These are tan, tiny moths (about one-third of an inch wingspan). They can be seen flying about the house during the day, whereas clothes moths, which are similar in size and color, shun light. The larvae develop within kernels of grain such as popcorn. Adult moths don't feed.

MITES AND PSOCIDS

A number of other pests, such as tiny scavenger mites and book-lice, also can infest stored food products. This is particularly true if the food is stored under moist conditions.

FOREIGN GRAIN BEETLE

This small, brown beetle can be found occasionally feeding on moist or moldy grain but is more likely found in newly constructed homes where the wood hasn't completely dried. Given time, this beetle should disappear on its own.

PREVENTION

The following procedures will help prevent infestations.

1. Purchase dried food in packages that can be used in a short time. Keep foods in storage less than two to four months. Use older packages before newer ones, and opened packages before unopened ones.

2. When purchasing packaged foods, be sure the containers aren't broken or unsealed. Check the packaging date to be assured of

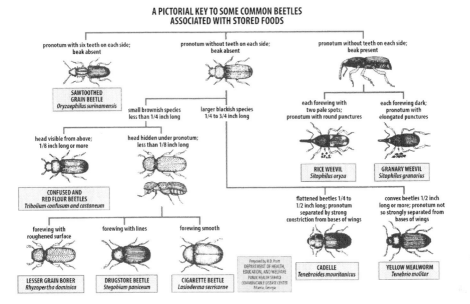

A PICTORIAL KEY TO SOME COMMON BEETLES ASSOCIATED WITH STORED FOODS

the freshness of the food. Packages with clear plastic or wax paper coverings should be checked for the presence of insects. Foods sometimes are infested before being brought into the home.

3. Store dried foods in insect-proof containers, such as screw-top glass, heavy plastic or metal containers. This will prevent entry or escape of insects. Ordinary metal kitchen canisters generally aren't tight enough to exclude insects. Some plastic containers with tight fitting lids might be acceptable. Cardboard, paper or plastic wrapping won't prevent insect infestations.

4. Storing dried foods in a home freezer will prevent pests from developing.

5. Keep food storage areas clean, and don't allow crumbs or food particles to accumulate because exposed food will attract insects. Cleanliness also is important in areas where pet food and birdseed are stored.

STEPS TO CONTROL BEETLES AND FLOUR MOTHS
1. Determine sources of infestation by examining all susceptible foods carefully. Properly dispose of any that are infested heavily. Small

amounts of highly susceptible foods can be kept in the refrigerator.
2. If infested material has further value or infestation is questionable, heat the material in shallow pans in the oven at 130 degrees for at least 30 minutes or place the material in a deep-freeze at 0 degrees for four days.
3. Empty and vacuum cabinets and shelves to pick up loose infested material; then wash them with soap and hot water.
4. Routine use of insecticides within food storage areas such as pantries and cabinets isn't recommended and normally will provide little additional control in the absence of an extensive cleaning program. Some household formulations of pyrethrins are labeled for use as crack-and-crevice treatments near food storage areas. There also are some formulations of pyrethroid insecticides that allow general use in the home and might help manage insects that are dispersed widely. Never allow insecticides to come in direct contact with food or food utensils. Remove all food and utensils during insecticide treatment to avoid accidental contamination. Treatment of cracks and crevices is more effective because insects might hide in these locations. Always read and follow label directions when using pesticides. This is extremely important when treatments are made around foodstuffs or food handling areas. Only products labeled specifically for use around food storage areas may be used for controlling insect pests around areas where food is stored.
5. If pesticides are applied, cover shelves with clean fresh paper or foil before replacing food or cooking utensils, etc.
6. Avoid spillage, and keep storage spaces clean.
7. Control moths or beetles flying around indoors by using a "flying insect" household aerosol insecticide. Total release aerosols containing synergized pyrethrins are also available for this use.

Insects infesting ornaments and decorations made from plant or animal products can be killed by placing the items in a freezer for three or four days. Insects in these items also might be killed by placing them in airtight containers along with aerosol fogs of the insecticides mentioned above. Leave the treated container closed for at least eight hours. Retreatment might be necessary if all insects aren't killed. Be careful when using plastic containers because some chemicals might react adversely with certain plastic materials. Pretesting the container with the insecticide to be used is always a sound practice.

Caution: If insects continue to appear, check other rooms in the home for possible sources. Tree seeds blown into ventilators or around windows may harbor these pests. Dermestids (carpet beetles) will develop in many products, including feathers, silk, wool, fur, stuffed animal skins, dead insects, lint and many other materials.

If insect problems persist, seek help from a professional pest control company.

PHEROMONE TRAPS

Use pheromone traps – only after the source of the infestation has been removed – to detect male moths that might remain in the house. Pheromones are chemicals – in this case a sex attractant – produced by an organism to affect the behavior of other members of the same species. The sex pheromone attracts adult male moths into the trap where they get stuck on the sticky sides. Moth traps designed to attract both sexes are available but must be combined with excellent sanitation for satisfactory results. Combination traps (moths and beetles) sometimes are available in certain local markets. Beetle aggregation pheromone and food attractants are combined with moth pheromone to create multiple species traps, which are most effective for monitoring the effectiveness of your sanitation program; they are not usually effective in controlling the insects.

To monitor, place the traps in the area of a previous infestation, and check them weekly. Most traps remain effective for about three months. Whenever you catch a new batch of moths in traps, it's time to inspect stored food packages again.

The large number of insect species and the numerous food products attacked make it important to hire a knowledgeable and experienced professional to handle the management of these pests. Perhaps even more important, is to have a knowledgeable professional using insecticides around food. Call a reputable pest management company to do the job, and avoid the worry and potential complications.

STORED FOOD PESTS

The pests of food products (and certain other stored products) are so numerous it's impossible to discuss all of them in this publication, so I'll focus on the major insect pests found in mills, warehouses, processing plants, homes and retail stores.

The stored food insects of concern to the public exist in specific conditions. Usually, they're found living in products such as:

* dried fruits
* spices
* flour
* bran
* peas
* dried vegetables
* dried flowers
* grain
* milled cereal products
* dog food
* nuts
* candy
* macaroni and spaghetti
* cheese

However, they also can be found in other stored products such as dried flowers, beans, seeds, plant arrangements, tobacco and pharmaceuticals. Additionally, animal products are subject to attack. These include:

* mounted or stuffed animals
* leather goods
* feathers
* furs
* hair
* silk
* rodent, bird and bat droppings or nests
* pet and bird food
* stuffing in upholstered furniture
* wasp nests and insect collections

Stored food pests are most important as pests of stored grain, damaging more than 10 percent of the world's grain production. They contaminate and eliminate for human consumption far more food than they eat. Stored product pests also are important in the household and retail stores as pantry pests that find their way into packaged cereals, spices and other foodstuffs.

Many stored food insects feed generally on all types of dried vegetables and animal matter, while others have more definite food preferences. Certain stored product pests originate in crops still growing in the field, while others infest food products during processing and storage. Stored product pests might fly into buildings, come from secluded areas indoors or migrate into uninfested items from infested sources, such as food refuse that collects in cracks and crevices. They also can be carried into a building on materials other than food products, such as furniture, rugs and bedding, as well as in or on almost any product of plant or animal origin. Be alert to these alternative sources of infestation when inspecting homes and offices.

Most pests of stored products are of tropical or subtropical origin. As a result, they live and reproduce best under warm conditions. With only a few exceptions, they can't live for long at low temperatures and usually don't hibernate. Almost all of them are adapted to living on foods with a low moisture content, although mites and psocids are exceptions. Few stored product pests can live and breed at temperatures above 95 F, and most do not lay eggs at temperatures below about 60 F. Certain insects and mites, however, can breed at temperatures of 40 F to 50 F if moisture conditions are suitable. Spider beetles, which might be serious pests in the Northern parts of the United States, are active at these temperatures.

Insects of stored products can be separated into four groups according to their feeding habits. Knowing the feeding habits of these pests, their biology and behavior, and the ability to identify the pests are invaluable.

※ **Internal feeders** – These insect larvae feed entirely within the kernels of whole grain and might remain undetected until adults emerge from the kernels. Examples: rice and granary weevil, lesser grain borer and Angoumois grain moth.

✳ **External feeders** – These insects feed on the outside of the grain. They also might chew through the outer seed coat and devour the inside. Examples: Indianmeal moth, drugstore beetle, flat grain beetle, cadelle, khapra beetle, and cigarette (or tobacco) beetle.

✳ **Scavengers** – Scavengers feed on grain only after the seed coat has been broken mechanically or by another insect. Examples: confused and red flour beetles, Mediterranean flour moth and sawtoothed grain beetle.

✳ **Secondary pests** – Secondary pests feed only on materials that are deteriorating, damp and have mold growth present. Some of them feed on mold rather than the food product. Examples: yellow mealworm, foreign grain beetle, some grain mites and psocids.

Occasional exceptions to these feeding habits might be found; however, as a general rule, each of these insects will feed as indicated.

Adult rice weevil emerging from a grain kernel after developing inside the kernel.

Photo courtesy of, and copyrighted by, Gene White, pmimages@earthlink.net

INTERNAL FEEDERS

Rice weevil

The rice weevil is known also as the black weevil. Adults are reddish brown and about one-eighth inch long. There are four light red or yellow spots on the wing covers, and the punctures on the pronotum are round. This weevil is distributed widely because of grain and food distribution. It can fly and frequently infests grain in the field and in storage. The rice weevil probably is the most destructive pest of stored grain.

The legless larva has a short, stout, whitish body and tan head. When viewed from the side, the body appears to be straight in outline on the underside and semicircular on the backside. The top surface of each of the first three abdominal segments has two transverse creases, so the segment is divided into three subsections.

Adults and larvae feed on various grains. The female bores a hole in a grain kernel, deposits an egg in this depression, and seals the hole with a gelatinous fluid. She might lay as many as 300 to 400 eggs in her average lifetime of four to five months. The larval and pupal stages are spent inside the grain, with the adult emerging through an irregular exit hole on emergence from the pupal skin. The exit holes usually are the first sign of grain damage, and by this time, serious damage might have been done to the entire lot of grain. The egg, larval and pupal stages might all be completed in as little as 26 days under favorable temperature and moisture conditions. Because the larvae and adults feed on the seed kernels, the grain is damaged beyond any use. Although it's seldom found in materials other than whole grain or seeds, the beetle has been recorded from solidified milled products, such as macaroni and caked flour.

Granary weevil

This chestnut brown or black beetle closely resembles the rice weevil. It's distinguished easily because it has no markings on its back, has no functional wings and the punctures on the pronotum are oval. The granary weevil has become so specialized it has no functional wings and is dependent almost entirely on humans for its distribution. It's found breeding only on grain in storage. The granary weevil is more common in the Northern states than Southern states, but it's found in all regions of the country.

The granary weevil larva appears similar to the rice weevil, but usually the first four abdominal segments bear two transverse creases on the top side. Larvae and adults feed on whole grain, such as oats, wheat, rye and barley that hasn't been milled. They occasionally infest beans and nuts, as do rice weevils.

Granary weevil adults are resistant to cold weather and might hibernate through the winter. Adults vary greatly in size, differing in this respect from most insects. Adult size usually depends on the size of the grain kernel. Large kernels produce large adults. The female drills a hole in the whole grain, buries a single egg in it, and seals the hole with a gelatinous plug in the same way the rice weevil does. Each female can lay as many as 250 eggs. Larval and pupal development take place inside the grain. When leaving the grain, the adult leaves an irregular, easily visible hole in the seed coat. Adults live an average of seven to eight months.

Angoumois grain moth

The Angoumois grain moth is next in importance only to rice and granary weevils as a pest of stored grain. It's frequently encountered in homes, warehouses and stores. It's distributed throughout the country but is particularly important in the Southern, Eastern and Central regions of the U.S.

In most cases, the Angoumois grain moth attacks only whole kernels of corn, wheat, and other grains and seeds. It's sometimes found in homes, emerging from decorative ears of corn or decorative boxes containing seed. Bird seed and cereal baits for rodents are subject to infestations if they contain whole kernels. Unusual infestations have been reported in cornmeal; flour; cashew nuts; hulled chestnuts; and dry, minced onions.

They lay eggs on or near grain in the field or after harvest. Upon hatching, the minute, white larvae bore into the kernels of grain and feed on the inside. When mature, the larva eats its way to the outer portion of the grain, leaving only a thin layer of the outer seed coat intact. Pupation takes place just under the seed coat. When the adult emerges from the grain, it pushes aside the thin layer of seed coat, leaving a small trapdoor covering its exit point from the kernel. The adult is small (wing spread about two-thirds of an inch), yellowish white, with pale front wings. The hind wings are pointed and fringed characteristically.

Lesser grain borer

The lesser grain borer is a dark brown, cylindrically shaped beetle about one-eighth of an inch long. The head is almost hidden by the thorax when viewed from above. The larva is thick bodied, cylindrical and grublike. It resembles the larva of the drugstore beetle, but the lesser grain borer larva has the head retracted into the thorax to about the level of the mandibles. Also, the body diameter of the lesser grain borer larva is largest in the thoracic region, in contrast to the drugstore beetle larva, which is largest in the abdominal region. Body setae (hairs) are short on lesser grain borer larvae.

This insect represents a transitional form insofar as its feeding habits are concerned. The eggs are laid singly or in clusters in the grain mass, and larvae might enter the kernels and develop within, or feed externally in the flourlike dust that accumulates from the feeding of the adults and their fellow larvae. Pupae might be found within the hollowed out grain or outside in the grain dust. Larvae and adults might bore into articles such as books and wood. The life cycle from egg to adult averages 58 days.

EXTERNAL FEEDERS
Drugstore beetle
The drugstore beetle is a brown, cylindrical beetle about one-eighth of an inch long. The adult closely resembles the cigarette beetle but doesn't have the hump-backed appearance of that beetle. The drugstore beetle has distinct longitudinal lines on the wing covers, which the cigarette beetle lacks. Adult drugstore beetles are good fliers.

The larva is about one-eighth of an inch in length, grub-shaped or C-shaped, and near white. The mouthparts and underside of the head are brown. There are numerous short, colorless setae on the head and body. There are no distinctive pigmented markings on the body, and the mouth opening is directed downward.

In the home, the drugstore beetle feeds on flour, breakfast cereals, red pepper or almost any food it can find. One of the most commonly infested materials is kibbled dog food. It's even been found in items such as books and pharmaceutical products, thus the name drugstore beetle.

Cigarette or tobacco beetle
The cigarette beetle is the most important pest of stored tobacco. It also might be a serious pest of items such as:
* books
* flax tow
* cottonseed meal
* rice

* ginger
* pepper
* paprika
* dried fish
* crude drugs
* seeds
* pyrethrum powder
* dried plants

Adults are light brown, about one-eighth of an inch long and fly readily. The head is bent downward, so the beetle has a distinct humpbacked appearance. The female lays about 30 eggs during a three-week period in newly harvested tobacco or other susceptible food items. The adults are good fliers and are most active during the early evening hours unless temperatures are below 65 F. During the day, they hide in dark places. Even though they're strong fliers, their primary means of spreading is through infested materials transported by humans.

The cigarette beetle larva resembles the drugstore beetle larva, but the body hairs of the cigarette beetle are considerably longer, giving it a more fuzzy appearance. The color is near white throughout, except for a distinctive group of yellowish-brown markings on the front surface of the head. The lower margin of the head is colored, and a series of four spots are arranged just above this area in such a way a pattern suggestive of a clownlike face is formed. Larvae feed on dried tobacco leaves, causing considerable damage.

Cadelle

The cadelle, also known as the bread beetle and bolting cloth beetle, can be found in rice and flour mills, in grain stored on farms and in country elevators. It's commonly found in packaged materials such as:

* ground cereals
* corn
* oats
* nuts
* spices
* fruits
* whole grains

Larvae and adults gnaw through sacks and even through wooden boards, leaving openings large enough for other insects to enter. Adults are shiny black and about one-third of an inch long. The pronotum is separated from the wing bases by a strong constriction, which is useful in identification.

The cadelle larva is strikingly marked and one of the most easily distinguished of the stored product pest larvae. It is about five-eighths of an inch long when completely grown and is dirty white. It has a dark brown head, and the mouth opening is directed forward. The prothorax has a dark brown hardened plate that covers most of the top surface of the segment. The second and third segments of the thorax have a pair of distinct brown spots on the top surface of each. The last segment of the abdomen has a dark brown plate on top, from which two distinct projections arise. Although a number of beetle larvae would fit this description, the cadelle is the only one of these likely to be found in stored grain and food products.

Eggs are deposited at random in flour or in crevices of food materials. A female will lay between 10 and 60 eggs in a batch and can lay as many as 3,500 in a lifetime.

The larvae feed on almost all grains as well as on flour, meal, bread, dried fruits, and similar foods. They also damage tobacco significantly by boring into it. In grain, the larvae often eat only the germinal portion of a grain, then move to another grain, damaging a large number of kernels. Moreover, cadelle damage provides the means of entry for other stored product pests that can't penetrate the seed coat on their own. Adults and larvae can be active in the winter, but they hibernate when the temperature gets too low.

Cabinet Beetles

The cabinet beetle and the larger cabinet beetle are well-known members of this group in the U.S. These two beetles have a similar appearance. Most specimens have well-defined areas of light brown markings on their dark wing covers. A distinctly indented notch on the inner margin of the eye of the larger cabinet beetle separates the two species. The larvae of all cabinet beetles have a similar appearance. When completely grown, they're about one-quarter inch long and about one-eighth inch

Indianmeal moth pupa, larva and adult (left to right).

wide at the middle of the body, which is tapered slightly at both ends and is yellow to medium brown. The last three or four abdominal segments bear dense clumps of darker setae that have distinctive spear-shaped tips. Larvae and adults of this genus are difficult to identify.

Indianmeal moth

Adults of the Indianmeal moth have a wingspread of about three-quarters of an inch. The front wings are tan on the front third and reddish-brown with a coppery luster on the back two-thirds. The mature larva is about one-half inch long and dirty white color with a sometimes greenish or pinkish tint. The larva feeds on all kinds of:

* grains and grain-based products
* seeds
* powdered milk
* dog food
* crackers
* candy
* nuts
* chocolate
* dried fruits
* almost all other dried foodstuffs around a home.

This moth is the most commonly found stored product moth in a home.

Larvae, when ready to pupate, leave their food supply and wander about in search of a suitable place in which to spin their white silken cocoons and pupate. During this period, they're frequently noticed by homeowners and mistaken for clothes moth larvae. It's important pest management professionals be able to distinguish between the larvae of clothes moths and Indianmeal moth to make proper recommendations and treatment for control. The Indianmeal moth is found in most any stored food product, feeds in or near a tunnel-like case with frass incorporated into it, and leaves extensive webbing matted over the surface of food products on which it feeds.

Adults, too, are frequently mistaken for clothes moths. The distinctive markings on the wings of the Indianmoth moth separate it from clothes moths. Adult Indianmeal moths live less than two weeks, are nonfeeding, and chiefly fly at dusk in the early evening. During the day, they prefer to rest in poorly lighted areas. If disturbed, they fly in an irregular zigzag pattern.

SCAVENGERS
Confused flour beetle

The confused flour beetle is a pest primarily in the Northern states. The adult is reddish-brown and about one-eighth of an inch long. It's often confused with the red flour beetle, but the antenna of the confused flour beetle is enlarged gradually to form a four-segmented club, whereas the antenna of the red flour beetle enlarges abruptly to form a distinct three-segmented club. The small size of the confused flour beetle enables it to work its way inside many sealed containers. It feeds on various foodstuffs and is an important pest in flour. It's also commonly found in cereal products, peas, beans, dried fruits, spices and other similar materials.

The adults of confused flour beetles don't fly. They can live as long as three years. Each female can lay as many as 300 to 400 eggs in her lifetime.

The larva is somewhat cylindrical in body shape and about one-eighth to one-quarter of an inch long. It's yellowish-white except for the darker mandibles and the pair of projections that arise from the last abdominal

Red flour beetles.

Photo courtesy of, and copyrighted by, Gene White, pmimages@earthlink.net

segment. There are no distinct darkened areas on the top side of the body segments. The head is flattened, so the mouth opening is forward.

Red flour beetle

The red flour beetle is primarily a pest in Southern states. It's similar in appearance, size and habits to the confused flour beetle. Adults can fly, which probably accounts for the much more frequent appearance of this beetle in farm-stored grain. The red and confused flour beetles, sawtoothed grain beetle, and Indianmeal moth are the most important pests of stored foods in retail stores and homes.

Flat grain beetle

The flat grain beetle is the smallest of the common grain-infesting insects. Adults are flattened, oblong, reddish-brown and about one-sixteenth of inch long. The antennae are slender and about two-thirds as long as the body.

The larvae is less than one-eighth of an inch long. The abdominal segments are about 1.5 times as wide as the thorax. The last segment of the abdomen bears a pair of distinctly sclerotized (hardened), hooklike structures joined at the base. These processes and the head are brown, in contrast to the remainder of the body, which is nearly white.

Sawtoothed grain beetle

The sawtoothed grain beetle is found in such foods as breakfast cereals, flour, dried fruits, macaroni, dried meats and chocolate. It's small enough that it can penetrate tiny cracks and crevices readily to get into packaged foodstuffs. When left undisturbed, a large population will develop rapidly.

The adult is a small brownish beetle about one-eighth of an inch long. It's easily identified by the six sawlike projections on each side of the thorax. The adult may live and breed for as long as three years. It doesn't fly. The female lays 50 to 300 white, shiny eggs. They're laid singly or in small masses in crevices in the food supply, although they're also laid freely in such items as flour.

The larva is less than one-eighth of an inch long and is long and narrow in body form. The head is somewhat flattened, and the mouth opening points almost straight ahead rather than downward. The antennae are about as long as the head. The last segment of the abdomen is tapered, and there are no large dorsal projections. The body is dirty white, and each abdominal segment bears a yellowish plate on the top side.

The larva nibbles on finely divided food particles because it can't feed on large particles, such as whole grain. So, the beetle and its larvae are found frequently along with other insects that feed on larger grains.

Sawtoothed grain beetles.

Mediterranean flour moth

The Mediterranean flour moth is a pest in the home and in food-processing plants such as feed mills. It infests such items as flour, nuts, chocolate, beans and dried fruits. Adults have a wing expanse of about 1 inch. The front wings are a pale grey with wavy black lines running across them. The hind wings are a dirty white. It can be distinguished from the Angoumois grain moth via the hind wings, which are rounded at the tips rather than pointed. The Mediterranean flour moth is recognized most easily by its characteristic pose when resting. The front of the body is raised, giving the wings a distinct downward slope with the tip of the abdomen protruding up between them. None of the other house moths have this characteristic pose.

Females lay their eggs in accumulations of flour or other milled products. The larvae hatch in a few days, and when mature, they measure about one-half of an inch long. They're white to pink, with a few small black spots on each body segment, from which the body hairs arise.

The larva spin silken threads as they move about. These threads fasten particles together in a dense mat that's characteristic of this insect. Larvae often are found away from the infested product, seeking a crack or crevice in which to pupate.

Species closely related to the Mediterranean flour moth include the tobacco (or chocolate), almond, and raisin moths. All are found throughout the U.S. and are similar in appearance and biology. They also might be found in similar habitats feeding on similar stored products. However, the tobacco moth is a significant pest of tobacco and isn't found often in homes. The raisin moth prefers dried fruits and often infests these fruits outdoors while they're drying. The almond moth prefers nuts and dried fruits and is a warehouse pest primarily.

SECONDARY PESTS

Yellow mealworm

Adults of the yellow mealworm are shiny dark brown or black, about one-half of an inch long, and most common in Northern states. Larvae are active and found in all sorts of unusual places, in addition to breakfast cereals and macaroni. The larva is the golden grub sold as fish bait in many parts of the country. When the larva is full grown, it's a little longer than an inch long. The body is elongate, cylindrical and has a harder body wall than the larvae of most other stored product pests. The body has a shiny yellow or light brown appearance with only a few scattered setae.

Mealworms (adults and larvae) usually are found in dark, damp places in spoiled grain products. In residences, they're commonly found in basements or at soil-grade level. The adults are confused with ground beetles easily, but examination of the hind leg reveals five tarsal segments on ground beetles and only four on mealworms. Also, a behavioral difference is that mealworm adults are slow moving, while ground beetles move rapidly.

Adult mealworms live only two to three months. Each female lays about 275 eggs, which hatch into larvae that grow to 1.25 inches long. The insect may remain in the larval stage for as long as 600 days, depending on temperatures.

Wing patterns of adult Indianmeal moth, Mediterranean flour moth, and Angoumois grain moth (top to bottom).

Dark mealworm

The dark mealworm is similar in habits and appearance to the yellow mealworm. Adult dark mealworms are the same size as yellow mealworms, but dark mealworms are dull black. Dark mealworm larvae are dark brown compared to the shiny yellow to light brown yellow mealworm. This insect is found throughout the U.S.

MISCELLANEOUS STORED PRODUCT PESTS

Many other pests are found in stored products. The corn sap beetle, which is common in the South, infests stored grain and flour. Spider beetles commonly infest flour, meal, seeds and similar products. Psocids, or book lice, are tiny, pale-colored insects that occur in great numbers on flour and in grain. Bean and cowpea weevils are found throughout the U.S. and infest all types of stored beans and peas. Foreign, rusty and squarenecked grain beetles are a small, reddish-brown family usually found infesting grains in poor condition. A number of other flour beetles – similar in biology and feeding habits to the red and confused flour beetles – are occasional pests of grain and grain products. Included in this group are the broad-horned, depressed, long-headed, slender-horned and small-eyed flour beetles. Moths of minor importance include the meal, rice, and wax moths, the European grain moth and the brown house moth. Grain mites frequently occur in large numbers in grain and flour. They're small and pale grey.

MANAGING STORED PRODUCT PESTS IN HOMES[1]

The source of a stored product pest infestation in a home usually is confined to areas where foods are stored, such as the kitchen. The entire infestation might be isolated within a cabinet or a single box of material. Before any control can be attempted, the source of infestation must be found and eliminated. This isn't always easy to do, but it's essential. Look carefully into all cracks and crevices where food debris might be accumulating – inside containers of such things as cereals, beans, peas, flour, dried fruits and spices, and any other material in which insects might live and complete their life cycle. Don't overlook the possibility a sealed container might be infested on the inside and loose enough to allow insects to escape. Also check under cabinets and open or accessible wall voids for spillage, such as pet food, which might harbor pests. Pet foods and birdseed might be a source of infestation, and they might be located in a room other than the kitchen. Nonfood items, such as ornamental seed and dried plant displays, ornamental corn, dried flowers, garden seeds, potpourri, and rodent baits, also might be infested. Pests of stored products such as fabrics (wool, fur, feathers, etc.) will be discussed in another chapter.

A stored food product might become infested at a processing plant, warehouse, in transit (trucks, train cars, etc.), at a grocery store or in a home. Many stored food insects are also pests of grain or other food crops and might be abundant outdoors. The outdoor insects often find their way inside homes, garages and storage sheds, and infest food and feed materials once inside. Food of any age can be infested, but when

[1] Prevention of food pests in homes and kitchens is discussed in the summary section of this chapter.

food products are left on shelves or the floor undisturbed for long periods, they become more susceptible to infestation.

Stored product insects are capable of penetrating unopened boxes, bags or other packages that are made of paper, cardboard, foil or cellophane. They may crawl in through seams or folds in the package, or they might chew their way into packages. Once inside the package, they begin to consume the food and lay eggs in it, and increase undetected into large numbers. The insects then spread to other stored foods or food particles that have collected in cracks, crevices and corners. All stages – egg, larva, pupa and adult – might be present in the infested products.

After removing infested material, remove the contents of drawers and cupboards in the area, thoroughly vacuum and clean these areas, and spray all cracks and crevices and other insect harborages with standard residual materials labeled for this use. After the insecticide has dried, cover all drawer bottoms and shelves with paper to avoid having food or food containers come in contact with the residual. It might take several days for insects not contacted during the treatment to come in contact with the residual to be killed. Control beetles or moths flying around indoors by using a flying insect household aerosol insecticide.

The application of insecticides for the control of pests in or around food requires considerable care for the homeowner. It's essential that no insecticide of any type come in contact with food products. No insecticide should be considered as nontoxic or suitable for use directly on any food product. When shelves are treated, food shouldn't be replaced on them until the insecticide is completely dry. Then shelf paper should be placed on the shelf to protect the food from direct contact.

7

BITING PESTS

SUMMARY: *BITING PESTS AND THEIR CONTROL*

There are many kinds of biting pests (insects and their close relatives) – mosquitoes, biting flies (such as black flies), bed bugs, fleas, lice, ticks, mites (such as chiggers) and spiders (covered in the chapter titled Occasional invaders). Most of these pests bite because they need blood to grow and reproduce (bed bugs), and a few others bite if you disturb them (spiders). By far, the most important group of pests that bite are blood feeders involved in disease transmission, such as certain mosquitoes as vectors of malaria and West Nile Virus. Control is best accomplished through prevention, such as using personal repellents and the removal of breeding and hiding areas. Insecticide use – other than a can of aerosol to kill a mosquito indoors – usually involves hiring a knowledgeable, experienced pest control company.

IMPORTANT GROUPS OF BITING PESTS

Mosquitoes – These biting insects annoy people and their pets and are the only known means of transmission of such diseases as yellow fever and dengue. Mosquitoes develop in various types of aquatic habitats, including standing water near homes (bird baths, flower pots, gutters, etc.). Adults lay their eggs on or near water, develop in water and eventually fly away as blood-feeding adults.

Mosquito control near the home can be accomplished best by eliminating any source of water where adult mosquitoes can lay eggs. To reduce the number of adult mosquitoes, mow tall grass and trim bushes where they may hide. Use repellents and protective clothing to avoid mosquito bites. Use aerosol sprays for adult mosquito control indoors. Outdoor insecticide use – which controls adult mosquitoes or larval mosquitoes in bodies of water – should be done by professionals. They'll know the best products to use and have the proper application equipment and experience to do a job safely and effectively.

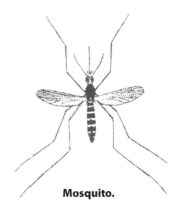

Mosquito.

Biting flies – The stable fly, horse and deer flies, black flies, biting midges and eye gnats are pests because of the painful bites they inflict when they suck blood. The stable fly looks like a house fly but has mouthparts adapted for blood feeding. They're common near livestock operations, stables and kennels.

Horse and deer flies feed on livestock, wildlife and humans. They range in size from 0.25 inch (some deer flies) to 1.25 inches (some horse flies) and breed in moist or wet areas. Females inflict painful bites.

Black flies are small (one-sixteenth to 0.25 inch long) and are usually black in color with a humped back. The females inflict a painful bite, sometimes making recreational areas unusable. They're associated with fast-running water.

Biting midges are small (one-sixteenth of an inch long), dark-colored flies that are associated with marshy conditions. The females are persistent feeders that constitute a serious economic problem in resort and recreational areas.

Eye gnats are small (less than one-sixteenth of an inch long) flies that come to the eyes of livestock, pets and humans. They're not blood feeders but feed on secretions. They're found in suburban areas bordering woods or fields, especially near livestock.

Biting fly control (prevention) is best accomplished by wearing clothing the flies can't bite through and by using personal repellents (DEET is most effective). Managing biting flies in their outdoor environment should be left to professionals because of the complex and often widespread nature of the environments they inhabit.

Bed bugs - These bugs (the common bed bug is the most frequent one) are an important human parasite because they depend on us for dispersal (suitcases and other personal belongings) and are found living and developing close to us in apartment complexes, hotels and other places visited by us (buses, cruise ships, etc.). The bugs lay their eggs and hide in cracks and crevices, especially near beds, and come out at night to feed on the sleeping host. Under favorable conditions,

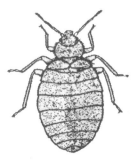

Bed bug.

they develop from egg to adult in one month. Adults are about 0.25 inch long and brown. Fecal and bloody spots can be seen on sheets and other surfaces on which they crawl. Although they don't transmit diseases, welts and itching associated with their bites can be annoying.

Prevention is the best control. When traveling, use a flash light to inspect mattress seams and cracks and crevices in headboards and bed frames. Don't stay in an infested room, and once at home, inspect and launder (hot, soapy water) all items taken out of the suitcase and carry bags. Inspect suitcases thoroughly. Be careful about bringing secondhand items (clothing, furniture, etc.) home with you.

Bed bugs can be difficult to eliminate once an infestation occurs. Thus, hiring a professional pest control service is essential to develop an integrated pest control program that uses nonchemical and insecticide treatments for successful control.

Fleas - Fleas are small (less than 0.25 inch long), reddish-brown, wingless insects with the ability to jump a foot or more if disturbed. They're usually associated with pets and their resting/bedding locations, emerging from these locations as blood-feeding adults to feed on pets or humans, mate and lay eggs to start a new generation.

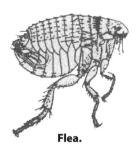

Flea.

The cat flea is the most common flea on cats and dogs (and humans) and isn't associated with any disease generally. Adult fleas can take several blood meals per day, usually in the ankle region of humans. Itching and scratching is the most serious problem associated with flea bites.

Flea control should be directed at cats and dogs to kill adult fleas and breeding sites (pet resting and sleeping areas) in and around the home to eliminate young and adult fleas. Pest shampoos, flea collars, etc., are available to rid the pet of fleas. The control of all flea stages in a home is complicated and usually involves thorough treatment(s) by professional pest managers.

Ticks – Ticks are close relatives to insects, are blood feeding parasites of many warm-blooded animals and are second only to mosquitoes as important vectors of disease (Lyme disease and spotted fever). Ticks frequently encountered by humans include the American dog tick, lone star tick, black-legged or deer tick and brown dog tick. The brown dog tick is the only one commonly found indoors. All others are associated with weedy, brushy and wooded areas where rodents and other wild animals (and occasionally humans) serve as blood meals for these ticks.

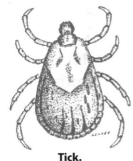
Tick.

Adult ticks are wingless, oval, have eight legs and are large enough to see with the naked eye (usually one-eighth to 0.25 inch long). People who spend time in recreational areas, weedy fields and woods often come in contact with ticks and become a blood meal.

Preventing exposure to ticks by avoiding tick-infested areas, wearing protective clothing, and using insect repellents (such as DEET) is the best way to avoid being bitten. Overgrown or weedy areas close to human activity and along hiking trails should be mowed or cut back to reduce tick encounters. Insecticides are available for use in tick control (including the indoor brown dog tick), but a professional should be contacted to do this work because tick control is often complex. Shampoos, collars, etc., are available for use on pets for tick control.

Lice - The head louse is the most common louse of concern in the U.S., although the pubic and body louse are problems occasionally. Head lice occur commonly on children, where they take blood meals daily by clinging to the base of hair shafts near the scalp. This results in itching and scratching, which can lead to a secondary infection. Children become infested by direct contact with other children and when hats, combs, brushes, coats, and sleeping or resting areas are shared.

Adult head lice are about one-eighth inch long, grayish, flattened and wingless. Their legs are claw-like, designed to hold onto hair. Lice eggs, commonly referred to as nits, are whitish, oval and the size of a pinhead. They're attached to the hair near the scalp. Head lice aren't found anywhere else on the body, aren't found on any other animal, and don't survive off a human host for more than a day or so.

The most effective control is prevention. If head lice are found at your child's school, inspect your children regularly. Start at the back of the neck and work forward, parting the hair to examine the base of the hairs

 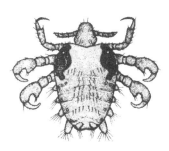

Human louse (left) and crab louse.

for head lice and nits. Watch for scratching and restlessness. Look for a black dandruff (louse feces) on your child's pillow. Encourage your children not to share combs, brushes, scarves and pillows.

Physical removal of lice and nits with a louse comb (available at pharmacies) is useful. Hair brushes, hats and other items closely associated with the child's head should be washed in hot, soapy water. Insecticide shampoos and other formulations are available over the counter, as well as physician prescribed. Louse eggs usually aren't killed by these treatments, so repeat applications may be necessary (follow label directions carefully).

Louse control on humans is a medical procedure. Thus, the only role a professional pest control company can play in louse control is educational, and they're usually happy to provide information about lice and their control.

Chiggers – The most frequently encountered, blood-feeding mite on humans is the chigger. Their bites cause red welts and severe itching. They're small and generally not visible to the naked eye. They usually inhabit areas where grass and weeds are overgrown and are found

Chigger.

throughout the U.S. but are more serious pests in the South.

Only the larval stage (newly emerged from the egg) feeds on blood, usually rodents and other wild animals; but if a human walks through an infested area, the chigger will attack readily. Chiggers almost embed themselves in the skin of the host, inject saliva into the wound that mixes with tissue and body fluids, which then are sucked. The feeding activity causes welts and intense itching for most people. Chiggers don't transmit disease in the U.S., but secondary infection occurs from scratching.

When going into potentially infested areas, professionals and homeowners should wear protective clothing and use personal repellents (DEET). Grass, weeds and brushy areas should be kept mowed or trimmed. When insecticide treatments are needed, it's best to contact a professional.

If exposed to chiggers, bathing in hot, soapy water as quickly as possible can reduce the number of bites. After welts appear, little can be done other than using local anesthetics to lessen itching.

Spiders - Some spiders can bite. The black widow and brown recluse are serious venomous spiders. Most spiders are beneficial predators and become pests as nuisances only when they're around or in buildings. Read more about spiders and their control in the chapter about occasional invaders.

There are many plant feeding bugs and predatory insects that will bite defensively (if humans disturb them). They're not blood feeders and are considered pests of buildings (usually outdoors in the landscape) occasionally.

Biting pests can be difficult, and even dangerous, to control. Call a professional pest control company to get the job done right.

Black widow spider (left) and brown recluse spider.

BITING PESTS

Many insects and their close relatives are pests because they bite. Such insects include mosquitoes, bed bugs, fleas, lice and biting flies, such as black, stable and deer flies. Close relatives to insects that bite include ticks, some mites such as chiggers and some spiders. Most of these pests bite because they need blood to grow and reproduce. Some of them may transmit disease organisms in the process of taking a blood meal. A few of the pests that bite – such as black widow and brown recluse spiders that inject venom into intruders that disturb them – do so as a defense mechanism. By far, the most important group of pests that bite are blood feeders involved in disease transmission, not only in man but pets and livestock as well. This focus will be on the biting pests of humans.

MOSQUITOES

Mosquitoes irritate and annoy people and can transmit many disease-causing organisms to humans. They're the only known means of transmission of such diseases as malaria, encephalitis, yellow fever, dengue and filariasis. All of these diseases, with the exception of filariasis, have been common in the U.S. Extensive control measures by

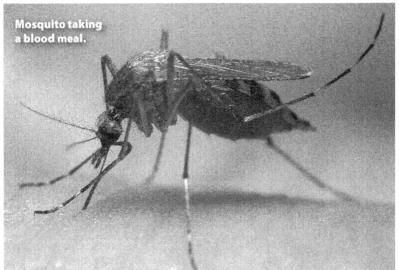

Mosquito taking a blood meal.

U.S. public health officials have almost eliminated all but encephalitis (such as West Nile virus) as a problem. However, mosquitoes are severe pests because they annoy people.

Mosquitoes always develop in water, but the type of breeding place varies with the species of mosquito. Common breeding places are flood waters, woodland pools, slow-moving streams, ditches, marshes and around the edges of lakes. Mosquitoes also can develop in tree cavities, rain barrels, fish ponds, bird baths, old tires, tin cans, guttering and catch basins – anything that holds water.

Mosquitoes have four distinct stages during their life cycle: egg, larva, pupa and adult. They can complete this life cycle in as quickly as eight to 10 days, depending on food availability, weather conditions and species.

Mosquito eggs can be laid individually, in clusters on the surface of water or individually in dry locations that are subject to periodic flooding. Some mosquito eggs can remain dormant in dry conditions for months.

Mosquito eggs hatch into larvae called wrigglers, which are seldom more than 0.5 inch long. Wrigglers have a small head, an enlarged thorax (center body section) and a long cylindrical abdomen. Wrigglers live in the water, and most of them feed on microscopic plants, animals and organic debris suspended in the water.

Mosquito pupae don't feed and spend most of their time at the water surface and tend to move only when disturbed. They're sometimes called tumblers because of their tumbling motion when disturbed in the water.

Adult males usually emerge from their pupal cases first and wait near the hatching point to mate with the females as they emerge. Most females must have a blood meal before they can lay fertile eggs. The adult female is the only stage that feeds on blood, which is a necessary source of protein for egg formation.

Adult mosquitoes typically live for a week to a month. Depending on the species, adult travel can be from 200 yards to longer than a mile from the breeding site. The ability of some species to travel long distances can create problems when managing a mosquito problem.

There are more than 150 species of mosquitoes in the U.S. Each species will differ in its biology, behavior, preferred breeding sites and proper identification. There are general control measure for use in backyards, but any long-term solution will require the expertise of a professional.

Control – The most effective control for mosquitoes around the home is to prevent them from breeding by eliminating egg-laying and larval development sites. This means eliminating standing water by disposing of old tires, cans, buckets and bottles that collect and hold rain water. Drain water from flower pots, birdbaths, rain gutters, pet dishes, etc., at least once a week. Empty plastic wading pools weekly and store indoors when not in use. Drain and fill stagnant pools, puddles, ditches, and swampy places around the property. Keep margins of ponds clear of vegetation and stock garden ponds with top-feeding minnows. Repair leaky pipes and faucets. Remove tree stumps that may hold water.

To reduce or prevent adult mosquitoes, mow tall grass and trim bushes and other vegetation where they might rest or hide. Keep window and door screens in good repair and make sure they seal around the frames. Mosquito species that are active at dusk can be avoided by scheduling outdoor activities at other times. Wear long, loose-fitting clothes to avoid mosquito bites.

When the female mosquito bites, histamine is released by our body at the site of the bite. This causes itching that can be relieved by a topical applied antihistamine. Check label directions for proper use. If an infection develops, seek proper medical attention.

Repellents are useful when protecting against mosquito bites. Products that contain DEET are the most reliable. Read and follow label directions carefully, especially when selecting a product for use on children. There are granular repellents available for use on lawns that provide some protection from mosquito bites.

Insecticide use outdoors to control adult mosquitoes, or larval mosquitoes in bodies of water, should be done by professionals because they'll know the best products to use and have the proper application equipment.

Space sprays and aerosols can be used to control adult mosquitoes indoors. Use these materials as directed on the label.

Mosquito transmitted diseases – Following transmission by an infected mosquito, West Nile Virus (WNV) multiplies in the person's blood system and can interfere with normal central nervous system functioning. It has been in the U.S. for more than 10 years and has moved from the East Coast across the country. More than 4,000 cases having been confirmed. More than 40 states have confirmed cases. WNV flu-like symptoms can develop three to 15 days after a bite from an infected mosquito. Severe disease is possible in older individuals or people with weakened immune systems, which can lead to encephalitis (inflammation of the brain), meningitis or paralysis. If you live in an area where WNV has been detected in birds, mosquitoes or humans and you experience flu-like symptoms, consult a doctor.

Mosquitoes feed on most warm-blooded animals, including dogs. Some mosquito species play a role in transmitting heartworm in dogs. During times of high mosquito infestation, keep pets inside the house or in a screened-in kennel or porch area. Avoid walking your pet during prime mosquito biting times. Check with your veterinarian for preventive medications.

BLOOD-SUCKING FLIES

There are numerous flies that will take blood from humans, have painful bites and disrupt outdoor activities. Other than their irritating bites, they generally aren't a public health concern.

The stable fly, similar in appearance to the house fly, can be distinguished by the long, pointed proboscis (feeding tube) that extends in front of the head. It's commonly found in association with livestock operations and stables, as well as along the seashore and shoreline of lakes and near dog kennels. Adults lay their eggs in decaying hay, straw and fermenting weeds, grass and seaweeds. In some areas, they're called biting beach flies and dog flies. Males and females use the proboscis to pierce the skin of a host and suck blood. The bite is painful, and outdoor human activity might be curtailed when many are around.

Horse and deer flies are pests of livestock and other domestic animals, and occasionally humans. Several hundred species are found in the U.S. Adults range in size from 0.25 inch to 1.25 inches long. They breed in moist or wet areas. Only females feed on blood. They use scissors-like mouthparts to inflict painful bites. Males feed on nectar, honeydew or other liquids. They're strong fliers and can be a serious nuisance in recreational areas.

Black flies, also known as buffalo gnats and humpbacked flies, are small (one-sixteenth to 0.25 inch long) and usually black. The area behind the head is humped typically. Females suck blood causing a painful bite, intense itching, and local swelling and inflammation. They're associated with fast-running water and laying their egg masses on stones or vegetation. They're a severe nuisance, often making recreational areas useless if the temperature is warmer.

Biting midges, also known as no-see-ums, punkies, black gnats and sand flies, are dark-colored, very small (about one-sixteenth of an inch long), and slender with blood sucking mouthparts. They're associated with marshy (salt and fresh water) conditions where eggs are laid in mud; plant debris; or in damp, rotten holes in trees. The females have sharp piercing mouthparts and are voracious feeders that aren't frightened. They're small enough to go unnoticed until they begin to pierce the skin. The bites can take longer than a week to heal. When many are present, people are forced to stay indoors. They constitute a significant economic problem in resort and recreational areas.

Eye gnats are small (less than one-sixteenth of an inch long) and are called such because they're frequently attracted to the eyes – as well as mucous and sebaceous secretions, pus and blood – of the victim. Eye gnats approach their human host quietly, usually alighting some distance from the feeding site. They crawl over the skin or resort to intermittent flying and alighting, thus adding to the annoyance of the host. They're extraordinarily persistent and, if brushed away, will return quickly to continue engorging themselves. They're nonbiting, but their mouthparts possess spines capable of producing small skin lesions.

Eye gnats can be found infesting just about any urban or industrial area but are more likely to be found in suburban areas bordering woods or fields, especially near livestock. The larvae develop in various materials such as decaying vegetation and animal matter. Eye gnats are bothersome to livestock and are suspected vectors of diseases such as conjunctivitis, yaws and bovine mastitis.

Control – Only a few of the biting flies will come indoors, but good screens on windows and doors work well against those that enter. Flying insect aerosols will kill the few that might get indoors.

Given the habitats occupied by blood feeding flies, outdoor protection from them means wearing clothing the flies can't bite through and using repellents that contain DEET. Read and follow label directions carefully.

Managing flies in their outdoor environments should be left to professionals because of the complex and often widespread nature of the environments they inhabit.

BED BUGS

There's been an increase in bed-bug problems during the past 10 years. These blood-feeding insects were all but eliminated from the U.S. after World War II by the insecticide DDT. These pests remained prevalent in other parts of the world, and have made a comeback in hotels, motels, apartment complexes, shelters, homes and modes of transport (trains, buses, cruise ships, airlines, etc.) recently. International travel, immigration, and the lack of good residual insecticides are factors suspected for the recurrence.

A mature bed bug is brownish, wingless and about 0.25 inch long. The common bed bug is the species most adapted to living with humans, although in the absence of a human host, it will feed on pets, birds and other animals. The sole food of bed bugs is the blood of warm-blooded animals. After feeding, the bug's body enlarges, becoming longer and much less flattened. Bed bugs, like most biting pests, have piercing-sucking mouthparts that enable them to pierce the skin and suck blood.

Bed bug eggs are white and small (about one-thirty-seconds of

Bed bug life cycle, from egg to adult.

Photo courtesy of, and copyrighted by, Gene White, pmimages@earthlink.net

an inch long), and under normal room conditions and with regular blood meals, a female will lay several eggs per day and several hundred eggs during her lifetime. Eggs are coated with a sticky substance that adheres them to objects on which they're deposited. The eggs hatch in one to two weeks, and the tiny white nymphs find a host and begin to feed. Bed bugs reach maturity after five molts, which, under favorable conditions, can occur in as little as one month. Cooler temperatures or limited access to a blood meal causes variation in the development rate. Nymphs and adults can survive months without feeding.

Bed bugs generally hide in cracks and crevices during normal daylight hours. They enter such areas easily because of their extremely flattened bodies. Typical hiding places are in the folds and tufts of mattresses, coils of springs, cracks and hollow posts of bedsteads, and upholstery of chairs and sofas (where they will be close to the human host). However, they aren't restricted to these places. In heavy infestations, bed bugs frequently are found in places such as behind loose wallpaper, behind pictures on the wall, under door and window casings, behind baseboards, and even in light fixtures or medicine cabinets.

Frequently, even when the bed bugs can't be found easily, their hiding places can be located by looking for the spots of fecal material they often leave in easily visible places. Fecal spots and the bloody spots left on sheets and pillowcases when engorged bugs are crushed serve as sure signs of infestation.

Bed bugs normally feed at night, but sometimes they'll feed during the day. They usually bite while people are sleeping, and then return to their hiding area. The human host doesn't know they're being bitten because the bed bug injects an anesthetic into the bite area. Many people who are bitten develop welts and irritation (similar to other insect bites), while other people might have no reaction. Antihistamines and corticosteroids will reduce allergic reactions, and antiseptic or antibiotic ointments will prevent infection. Though not known to transmit diseases, bed bugs can reduce the quality of life by causing discomfort, sleeplessness, anxiety and embarrassment.

Control – Prevention is the best control. In hotels and other boarding locations, be careful to inspect cracks and crevices in headboards, seams in mattresses and box springs, and sheets and bed spreads for signs of bed bugs. If bed bugs or their signs (dark fecal spots or bloodstains) are found, move to another room in another area of the building. Keep suitcases and personal items off the floor and on a luggage stand, tabletop or other hard surface. Inspect items as they're removed from a suitcase at home, and launder or dry clean these items to keep bed bugs from gaining entry into new locations.

Used beds, couches, and other furnishings should be closely inspected before bringing them home. If secondhand items can be laundered or placed in a dryer, bringing bed bugs home is reduced greatly. Items from curbside, trash piles and landfills should never be brought home.

Hotels, apartment buildings and other places where many people come and go need to have preventive inspections by tenants, housekeeping staff or pest management personnel. Early stage infestations can be detected and controlled before an infestation becomes established and spreads.

Bed bugs can be difficult to eliminate once an infestation occurs, so hiring a knowledgeable, experienced professional is essential to successful control. Experienced companies know where to look for bed bugs and can develop an integrated program (using nonchemical controls such as vacuuming and heat treatments) and insecticide treatments.

OTHER BUGS CLOSELY RELATED TO BED BUGS

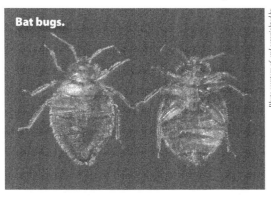

Bat bugs.

Photo courtesy of, and copyrighted by: Gene White, pmimages@earthlink.net

Bat bugs are pests of bats that roost and nest in houses that will feed on humans when bats leave their roosting and nesting areas. They look like the common bed bug, so a professional pest control company should be called to seal all openings so bats can't re-enter the home. Then an insecticide application can be made to eliminate the bat bugs.

Other similar bugs, such as swallow, pigeon and poultry bugs, are associated with birds nesting in homes. Bird proofing the home is the first step, then insecticides can be used to control the bugs.

A number of bugs (the bloodsucking conenose, masked hunter and wheel bug) can inflict painful bites on people. Most of these species are predaceous on other insects, but some also are adapted to blood feeding. They're vectors of the organism that causes Chagas disease, which is significant in Latin and South America. The elimination of bugs, their harborage areas, and the harborage areas of rodents and birds that host the bugs are essential for control. A professional service usually is needed.

FLEAS

Adult fleas are small (shorter than 0.25 inch), wingless insects that are dark reddish-brown. They have laterally compressed bodies enabling them to move easily through body hairs or carpet nap. They have three pairs of legs with the back pair modified for jumping and piercing-sucking mouthparts that penetrate the skin of the host and suck blood.

Two adult fleas.

Photo courtesy of, and copyrighted by, Gene White, pmimages@earthlink.net

Flea larvae are small, active, maggot-like creatures that emerge from light-colored eggs that can barely be seen. Because flea eggs aren't attached to the host animal, those laid on the host will fall off and hatch on the ground or in bedding, carpets, etc. Slender, white, legless larvae emerge from the eggs in a few days to scavenge on dried blood, adult flea feces and other organic debris. In a couple weeks, the grown larvae change to pupae, which, in turn, emerge as adults within a week or two. The adults immediately search for animals (including humans) on which to feed.

Pet owners returning from vacation often find themselves besieged by hungry adult fleas. Homeowners or new tenants moving into vacant homes or apartments where previous occupants had dogs or cats also might experience an adult flea explosion.

Fleas – some species that are parasites of rodents – are important carriers of disease such as plague or typhus. However, the most common pest flea is the cat flea, which is found in association with pet cats and dogs in and around homes. It's generally not associated with any diseases. Itching and scratching are the most common hazards associated with adult fleas and their bites. Bites on humans usually occur on the ankles and calves. One flea may take many blood meals each day.

Control – Flea control should be directed at cats and dogs to kill adult fleas and breeding sites in and around homes to eliminate young and adult fleas. Cat flea breeding sites include in and around those areas where pets are active and where they sleep and rest, such as pet bedding, carpeting, upholstered furniture, crawl spaces under homes, etc.

Flea control often is difficult because it involves killing fleas on pets as well as in the home. Pets can be treated with insecticide sprays, dusts, foams, shampoos, collars, feed additives, spot-on treatments and pills. Check with veterinarians for specific products and formulations.

Always read and follow insecticide label directions. Don't use any insecticide on a pet unless the label specifically states it can be used on that pet species. Follow restrictions such as the age of the animal to be treated and precautions such as not treating sick animals or using insecticides in conjunction with other medications.

Other products, such as pet collars equipped with electronic sounding devices and combs for mechanical removal of fleas, are available for flea control. These devices haven't been proven to repel or kill fleas and aren't recommended. Also, brewer's yeast, B-complex vitamins and garlic aren't effective flea repellents.

Control in homes and other buildings is complicated and might require more than one insecticide, as well as multiple treatments, especially if the infestation is in multiple areas of the home and involves numerous flea bites each day. A professional pest control company should be contacted to handle most flea infestations.

Before treating for flea control, it's advisable to vacuum the premises thoroughly, especially pet resting areas, to remove developing fleas. Be sure to dispose the vacuum bag after vacuuming. If bedding, rugs, etc., can be laundered in hot soapy water, all flea stages will be killed. The entire house should be vacuumed, especially carpets, under furniture, in cracks and crevices, along walls and upholstered furniture. Some pest control companies will provide a vacuum service.

A professional pest control company will have numerous insecticides available to use for fleas. Spray formulations will be applied as a light mist to infested areas. Dusts will be used in protected areas that can't be reached with sprays. Insect growth regulators will be used to prevent flea eggs from hatching and larval fleas from pupating into adults that reproduce. Often a product containing an insecticide to kill adults and an insect growth regulator to keep flea eggs from hatching and larval fleas from becoming biting adults will be used. Multiple applications might be needed to kill fleas in well-protected areas, including outdoor areas frequented by pets.

TICKS

Ticks are close relatives to insects and are well-known bloodsucking external parasites of humans, pets, livestock and wild animals. They're vectors of various disease-causing organisms that infect humans and other animals and are second only to mosquitoes in public health importance.

More than 90 species of ticks are found in the U.S. The most frequently encountered outdoor species is the American dog tick, also known as the eastern wood tick. The lone star tick, and more recently, the deer tick (also known as the black-legged tick and the Lyme disease tick) also might be found occasionally in outdoor, wooded areas. Another species, the brown dog tick, sometimes might become a problem indoors, primarily in association with dogs.

Ticks are wingless as adults and possess a flat (except when filled with blood), oval body region. Adults have eight legs, although some immature forms have only six legs

An American dog tick.

Photo courtesy of, and copyrighted by, Gene White, pmimages@earthlink.net

(as do insects). Most people encounter adult, female ticks outdoors in fields and wooded areas, where ticks rest on grassy or bushy vegetation until a host (deer, livestock, dogs, humans) comes in contact with them. Ticks attach to the host and take a blood meal during a period of a few days to a week. If the tick is infected with a disease pathogen, it might transmit the pathogen to the human host during the feeding period.

The American dog tick is found in woods, grassy fields and other areas of wild vegetation. Adults are dark brown to black, with short, rounded mouthparts and white markings on the top side. In the spring and early summer, adult ticks are numerous along paths used by animals, feeding on many wild animals, as well as dogs and humans. This type of tick is the primary vector of spotted fever (also known as Rocky Mountain Spotted Fever) in the U.S. Symptoms start soon after the tick bite and include fever, chills, headache and muscle aches. A rash appears usually one to three days after the onset of the fever, spreading from wrists and ankles to the rest of the body. Treatment with broad spectrum antibiotics usually will cure the illness.

The lone star tick also is found in wooded areas, especially where deer are established. Adults have long mouthparts and a distinct white spot on the top side. The tick feeds readily on various animals (including humans and ground feeding birds) and is most active generally in the spring and summer. The lone star tick isn't considered an important vector of diseases.

The black-legged tick (deer tick) also is common in wooded areas occupied by deer. Adults are small and dark brown in color, with no white markings on the top side. Deer, dogs, humans and birds are common blood hosts for this tick. The black-legged tick is the primary vector of Lyme disease caused by a spirochete (bacterium) it carries. Early symptoms of Lyme disease can be mild and overlooked. Flu-like symptoms, chills, fever and fatigue are experienced often. A diagnostic symptom is a red, expanding rash (sometimes resembling a bull's-eye – circular with brighter red outer margins and a partially clear center). More than one rash might appear. They don't always occur at the site of the tick bite – the rash might occur anywhere on the body. More severe symptoms might occur weeks to years later in the form of severe headaches, arthritis and nervous system or cardiac abnormalities, which result from the spread of the spirochete to various parts of the body. Thus, early detection and treatment are most important to avoid the debilitating effects of the disease. Personal protection and prevention of tick exposure are discussed later under tick control.

The brown dog tick differs from other ticks because it feeds primarily on dogs, and it's common indoors in and around pet bedding. After feeding, the tick drops off a dog and hides in any available cracks and crevices. Because of their strong tendency to climb, they're often found behind cove moldings and window frames and often are seen crawling up walls and curtains.

Control – Preventing exposure to ticks involves avoiding tick-infested areas and wearing protective clothing. Stay on established trails and avoid brushing against vegetation. Wear light-colored clothing (so ticks can be seen more easily), long pants and long-sleeved shirts. Tuck in your shirt, and pull your socks over your pant cuffs.

Use an insect repellent such as DEET or permethrin and apply it according to label directions. Children formulations of these repellents are available. Occasionally, check yourself and your children for ticks, emphasizing the head and neck, groin, underarm and waistline areas. Warm, soapy showers after coming indoors will help remove ticks that have not yet attached to the skin. Inspect pets after they've been outdoors, and remove ticks.

The safest and most effective way to remove an attached tick is to use forceps or tweezers to grasp the tick as close to the skin as possible, pulling gently and steadily until the tick releases its hold. Take care not to squeeze, crush or puncture the tick because body fluid can enter the tick-bite wound. Wear latex-type gloves to avoid contact with any tick fluids. After removing the tick, disinfect the attachment site with warm soapy water and rubbing alcohol. Consult a physician immediately if a rash or flu-like symptoms develop. Don't attempt to remove a tick with chemicals, medications or by applying heat. The use of these methods can cause the tick to regurgitate body fluids into the wound.

To control ticks outdoors, keep overgrown and thick vegetation cut and cleared in areas where ticks occur. Eliminate or at least cut back unwanted vegetation around yards, along the edge of woods and along paths in woods leading into the yard. Remove leaf litter at the edge of woods and in flowerbeds. Insecticides that are labeled for tick control can be applied according to the directions on the label. Be sure to keep children and pets off treated areas until they're dry. A professional pest control company will have the knowledge and equipment for making these treatments safely and effectively.

Indoor tick (usually the brown dog tick) control is difficult because there are so many possible hiding places and tick eggs might hatch throughout a five-month period. More than one treatment might be needed, so a professional pest control company can handle indoor tick control the best.

Tick control products (shampoos and collars) are available for pets, and most veterinarians can apply tick removal products to infested pets. Pest control companies can't perform pet treatments.

HUMAN LICE

Head lice are blood-sucking nuisances that cause social embarrassment. In the U.S., the head louse is the most important because of its common occurrence, especially among children. Fortunately, they don't transmit disease. Head lice inject saliva into their host as they feed to prevent blood from clotting. This results in itching, which is bothersome, but more importantly, can result in infection. Anyone can become infested through direct contact with an infested person or indirectly when infested items such as hats, scarves, coats, combs and brushes are shared. Thus, school-age children are at risk especially.

Other human lice include the pubic and body louse, which aren't as important in the U.S. as they are in other parts of the world.

Adult head lice are about one-eighth-inch long, grayish, flattened and wingless. Their legs are claw-like, designed to hold onto hair. Lice eggs, commonly referred to as nits, are whitish, oval and the size of a pinhead (one-thirtieth of an inch long). They're attached to hair near the scalp. Nits found further than 0.5 inch from the scalp almost always have hatched or died.

Head lice live in close association with humans (young children) and are found on the head where they take blood meals daily. Head lice cling to hair shafts near the scalp, often on the back of heads. Eggs hatch after five to 10 days. Young lice are mobile (but can't jump or fly) and molt three times (each after a blood meal), developing into adults in about three weeks. Adults mate and lay eggs after seven days and live for about four weeks. They don't survive off a human host for more than a day or two, and they won't feed on animals.

Control – The most effective control is prevention. For example, if head lice are reported from your child's school, inspect your children regularly. Watch for scratching and restlessness. A black dandruff might be visible on their shoulders and pillows. When inspecting your child's head, start at the back of the neck and work forward, parting the hair to examine the base of the hair shaft for head lice and nits. Children can help prevent infestations by not sharing combs, brushes, clothes, scarves and pillows.

Physical removal of lice and nits with a nit comb or cat flea comb is useful. Combs are available from pharmacies. Additionally, all infested items (hair brushes, hats, pillow cases and other bedding) must be sanitized in hot, soapy water. Insecticide shampoos and other formulations are available over the counter, as well as physician prescribed, for louse control. Apply these products specifically as labeled. Louse eggs typically aren't killed by these treatments, so repeat applications might be needed.

Home remedies such as vinegar, rubbing alcohol, olive oil, mayonnaise, melted butter and petroleum jelly aren't effective, and some are difficult to remove from the hair.

Patience and persistence are key to removing head lice from a human host. Reread the product directions to make sure it's used properly. Check all family members for head lice, and treat them if they're infested. If you continue to see head lice after two applications and don't feel you're using an effective product, switch to a product containing a different active ingredient. Follow labels carefully, and don't apply the product any more frequently than recommended. Always keep the individual's safety as a top propriety.

Because louse control is a medical problem, professional pest control companies can play no role in their control, other than providing educational information.

CHIGGERS

Some mites are blood feeders. A chigger is a tiny parasitic mite and is the most problematic blood-feeding mite humans encounter. It attacks people, birds and other animals, causing red welts and severe itching. Chiggers generally aren't visible to the naked eye unless they're completely engorged with blood. They're found in all states but are a much more serious pest in the southern states. They usually inhabit areas where grass or weeds are overgrown.

Eggs are laid on the soil, and after hatching, the larvae crawl about over vegetation until a suitable host approaches. Larvae crawl onto people and generally move upward until reaching a place where clothing is tight against the skin, such as around the ankles, waist and armpits. They usually remain on the host for two to four days and then drop off to become nymphs and later adults. Only the larvae are blood feeders.

Chiggers feed by piercing the skin and injecting a fluid (saliva) that mixes with tissue and body fluids sucked up for food. This results in irritation (red welts) and intense itching with some people being more susceptible than others. Secondary infections might occur as a result of scratching. Chiggers aren't known to transmit disease in the U.S.

Control – If you enter chigger-infested areas (woods or fields, parks, campgrounds, etc.), personal protection can be gained by using repellents such as DEET. Follow all directions and precautions when using repellents.

By keeping grass, weeds and brush mowed, chigger prevention and control can be accomplished. Rodent populations, on which chigger populations build, also can be reduced by mowing. Insecticide sprays and dusts also are available for treating vegetation where these mites occur. A professional pest control company is best equipped and has the knowledge and experience to make these treatments.

If exposed to chiggers, bathing in hot, soapy water as soon after exposure as possible will reduce the number of bites. Once welts appear, little can be done, although a physician can prescribe local anesthetics to lessen irritation and itching.

SPIDERS AND OTHER BITING PESTS

Some spiders will bite, and some that bite are venomous (black widow, brown recluse, etc.). Because many spiders don't bite and generally are nuisance pests when they get indoors, they're discussed in the chapter about occasional invaders.

8

STINGING PESTS

SUMMARY: *STINGING PESTS AND THEIR CONTROL*

Stinging insects mainly belong to the group that consists of wasps, bees and ants, although most ants don't sting. There also are a few moth larvae (caterpillars) covered with stinging or nettling hairs that produce a stinging sensation and a temporary but painful rash when the caterpillars contact the skin. Scorpions – closely related to insects but with four pairs of legs – also will sting. The most problematic stingers are the social wasps and bees – social indicating they live in colonies. They become serious pests in and around parks and recreational areas, as well as homes and other structures. Stinging ants also are social insects. Most ants don't sting, and the ones that do are found only in certain parts of the U.S.

Stinging pests are encountered from time to time, especially during warmer periods of the year. All bees and wasps, and some ants, are beneficial as pollinators of crops and other plants and predators of other insects and should be conserved unless they constitute a stinging threat in areas of human activity. Colonies found in seldom-used areas or high in trees that aren't a threat to people should be left alone.

Controlling bees, wasps and stinging ants in and around buildings and recreational areas might be difficult and possibly hazardous. Some people are hypersensitive to their venom, and others are afraid to be stung.

Although all female bees and wasps are capable of stinging (males are harmless), only the social species aggressively do so when defending their colonies. Solitary species rarely sting, typically only if they're

mishandled. Accordingly, it's important to
distinguish social bees (honey and bumble
bees) and social wasps (paper wasps,
hornets, yellow jackets) from their solitary
relatives such as carpenter bees, cicada
killer, mud daubers, etc.

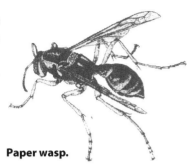

Social bees and wasps exist in
colonies associated with an elaborate
nest. Colonies are recognized easily
by the great amount of activity in and out of a nest site. Solitary bees
and wasps, although sometimes existing in aggregations, build a small
burrow in which a female raises a few young by herself. Such females
don't defend their solitary nests.

Paper wasp.

Bees and wasps can be distinguished by their appearance and the
type of nest they build. Almost all bees gather pollen to feed their young
and possess robust, hairy bodies with flattened, hairy hind legs to assist
in pollen transport. In contrast, wasps capture insects to feed their
young and are much less hairy and have a slender body. They also lack
the flattened, hairy pollen basket on the hind leg.

Wasps and most bees have annual colonies that last for only one year.
The colony dies in the fall, and only the newly produced queens survive
the winter (under loose bark, under siding, etc.). Queens become active
the following spring when temperatures warm and begin searching for
favorable nesting sites to construct new nests. They don't reuse old nests.

Honey bees are perennial insects with colonies that survive more
than one year. Honey bees form a cluster when hive temperatures
approach 57°F. As the temperature declines, the cluster of bees becomes
more compact. Bees inside this mass consume honey and generate heat
so those in the cluster don't freeze. As long as honey is available in the
cluster, a strong colony can withstand temperatures as low as -30°F or
lower for extended periods.

Wasps and bees sting to defend themselves or their colony. Stinging
involves the injection of a protein venom that causes pain and other
reactions. Wasps and bumble bees can sting more than once.

Honey bees have barbs on their stinger, which remain hooked in the
skin. The stinger, which is connected to the digestive system of the bee,

is torn out of the abdomen as the bee attempts to fly away. As a result, the bee soon dies. If you're stung by a honey bee, scratch out the stinger (with its attached venom gland) with your fingernail as soon as possible. Don't try to pull out the stinger between two fingers. Doing so only forces more venom into your skin, causing greater irritation.

Most people have only local reactions to wasp and bee stings, although a few may experience more serious allergic reactions. Local, nonallergic reactions range from burning, itching, redness and tenderness to massive swelling and itching that can last as long as a week. These local reactions can be treated with ice, vinegar, honey, meat tenderizer or commercial topical ointment to relieve the itching. An allergic reaction might include hives or rash, swelling away from the sting site, headache, minor respiratory symptoms and stomach upset. These allergic reactions usually aren't life-threatening and can be treated readily with an antihistamine.

It's rare that a person will suffer a life-threatening, systemic allergic reaction to a bee or wasp sting, which can cause anaphylactic shock (fainting, difficulty breathing, swelling and blockage in the throat) within minutes of being stung. These systemic symptoms are cause for immediate medical attention. People with known systemic allergic reactions to bee or wasp stings should consult with their physician to obtain an Epi-Pen or sting kit to carry with them at all times. The venoms of bees and wasps are different, so having a severe reaction to a wasp sting doesn't mean a person will have the same reaction to a bee sting.

WASP AND BEE CONTROL

The best time of year to control wasps is in the spring after the queen has established a colony and while the colony is still small. It's best to conduct the operation at night, when all the members of the colony have returned, and on cool nights when they're less active. There are ready-to-use aerosol wasp-and-hornet sprays as well as dusts that can be applied directly to the pests or applied into the entrance of ground-nesting wasps and bees. Follow label directions carefully, and if protective equipment is recommended, be

Honeybee.

certain to obtain the equipment before treating. Dust applications usually are best for hidden nests – where wasps or bees can be seen flying back and forth through a crack or hole in the building – because the dust particles will be tracked by the pests into the nest to kill the colony.

Wild honey bees nesting in walls or attics can be a challenge. You not only have to kill the bees (with an insecticide dust preferably), but the honey and honeycomb need to be removed to avoid having honey seeping through ceilings and walls. Protective equipment is essential.

During late summer and fall, wasps and bees (mainly yellowjackets and honey bees) become aggressive scavengers and disrupt outside activities where food and drink is served. One of the best methods of reducing contact with these pests in urban, residential and recreational areas is to keep foods covered until immediately before consuming them. If a wasp or bee flies to your food, wait for it to fly away or gently brush it away. Additionally, remove and handle garbage in such a way to make it less available to foragers. Garbage should be cleaned up regularly, and receptacles should have tight-fitting lids. During periods of heavy pest activity, trash receptacles should be relocated away from open doors or where people congregate. There are traps that can be purchased, but usually not enough of the pests are captured to reduce the population noticeably.

Wasp and bee control can be complicated and dangerous. Contact a professional pest control company for difficult problems.

SOLITARY BEES AND WASPS

The majority of species of bees and wasps aren't social insects and aren't a medical risk. Considered solitary, they include numerous common examples such as carpenter bees, the cicada killer, mud daubers and spider wasps. Solitary bees and wasps don't exist in colonies consisting of numerous workers and almost never sting in defense of their nest. Their venoms cause nothing more than burning pain that persists for a minute or two. No control measures are needed for these bees and wasps.

ANTS AND THEIR CONTROL

Few ants are as important as stingers. Ants of greatest medial risk in the U.S. are the so-called fire ants, all of which are limited to southern, southwestern, and western states. Fire ants can be common in certain habitats, and their colonies typically consist of thousands of workers. If their colony is disturbed, workers can deliver a sting that produces an intense burning sensation, which is the basis for the common name fire ant. Allergic reactions are reported in an estimated 1 percent of individuals who are stung.

Where fire ants are present in large numbers (many mounds), professionals should be called to handle the problem. For the occasional fire ant mound, baits and sprays are available in retail stores. Follow label directions carefully.

In the southwestern U.S., harvester ants commonly inflict stings that are extremely painful, lasting several hours. There are no reports of allergic reactions to these stings, however.

STINGING CATERPILLARS

The bodies of Io moth larvae, saddle back caterpillars and puss caterpillars are covered with stinging or nettling hairs that produce a stinging sensation and temporary rash when the caterpillars come in contact with the skin. These moth larvae feed on various plants and are common during the summer. If caterpillars with spines (nettling hairs) are encountered, it's best to avoid contact with them. If they occur in large numbers, contact a professional pest management company.

SCORPIONS AND THEIR CONTROL

Scorpions are common in the southern and southwestern U.S. Certain species in the desert Southwest can be dangerous, especially to sensitive or allergic individuals. In houses, they're most often found in undisturbed areas, such as closets or storage areas.

Removing hiding areas (rocks, boards, etc.) around and beneath buildings reduces the number of scorpions in an area. Treating indoor and outdoor hiding areas with an appropriately labeled insecticide can be useful when quick control is needed.

Scorpion.

Call a professional pest control company to deal with these dangerous pests. Professionals will have the expertise and equipment to get the job done safely and effectively.

STINGING PESTS

Wasps, bees and ants are the principal stinging insects that can become problems around homes and other structures and recreational areas. Because they're mostly outdoor pests, they occur mainly during warmer periods of the year. Some are pests because people are disturbed by their presence; others are important because their presence in or near inhabited structures represents a health and safety risk to people and pets.

Photo courtesy of, and copyrighted by, Gene White, pmimages@earthlink.net

Face of a bald-faced hornet.

There are a few other stinging pests that are not as important. A few moth larvae (caterpillars) are covered with stinging or nettling hairs that cause discomfort when the caterpillars come in contact with the skin. Scorpions, closely related to insects, also will sting. However, the social wasps and bees, living in colonies, are the most important stingers. Stinging ants also live in social colonies, but only a few ant species sting, and most of them are southern species.

Some wasps are social and live in colonies, while others are solitary. Social bees and wasps develop colonies similar to those of ants. These colonies have a queen that produces all the eggs, workers and brood.

Solitary wasps don't have a colony group. The adult female builds a cell for each egg that she lays and provisions each cell with insect or spider prey for the larva to eat. There are several families of solitary wasps, but the most commonly encountered species include the mud daubers and digger wasps.

As with bees, female wasps have their ovipositor, or egg-laying structure, modified into a stinger. Wasps differ from bees in that most feed their young on animal matter, such as insects, spiders or meat

Yellow jacket colony.

Photo courtesy of, and copyrighted by, Gene White, pmimages@earthlink.net

particles and not on pollen. Bees also have hairy, robust bodies, while wasps tend to have sooth, slender and hairless bodies.

The most common stinging pest species that might harm people directly include social bees and wasps. In contrast to most of our North American ants (except fire ants and harvester ants), these bees and wasps frequently are dangerous because of allergic response to their painful stings.

Stinging behavior is generally a defensive reaction, which can occur when the colony is threatened near the nest area or the individual bee or wasp is trapped and threatened. Foraging wasps of some species are more likely to sting people at some times of the year than others. For example, yellowjacket workers are more apt to sting people during the latter part of their annual cycle, in August or September, for much of the northern region of the U.S.

The stinging process includes injection of rather potent venom. For some species, especially solitary wasps, the venom serves the function of paralyzing or subduing prey, but stings of these wasps aren't dangerous to people. The venom of social wasps and bees is a defensive material used to drive off intruders when the nest is threatened. In addition to causing intense pain, these venoms contain proteinaceous materials that can cause severe allergic reactions in some people. Some people might even go into shock and die of suffocation as their lungs fill with fluid after being stung by a social bee or wasp. Fortunately, the percentage of the population allergic to these venoms is quite low, probably less than 1 percent.

Wasps and bees are considered beneficial insects in most circumstances. Control measures are justified only on the basis of problems these insects might be causing in each instance. Control usually becomes necessary when a nest is located in a poor location relative to the safety, comfort or other interests of people. There will usually be little need to control a hornet nest high in a shade tree or a paper wasp nest on a high, remote eave of a house. In these locations, the colony is unlikely to be disturbed by the activities of people or pets near ground level. However, when social wasps or bees are nesting in locations such as under the front steps of a home, in a school playground, or near the pole supporting a clothesline, an imminent hazard is created, and control is warranted.

WASPS, HORNETS, AND YELLOWJACKETS

These wasps are the most dangerous stingers and are social insects that build nests of a paper-like material, called carton, which is a mixture of wood fibers and the salivary secretions of the female wasps. In northern, temperate regions of the world, including the U.S., new colonies must be founded each year because only the mated queens from the previous year's colonies overwinter. Queens are inactive during the winter, hiding in protected niches under tree bark or in stonewalls, attics and other sheltered places.

In early spring, overwintering queens – called foundresses, since they establish, or found, the new nests and colonies each year – visit exposed wood surfaces, such as raw and weathered wooden fences or siding, or dead tree limbs where the bark has sloughed away. They chew wood fibers and combine them with salivary secretions to form the paper-like carton for nest construction.

Only one egg-producing queen will be present in the colony. The workers protect and maintain the nest, forage for food and water, and care for the immature stages, or brood (i.e., the eggs, larvae, and pupae). Adult males and newly produced queens leave their parent colony during late summer into early fall. The colonies die off, and only the

Paper wasps on their nest.

newly mated queens will find a protected location to overwinter. The following spring, the nest building process begins again.

Paper wasps build simple nests, usually consisting of only one tier or layer of cells, which open downward and aren't covered. Collectively, this layer of cells is called

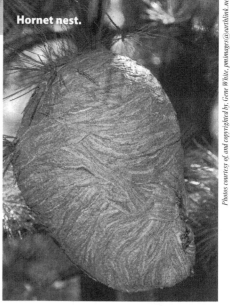

Hornet nest.

a comb. Nests are usually suspended beneath horizontal surfaces, commonly hanging from the eaves of houses and beneath window ledges or porch roofs. Their nests are rather small, rarely more than 6 to 8 inches in diameter, so there are seldom more than 100 to 200 workers on the nest at any one time.

Hornets build some of the most recognized and frightening nests, which are the large, grayish-brown carton structures often seen hanging from a tree or bush. These nests generally resemble large, inverted teardrops or bloated soccer balls. The nest consists of several tiers of carton cells. A continuous paper envelope surrounds the whole nest. There's an opening at the lower tip of the nest. As the nest approaches its final size, the new combs are built below the level of this opening, which will then be positioned on the side of the nest.

There are two species of hornets commonly found in the
U.S. The bald-faced hornet has a black body with white markings
on the body and front of the head. It is about 1.25 –inches long.
The European hornet is 1.5 inches long, brownish with
orange markings.

Yellowjackets are about a half inch long and are so called because
of the extensive yellow markings on the body. Most species typically
build their nests underground, so workers will come and go from the
nest via an earthen tunnel that ends in a hole at the soil surface.

A species that commonly nests in structures has spread widely
throughout the Northeast and Midwest U.S. and is also established in
the western U.S. – Washington, Idaho and California – is the German
yellowjacket, which was introduced from Europe into the northeastern
United States. German yellowjackets are often found nesting in wall
voids, attics, or crawlspaces, and they use an available hole or crack in
the exterior facing of the building as an entry point.

Whether in the ground or a wall void, yellowjacket nests are made
of carton. As many as several thousand workers might be produced in a
colony in one season. The tendency to scavenge at human food sources
puts these yellowjackets in frequent conflict with people in picnic areas,
parks, backyard patios and other outdoor areas. They're troublesome
during the late summer and early fall when the number of workers out
foraging for meat and sugars is at its peak.

Most serious stinging incidents occur when the nest is disturbed.
Foraging workers also will sting, but only when they're accidentally
trapped against the body, such as in the mouth when swallowing a
beverage from a container with a foraging worker in it. Yellowjackets
are considered the most dangerous of the stinging insects because
of their nesting and foraging behavior and the potential for life-
threatening allergic responses in some sting victims.

The dominulus paper wasp builds an exposed paper nest but
closely resembles a yellowjacket. However, unlike other paper
wasps, it might reuse and add to nests built in previous years.
This paper wasp has spread westward during the past 30 years
to the Midwest. It's active on its nest but won't sting aggressively
until the intruder is close.

Cicada killer carrying a cicada.

Photo courtesy of, and copyrighted by, Gene White, pmimages@earthlink.net

NONSOCIAL (SOLITARY) WASPS

Solitary nesting species include those of which a female builds a nest with several to many cells in which eggs are laid and the young develop. Each cell is provisioned with prey paralyzed by a sting, usually another insect or spider. An egg is laid on the prey before the cell is sealed. The nests are usually in the ground (cicada killer) or are built from mud plastered inside attics, garages or outbuildings (mud daubers).

The cicada killer is a large (2 inches long) wasp that's dark colored and striking yellow markings. It provisions its young with cicadas as prey. It's a large and frightening wasp, but it won't sting unless someone grabs a female.

Mud daubers are seen frequently in the summer months visiting mud puddles to gather mud to make their nests. They typically prey on spiders, which are used to provision their young inside the mud nests. The chances of being stung by a mud dauber are remote.

HONEY BEES

Wild or domesticated European honey bees can become a serious pest when they establish a nest in or on a structure. The most serious problems result when a swarm of honey bees locates a small opening in an exterior wall, down a chimney or behind a faulty flashing of a home, and then nests in a wall void or other interior area.

Honey bees might be various shades of yellow, black, brown or orange, with the head, antennae, legs and a portion of the abdomen dark. The body is covered with light-colored hairs. Worker bees are usually about two-thirds of an inch long. This is a social species with three adult castes: queens (only one lays eggs in each colony), drones (males) and workers (sterile females). Individual colonies can have 20,000 to 50,000 bees, and they can survive through the winter.

Africanized honey bees, which have become established in parts of Texas, are similar to the common wild and domesticated honey bees of the United States in appearance, except they're slightly smaller on average. However, Africanized honey bees are different in key aspects of their behavior. First, they're more aggressive than the other strains of honey bees, so they gradually displace other strains in regions where the Africanized strain becomes established. Second, colonies of Africanized bees are more likely to abscond, or change location, than the domesticated honey bees. Third, Africanized honey bees are much more aggressive when attacking animals, including humans, that disturb the colony. Workers from the nest will attack in great numbers, stinging the threatening animal or human. The attack will persist much longer than that of non-Africanized honey bees.

BUMBLE BEES

Bumble bees are social insects that generally nest underground. They don't make holes or tunnels in wood but will nest in abandoned mouse burrows and under piles of grass clippings, leaves, stones, logs, or other such locations. They seldom become a problem of consequence except in situations where the nests are established close to a sidewalk, near a building foundation, or in another location where conflict with people or pets is inevitable.

CARPENTER BEES

Carpenter bees resemble large bumble bees but have different nesting behavior. They bore long tunnels into wood and divide the tunnels into cells where individual larvae will develop. While several to many females might be nesting in wood of the same structure, each is acting in a solitary fashion because they're nonsocial bees.

Carpenter and bumble bees can be distinguished by yellow hair on the top side of the bumble bee abdomen, which is lacking on the black, shiny carpenter bee.

The typical carpenter bee gallery has an entrance hole on the wood surface that continues for a short distance. It then turns sharply and runs in the same direction as the grain of the wood. The female provisions each cell in the gallery with a ball of pollen on which an egg is laid. These galleries are made often in the wood siding, eaves, porch ceilings or window trim of homes, eventually causing the loss of structural strength of the wood. Unpainted or well-weathered wood is more susceptible to attack than hardwood or well-painted timbers. This bee isn't a threat to sting unless handled.

STINGING ANTS AND THEIR BEHAVIOR

There are a number of fire ants found in the U.S., but the red imported fire ant is the most serious stinger. Their stings cause intense irritation and can cause severe reactions, and even death, in sensitive people. Fire ants are active and aggressive and can kill young wildlife and livestock or produce sores and nausea in humans.

Fire ants are found in southern states from the East Coast to the West Coast. Their presence in lawns, parks, athletic fields and similar urban areas brings them into direct conflict with people, where its aggressive stinging behavior makes it intolerable in most situations.

When mounds of fire ants are disturbed, worker ants appear to boil out of the ground, aggressively stinging any intruding animal repeatedly. These worker ants are dark reddish-brown and vary in size from one-fifteenth to 0.25 inch long. Typical yards might contain many mounds.

Harvester ants are found in the warmer and drier regions of the West and South most often. They're large, red to dark brown ants, ranging from 0.25 to 0.50 inch long. They have characteristic long hairs that form a brush under their heads.

Normally, they're found in fields and lawns where they clear large areas of vegetation around their nest openings. Their severe stings make them serious pests. Fortunately, they rarely invade homes.

These stinging ants can be controlled by eliminating their mounds. A spray or drench of insecticide solution generally will be effective.

Insecticide granules can be applied to mounds and then thoroughly watered in. Several gallons of drench might be required. Baits also are available for fire ant control.

SOCIAL WASPS AND BEES - CONTROL

Wasps and bees are active during the daylight hours, so control measures should be implemented at night because all members of the colony will be present. The open-faced nesting paper wasps can be controlled during the day because they're less aggressive then other wasps and bees and their colonies usually are smaller in the number of wasps present.

Although spray formulations are available over the counter for individual use, it's advisable to employ a professional with protective equipment and experience in dealing with wasps and bees to handle the problem safely. Heavy-duty ladders are used for aerial nests, as are heavy-duty wasp suits. Dealing with ground-nesting wasps or wasp and bee nests in the walls or ceilings of structures requires professional specialists as well. Entrance holes should be sealed after treatment. When controlling honey bee colonies, consider removing melting wax, honey and rotting bees.

Solitary bees and wasps can be controlled using appropriate sprays and dusts to treat the burrows, galleries and entryways used by these pests. Follow this same procedure for applying insecticides into the gallery entrance of carpenter bees, and plug the holes securely with pieces of wooden dowel coated with carpenter's glue to kill bees in the gallery. Wood surfaces in the area of the entrance holes can be treated with a residual spray to control any bees that might return to the area.

SCORPIONS AND THEIR CONTROL

Scorpions are found in the more temperate (southern and southwestern) parts of the U.S. Most species prefer dryland habitats. They'll sting when disturbed.

Scorpions have long, slender bodies with a five-segmented tail that can arch over their backs. The last segment of the tail is a bulb-like poison gland or stinger, which is used to paralyze prey and for defensive purposes.

Scorpions are active at night and emerge from hiding in and under objects in their environment to hunt for food such as insects, spiders, and earthworms. They're found in a wide variety of outdoor and indoor habitats, with species preferring different geographic habitats.

Scorpion stings varying in terms of pain and physiological response of the recipient. The sting can cause allergic reactions, so a person who's been stung should be watched closely for adverse reactions. An ice pack applied to the affected area will relieve some pain. Seek medical attention if pain persists or if breathing difficulties occur.

In areas where scorpions are prevalent, environmental modifications should be used. Remove trash, boards, stones and other objects from around the residence. Keep grass, shrubs and trees pruned away from the house. Don't store firewood close to the house or indoors. Maintain tight fitting doors and screens, and caulk eaves, pipes and other cracks leading into the home.

Use appropriately labeled insecticides around the perimeter of buildings and around doors, eaves and entry points. Treat indoors around cracks and crevices where scorpions can hide, as well as entry points into the structure. Follow all label directions carefully.

9

PESTS OF DRAINS, SEWERS AND DAMP LOCATIONS

SUMMARY: *PESTS OF DRAINS, SEWERS AND OTHER DAMP LOCATIONS AND THEIR CONTROL*

Many insects, and some of their close relatives, live in, lay eggs in, or spend a portion of their lives in moist or wet areas. The moisture needed by such pests can come from many sources – leaky roofs, poor flashing, plumbing leaks, condensation problems around windows, plumbing, wet basements, crawl spaces, air conditioning, clogged drains and green lumber. In many cases rain water isn't properly directed away from buildings, leading to moisture problems. In other cases, moist, decaying organic matter serves the needs of pests.

In the immediate surroundings of buildings, such as mulched flower beds, planters, and other landscape areas, moisture often is plentiful and supports many pests. Sowbugs, pillbugs, millipedes and earwigs are found in the moist areas but aren't pests that deliberately infest damp locations in or around the home. They enter buildings as accidental intruders and can't survive and reproduce there.

Filth fly.

Flies' eggs are laid in moist situations, and their larvae develop on decaying organic matter. Quite often, animal manure, including in livestock operations, is the breeding source for many flies, which often are referred to as filth flies (except for biting species).

It is usually best to contact a professional pest management company. They have the knowledge and equipment to handle the problem.

SPRINGTAILS

Springtail.

Springtails often are found in homes, although they occur outdoors most commonly. They're tiny insects – less than one-twelfths of an inch long – and have a forked appendage at the end of their body that enables them to jump several inches, hence the name springtail. They have rounded, soft bodies; are easily crushed; and are white or gray. They're associated with dampness in bathrooms, basements and kitchens, or in the soil of houseplants.

To control springtails, it's best to eliminate the moisture problem. Using a fan or dehumidifier is helpful. Crawling-insect-control sprays will help reduce large numbers of the pest, but permanent elimination requires moisture control.

FUNGUS BEETLES

Fungus beetles are tiny – less than one-tenth of an inch long – and are reddish-brown. They're nuisance pests that feed on molds (thus the name fungus beetles) generally and can occur in large numbers near plumbing leaks, ventilation problems and other moisture accumulations. They can be eliminated through moisture control.

Foreign grain beetles also are tiny reddish-brown beetles that feed on mold. They're found in large numbers, usually in association with new construction. Mold and mildew might grow on wood that hasn't been dried adequately before construction. Crawling-insect-control sprays usually will kill the beetles, but they might recur until the wood dries out and no longer supports mold and mildew growth.

SMALL FLIES

This group includes fruit flies, humpbacked flies, moth or drain flies, and fungus gnats. They're generally one-eighth to one-sixteenth of an inch long and commonly are found in areas of moisture and decaying organic matter.

Moth fly.

Fruit flies have red eyes, humpbacked flies have a humped mid-section on the topside, and moth flies have long legs and hairs on their wings that give them a moth-like appearance. These pests feed and lay eggs on rotting fruits and vegetables, garbage, in drains and on contaminated soil. They're common in kitchens where grease or food accumulates in cracks, crevices, appliances, etc.

Control is best accomplished by removing moisture, food and other organic matter associated with food and filth. Drains must be cleaned with a brush and an industrial strength drain cleaner so all food residues, sewage and other organic matter are removed completely. After breeding sites are removed, caulk cracks and crevices and use flying-insect aerosols to eliminate adults.

FILTH FLIES

House, blow, bottle and flesh flies are the most common filth flies that invade homes and offices. They're a nuisance problem primarily, but when found in association with food-preparation areas, they're important carriers of disease because of their filthy habits.

The house fly is about 0.25 inch long and has four dark longitudinal stripes behind the head. Blow and bottle flies are slightly larger, but are metallic blue and green. Flesh flies are large gray with a checkerboard pattern on top of the abdomen. All these flies are associated with garbage and filth. All but the flesh fly will breed (lay eggs) in decaying organic matter. Blow, bottle and flesh flies will also lay eggs in dead animals, while house and flesh flies also will deposit eggs in manure. Larvae typically leave the breeding site to seek drier areas to pupate. Adult flies move inside from garbage, dumpster and manure areas, such as pet and livestock areas.

Control is accomplished through extensive sanitation, such as cleaning garbage and manure areas, and sprays or baits labeled for fly control. Exclusion – tight fitting window screens and doors, caulking other entry ways, etc. – is essential to keeping adult flies outdoors.

NUISANCE FLIES

These flies, including cluster and face flies, become pests after spending the winter in walls and attics of buildings. However, when warm weather arrives, the flies become active and find their way indoors. The cluster

fly is slightly larger than a
house fly, with golden hairs
on the top of the thorax.
The face fly is similar in
size and appearance to the
house fly.

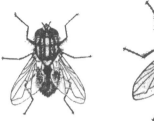

Cluster and face flies
are attracted in the fall to
warm walls of buildings,

House fly and cluster fly.

often south and west sides. Most infestations occur in attics and other
upper areas. When the flies warm up in late winter and spring, they're
attracted to light
or windows.

The most effective control is to prevent the flies from entering walls
or attics and sealing all cracks and crevices. A residual insecticide
application to exterior surfaces where flies will land in the fall will
kill them before they enter.

MIDGES

Midges, sometimes referred to as Chironomid midges, are attracted
to lights at night, usually on buildings that are close to polluted water,
where midge eggs and larvae are found. The larvae feed on algal growth
that occurs in polluted water. Midges come in all sizes, from tiny to
the size of mosquitoes. They have the same general appearance as
mosquitoes but aren't blood feeders.

Midge invasions might be abated by avoiding the use of outdoor
lighting. For midges that are still able to find their way indoors, flying
and/or crawling insect sprays can be used as appropriate.

Flies and other pests found in damp locations can be difficult
to control. Usually it is necessary to find where the pest problem is
located and finding that source is difficult. Contact a professional pest
management company to eliminate these hard to control pest problems.

PESTS OF DRAINS, SEWERS AND OTHER DAMP LOCATIONS

Moisture is needed by all insects; however, some spend all or most of their lives in wet areas. Some need free water while others live in moist environments such as soil, decaying wood and other organic matter, manure and almost any wet environment. Most of the moisture-loving insects are difficult to eliminate.

SPRINGTAILS

Springtails sometimes are found in houses, although they occur most commonly outdoors. They're small, usually less than one-twelfth of an inch long. The body may be white or gray. In most species, a forked appendage is attached to the lower back of the abdomen and can be moved away from the body suddenly, causing the insect to jump. Jumping and its unique mechanism result in the common name of springtails, which have no wings.

Springtails feed on algae, fungi and decaying vegetable matter, although a few species might feed on living plants – especially tender seedlings – and dead animal matter. They can develop in large numbers in mulched areas and thatch of lawns surrounding homes. During periods of favorable weather, such as after rain, they can become so abundant they form floating mats or scum on surfaces of swimming pools and enter homes in significant numbers.

Indoors, springtails sometimes are found in damp places such as kitchens, and bathrooms, around drains, in moist basements, on damp walls, in the soil of potted plants, in stored plant bulbs and around window moldings. Springtails do no damage generally, but homeowners consider them pests because they're often encountered in large numbers.

SPRINGTAIL CONTROL

The best means of obtaining springtail control is to institute measures that will lower the humidity, condensate or other moisture availability. In many cases, providing simple ventilation or airing of the room is sufficient. Using a fan to keep the air moving through the infested area might have the necessary drying effect. Any procedure that eliminates moist places of concealment likely will be of value managing springtails. Springtails are easy to control if the dampness and organic matter that allow them to build populations can be eliminated. Prevention of invasions from outside areas is more difficult. Residual applications of one of the pyrethroid insecticides (crawling insect sprays) should be applied to surfaces where springtails occur, either indoors or outdoors. If insects are under debris, loose soil, mulch, or other protective materials, a thorough treatment should be made to penetrate into these areas. Contact applications of crawling insect sprays also are useful where these insects are exposed.

FUNGUS BEETLES
Fungus beetles are tiny – one-twenty-fifth to one-tenth of an inch long – and reddish-brown. They're sometimes found in large numbers inside buildings. They're nuisance pests that feed on molds generally.

These beetles are associated will fungi, such as molds and mildew. Larvae and adults often accumulate in large numbers around windows and lights. Because a good moisture source is necessary for the growth of fungi, the beetles are found often where there are plumbing leaks, ventilation problems or other accumulations of indoor moisture. These beetles usually can be eliminated with appropriate moisture control.

One of the most commonly encountered species with this behavior is the foreign grain beetle. Adult beetles of this species are only about one-tenth to one-eighth of an inch long and reddish-brown. They often become a serious nuisance problem in newly constructed homes and homes where exterior wall voids or other spaces contain unusually high levels of moisture, which fosters growth of surface molds and mildew.

In new construction, this mold and mildew might be caused by use of wood that wasn't adequately dried before construction or had been left out in the rain before use. Newer homes might also be heated inadequately during cool or cold periods before occupancy, which can create temporary moisture problems within wall voids or basements because of condensate formation.

Tight building and insulation techniques and overuse of humidifiers often contribute to excessive moisture problems in certain localized voids or other areas. These factors and conditions foster buildup of foreign grain beetle populations until the home's heating system and natural ventilation can dry out all the voids where moisture has built up. Thus, foreign grain beetle infestations in new home construction often fade away as the mold and mildew films that are the source of food for the larval stages of this species disappear because of adequate heat and ventilation.

FUNGUS BEETLE CONTROL

Immediate control can be obtained with crawling insect sprays, unless the beetles are inside walls or floors and can't be reached with the spray. Control using insecticides will be enhanced if the moldy areas that are the source of the infestation can be found and the problem corrected. It might be necessary to call a professional to solve the problem.

SMALL FLIES

Fruit flies, humpbacked flies, moth or drain flies, and fungus gnats are a group of small flies that are pests in kitchens, bathrooms and other areas where moisture is commonly found. These flies, as is the case with all flies, only have one pair of wings as adults, and the immature forms, the stage most often found in wet areas, often are called maggots.

Fruit fly.

Photo courtesy of, and copyrighted by, Gene White, pmimages@earthlink.net

Fruit flies, also known as vinegar flies, most often are associated with overripened fruits and vegetables. These insects are of concern as nuisance pests and contaminators of food. Large populations can build up quickly in food service establishments. Food processing plants, such as wineries, pickle plants, and canneries, consider them to be their most bothersome pest.

Adults are about one-eighth of an inch long. Their eyes are red, the thorax is tan, and the abdomen is black on top and gray underneath.

Eggs are laid near the surface of fermenting materials, such as fruit, dirty garbage containers, rotten vegetables or slime in drains. Minute larvae hatch from the eggs in about 30 hours and feed near the surface of the fermenting mass on which the eggs were laid. When mature, the larvae move to a drier area and pupate.

Each adult female lays about 500 eggs. Because these flies require a period of only nine to 12 days to develop from egg to adult, their reproductive potential is tremendous. Large numbers can appear in a short time.

Adult flies are strong fliers. They've been known to travel as far as 6.5 miles within 24 hours. Populations tend to build during the summer, becoming abundant at harvest time. Indoor, they're frequently active at all times of the year. They're readily attracted to various material, including ripened fruits and vegetables, fermenting products, empty bottles and cans, drains and garbage disposal areas, and any area where moisture has collected, including mops and cleaning rags.

Humpbacked flies are small flies that resemble fruit flies. The adults are fairly common in many habitats but are most abundant around decaying plant and animal matter. Those of importance in structures can be found breeding wherever moisture exists, such as around plumbing and drains in bathroom and kitchen areas, garbage containers, crawlspaces and basements. These breeding areas are difficult to locate occasionally.

Adults can be found flying about in most areas of the house. They're active even through the winter months, although they're most abundant in the warmer months of the year.

Moth flies, also known as drain flies, are found on bathroom, and less frequently, kitchen walls in homes and other buildings. These flies can become nuisance pests.

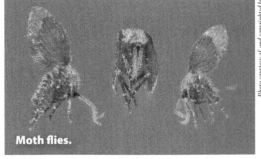

Moth flies.

Photo courtesy of, and copyrighted by, Gene White, pmimages@earthlink.net

Adults are about one-sixth of an inch long. They have a light gray or tan body and lighter-colored wings. The body and wings are covered densely with long hair that gives the body a fuzzy appearance – hence the name moth fly. When at rest, the wings are folded over the body in a characteristic rooflike manner.

Eggs are laid in irregular masses in the stones of sewage plant filters, dirty garbage containers, water traps in plumbing fixtures, built-in sinks and garbage disposal units, and almost anywhere decomposing organic materials are found. Larvae and pupae live in the decomposing film, with breathing tubes extending through the surface. Under favorable circumstances, the flies can go through one generation as quickly as a week, although two or three weeks is more typical. Some activity might occur during the winter.

Adults often are found in homes. Usually only a few are seen at a time, because old ones die and new ones are emerging continually. They're poor fliers and are seen commonly walking or running on walls and other resting surfaces. When they do fly, their flight covers only a few feet and is in short, jerky lines characteristic of these flies. During the day, the adults rest in shaded areas, walls near plumbing fixtures, or on the sides of tubs and showers. Most of their activity occurs during the evening, when they can be seen hovering about drains and sinks.

Fungus gnats are small, about one-tenth of an inch long, with threadlike antennae and long, slender legs. Resembling mosquitoes, they can be black, brown, red or yellow as adults and are found throughout the world. Larvae develop in high organic, moist environments; feed on fungi, thus the common name, and decaying plant matter; and can damage plant roots when prolonged infestation occurs.

Adult gnats are harmless to humans, although they can be a persistent nuisance. They're attracted to light and swarm around windows in homes.

SMALL FLY CONTROL

Sanitation and habitat elimination are the keys to managing this group of flies. Damp organic matter in and around drains, sinks, bathing areas, mop closets, washing machines and potted plants needs to be cleaned up because it serves as a breeding source for these flies. In many instances, locating the source of the infestation can be difficult because the flies can be well concealed in and around plumbing or any area where moisture might collect. There are often numerous breeding sources in infested areas. In homes, breeding sites in sinks and floor drains can often be eliminated by means of caustic drain cleaners available for home use.

House flies.

When the source of the infestation can't be found and eliminated, crawling-insect and flying-insect sprays can be used to control the adults, but repeated applications will be necessary as long as the breeding source remains.

To control fruit flies, the elimination of the attractants – decaying or overripened fruits and vegetables – is important. Removing these breeding sites often is enough to solve the problem.

FILTH FLIES

Filth flies live in close association with humans, are typically found around and within structures, and can become annoying by their constant presence. Pathogenic organisms are picked up by these flies from garbage, sewage, manure and other sources of filth and transferred to human and animal food.

The common house fly is a worldwide pest. The adult has four lengthwise dark stripes on the top of the thorax and is about 0.25 inch long.

Each adult female begins laying eggs a few days after hatching, laying five to six batches of 75 to 100 small, white oval eggs. In warm weather, these hatch in 12 to 24 hours into cream-colored larvae that burrow into the food material on which they hatched. These larvae grow and pupate in four to seven days in warm weather.

House fly eggs are laid in almost any warm, moist material that will furnish suitable food for the growing larvae. Animal manure, human excrement, garbage, decaying vegetable material and ground contaminated with such organic matter are suitable. Although they're attracted to various food materials, adult house flies have mouthparts that enable them to ingest only liquid materials. Solid food is liquefied by means of regurgitated saliva. This liquefied food then is drawn up by the mouthparts and passed into the digestive tract.

Bottle and blow flies are common in areas near garbage and garbage dumps. Single garbage cans have produced more than 30,000 flies in a week. These flies have feeding habits and mouthparts similar to those of the house fly and are mechanical carriers of disease organisms. Adults are usually large flies with a metallic blue or green color. Eggs usually are laid on meat or dead animals, although they can be placed in decaying vegetable materials when meat isn't available. They're frequently found in meat scraps or waste contained in garbage.

Flesh flies often are numerous in populated areas but seldom enter houses or food-handling establishments in significant numbers. Females of many species lay living larvae on meat scraps or dog excrement. Adult flies frequently are annoying outdoors near dog runs.

Flesh flies are larger than house flies (two or three times larger) and are grayish in color. Adult flesh flies have a familiar gray and black checkerboard pattern on their abdomen.

FILTH FLY CONTROL

Good sanitation is a basic practice in managing these flies. Whenever possible, food and materials on which the flies can lay their eggs must be removed, destroyed as a breeding medium or isolated from the egg-laying adult. Killing adult flies will reduce any infestation, but elimination of breeding areas is necessary for effective management. Where flies are a problem in buildings, the owner or occupants might be able to do this work. A pest management professional's job is to seek out the breeding places and implement a management plan. Removing materials in which flies breed is essential. Thus, twice-weekly garbage removal is most important. Practical sanitation often will make other control measures unnecessary.

Tight fitting screens and doors help keep adult flies at bay. When adults do manage to get in, crawling insect sprays can be used on places where flies are resting, including outdoor areas such as garbage cans.

Insecticide baits kill flies rapidly, but their effectiveness is short lived unless treatments are repeated. Baits are best used to supplement a spray program. Wet baits can be sprayed or sprinkled on fly resting surfaces outside the home. Dry baits can be scattered around garbage cans or placed in garage windows or near other fly resting surfaces. Fly baits can be purchased in ready-to-use forms.

Contact sprays (flying insect control) can be used outdoors for quick knockdown of flies, but they have no lasting effect. Be careful not to contaminate surfaces that humans, pets or food will come in contact with.

NUISANCE FLIES

The cluster and face fly often are nuisances around homes and other buildings when they start looking for a place to spend the winter in the fall of the year, and especially in late winter or spring when they attempt to find their way out of a structure. These flies are similar to house flies, although they're slightly larger and don't fly as well. They also differ from the house fly because they're darker in color and cluster flies have yellow hair on the thorax.

Photo courtesy of, and copyrighted by, Gene White, pmimages@earthlink.net

Cluster flies.

Face fly eggs are laid on fresh undistributed cow manure in pastures during the summer. The yellowish larvae live in the manure until they're mature and then pupate in the soil or on the surface of the soil under the manure. Adults feed on mucous and watery secretions around the eyes and nostrils of horses and cattle, causing considerable annoyance to animals.

During the fall and winter months, adult face flies may hibernate in the walls of buildings similar to cluster flies. On warm days, these hibernating flies become active and frequently move to the inside of the building in large numbers.

Cluster fly eggs are deposited at random in cracks in the ground. Newly hatched larvae enter the bodies of certain earthworms, where they develop for 11 to 14 days. When mature, they leave the body of the earthworm and pupate in the ground.

In the fall, adults congregate in the voids of houses, particularly in the walls. They can enter through numerous small openings; therefore, good screens are often of little value in excluding them. On warm days during the winter, or the beginning of spring, they leave these voids in larger numbers and are frequently trapped inside the building. They'll also be found frequently outside buildings on warm sunny days, particularly on the south and east walls, which have been warmed by the sun most of the day. They're of no particular harm but are a nuisance because of their large numbers. Mixed infestations of cluster flies and face flies aren't uncommon.

CLUSTER AND FACE FLY CONTROL

Killing the flies indoors with sprays usually doesn't result in satisfactory control because new flies constantly emerge from the wall voids. Effective treatment requires the introduction of insecticide into the wall voids. All openings through which flies are entering the building must be located and treated. These usually are openings around window pulleys, window and door casings, under baseboards, or between the tops of wall studs.

Using sprays in attics and other areas where flies are seen, as well as spraying outside the structure, especially in areas beneath the eaves and around windows, requires the experience and equipment of a professional.

MIDGES

Midges are a group of minute to medium-sized flies. Adult midges are slender, usually less than 0.25 inch long, and feature long, slender legs and wings. They resemble mosquitoes superficially, but their mouthparts are short and not adapted for sucking blood.

Midges lay their eggs on water. The larvae usually are aquatic – found in lakes, ponds, reservoirs and tanks – and bottom feeders. Polluted water apparently favors their growth and development. In the summer, eggs will hatch in about three days, and larvae will reach adulthood in about four weeks.

During peak emergence, large numbers of midges fly into residential and industrial areas, causing annoyance and damage. They're attracted to lights at night, and thousands will rest on the outside of buildings and enter homes through the slightest crack. They fly into people's eyes, ears and mouths and are sometimes inhaled. They contaminate everything.

MIDGE CONTROL

Midge populations thrive in polluted, algae-infested waters. There are insecticides that can be applied to water to kill midge larvae, but if the algae that serves as food for these flies isn't removed, the source of the problem remains.

When water management techniques aren't practical and the treatment of larval breeding waters isn't feasible, fogging for adult flies might provide temporary relief. However, fogging provides limited results unless the entire residential area is treated.

Midge invasions also might be abated by avoiding the use of outdoor lighting to the greatest possible extent, especially during early evening hours. For those midges that are still able to find their way indoors, crawling- and flying-insect sprays can provide relief temporary.

10

OCCASIONAL INVADERS AND MISCELLANEOUS PESTS

SUMMARY: *OCCASIONAL INVADERS AND THEIR CONTROL*

Occasional invaders include those pests that usually enter homes and other buildings from outside accidently because the building is in the path of the pest, they're attracted to lights at night and they're seeking a protected harborage from harsh environments.

Because this is a widely diverse group (insects, millipedes, sowbugs, slugs, mites and spiders) with varying biologies and behaviors, no one general management method exists for all these pests. Each case must be diagnosed properly.

The Asian lady beetle, although it feeds on many plant pests, has become a significant home invading pest. The beetle is about one-third of an inch long and features different color variations and spots. A black "M" design just in front of the wing covers is the best diagnostic tool. These beetles become pests when they begin congregating in late fall in large numbers, looking for a place – in wall voids, under siding and other

Lady beetle.

protected spots – to spend the winter. During warm days, they emerge, creating a considerable nuisance. As winter sets in, the beetles move deeper into cracks and crevices to hibernate for several months. Then, as the warm days of spring approach, the beetles emerge in mass – often into homes and buildings – creating a considerable nuisance, pinching people on their skin with their mouthparts, releasing a foul-smelling odor when disturbed or crushed and causing allergies if accumulations of dead beetles aren't cleaned. Sweeping or vacuuming them might be the best option. Using residual insecticides in late fall on a home's exterior when the beetles start to congregate also is useful. Preventing beetles from entering by caulking and sealing cracks, crevices and openings around windows, doors, plumbing and rooflines always is an important control measure. In most cases, a combination of these methods work best.

The clover mite is a tiny (smaller than a pin head) creature that appears in the spring – sometimes fall – around homes that have newly established lawns and lush grass. They don't bite and occur in large, annoying numbers, leaving a red stain when crushed. They'll crawl into cracks and crevices to molt and lay eggs, as well as escape hot or cold weather. Eventually, they'll find their way indoors in large numbers. Keeping the mites from entering is important because they're difficult to control once they penetrate the interior hiding places within the dwelling. An 18- to 24-inch-wide, plant-free barrier will prevent access. Spray a barrier strip and foundation walls around the house with a residual pyrethroid miticide. Follow label directions for the conditions, such as whether you have

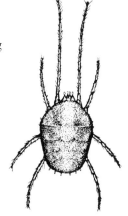

Adult clover mite.
(Greatly enlarged.)

a plant-free barrier. Treat all potential entry points. Indoors, mites can be vacuumed or wiped with a damp cloth. A spray containing synergized pyrethrins will kill those mites directly contacted. Because there's no residual activity with this spray, frequent applications might be necessary.

Millipedes, sowbugs and pillbugs are closely related to insects and become pests as their numbers increase and they invade homes.

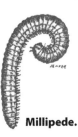

Millipede.

Millipedes have two pairs of short legs on each body segment, and they're 0.5 to 1.5 inches long, gray or brown, and curl when disturbed. Sowbugs and pillbugs are gray and have flattened bodies and seven pairs of legs. They can be as long as 0.5 inch. When disturbed, pillbugs can roll themselves into a ball. Sowbugs can't. Prevention and control

measures are similar to those for lady beetles and
clover mites except millipedes, sowbugs and pillbugs
feed on decaying plant materials and are found in
mulched flower beds, thick thatch layers in turf, leaf
or compost piles, as well as trash, rocks, boards
and other poorly maintained outdoor areas. These
areas, along with any other hiding places around
a structure, have to be cleaned. A more thorough

**Sowbug (left)
and pillbug.**

outdoor insecticide treatment might be needed. Sprays must be applied
in a 5- to 20-foot wide perimeter barrier around the structure and applied
thoroughly enough to be certain the insecticide penetrates the soil surface.
Other insecticide (indoor) treatments and nonchemical – caulking and
exclusion techniques and sweeping and vacuuming the pests – methods
are the same as they are for lady beetles and clover mites.

There's an extensive list of other pests that come into buildings:
* crickets
* earwigs
* boxelder bugs
* elm leaf beetles
* house centipedes
* slugs
* snails
* chinch bugs
* hackberry psyllids
* thrips
* root weevils
* ground beetles
* picnic beetles
* fungus beetles
* daddy longlegs
* insects attracted to lights at night
* house dust mites
* spiders
* silverfish
* firebrats
* dermestid beetles

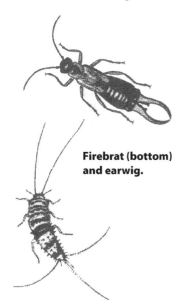

**Firebrat (bottom)
and earwig.**

Prevention and control will be similar to those measures used for lady beetles, clover mites, millipedes, sowbugs and pillbugs. For some, there might be a factor or stimulus that's resulting in the pest problem. This is the case for light-attracted pests. Manipulation of lighting might give the most satisfactory long-term relief. For boxelder bugs that feed on boxelder trees, removing this tree will eliminate the bug's habitat, as will the relocation of firewood piles that are a source of a pest infestation indoors.

Contact a professional pest management company if their assistance is needed.

OCCASIONAL INVADERS

Occasionally invading pests include a diverse group – insects, millipedes, sowbugs, slugs, mites and spiders – that usually come into homes and buildings accidentally. Many of these pests enter buildings because they're stimulated by environmental extremes – too wet, dry, hot or cold. Some pests are attracted to lights around buildings and accidentally enter through openings in the structure. On other occasions, the number of pests will increase significantly when conditions are favorable to their development and as they look for food, water and harborage. Although occasional invaders might enter in large numbers, they usually cause little damage; but because they create such a nuisance, measures must be taken to prevent and/or eliminate them from a home or building.

This group of pests has significant differences in their biologies and behaviors. Once the pest is identified properly, a thorough inspection will identify access routes through the building's exterior, where exclusion techniques might be helpful. These include caulking or sealing cracks and voids around utility entrances, the use of screening over or under vents, and weather-stripping around doors and windows. Many of these pests can be managed effectively by eliminating conditions that allow them to harbor and build great numbers near the structure. Usually, this involves sanitation, such as keeping vegetation cut and away from direct contact with the structure, removing trash and debris, and managing mulched areas or compost piles that are attractive to pests. In some cases, sprays of residual insecticides can be used on exterior surfaces or along the soil perimeter of the foundation to keep pests from entering the structure.

CLOVER MITE

The clover mite is a common nuisance in and around homes, especially where new lawns are being established or where well-fertilized grass grows close to foundation walls. They also can be found on clover and other plants in lawns. Although most abundant in spring and fall, they might be troublesome in the winter on warm, sunny days. Inactive during hot or cold weather, the mites migrate into homes when these weather extremes occur or when their numbers have grown so large they have to disperse to find food, water and hiding places.

Clover mites usually appear first around windows but eventually might be found throughout the home. The red to reddish-brown mite is slightly smaller than the head of a pin, hiding in cracks and crevices around windows or in foundation walls and under siding where they'll molt and lay eggs. They'll congregate on the sunny side of the structure. They don't bite but are annoying and will cause a red stain when crushed. During the advent of spring, the mites become active again and return to the lawn to feed.

Control – Mites in the home are difficult to control. They can be vacuumed or wiped with a damp cloth, or sprayed with synergized pyrethrins commonly found in aerosol cans, but direct contact is necessary. Permanent control can't be assured with any of these methods.

The best answer to the problem is to prevent the mites from entering the structure using a barrier of cultivated soil (or pea gravel) next to the foundation. Mites don't readily cross cultivated, grass-free soil. An 18- to 24-inch band around the perimeter of a house serves as an excellent deterrent. Flower beds in bare soil can be used if the soil around plants is free of grass, weeds and leaves.

A miticide can be used to spray the barrier strip and the foundation walls, as well as the lawn for 25 feet out from and around the house. Use a drenching spray during the warmest time of the day when the mites are most active. If the mites are discovered before invading the house, paint or spray window and door channels and outside frames with one of the labeled miticides.

ASIAN LADY BEETLE

Lady beetles are considered beneficial insects to farmers and gardeners. They feed on aphids and other soft-bodied insects that can damage plants, such as crops, gardens and landscapes. However, the multicolored Asian lady beetle has become a considerable nuisance pest in many parts of the U.S., especially Eastern and Midwestern states, because of its habit of congregating in large numbers inside homes to spend the winter.

Adults of this species look like most other lady beetles – oval, convex and about one-third of an inch long. However, many different color variations can be found, even within a handful of overwintering adults. They can be yellow, red, reddish-brown or any shade in between. Many beetles will have black spots – as many as 19 – on their wing covers (elytra). Some have no spots. The most common and useful identifying characteristic is the presence of a dark or black M-shaped mark on the upper surface of the thorax, just in front of the wing covers. The mark is more readily apparent on some than on others, but it's usually visible and is diagnostic for this species.

After feeding on trees and soybeans throughout most of the summer, large numbers of adult beetles are attracted to light-colored buildings in the late autumn for overwintering. They orient to homes or buildings that are illuminated and warmed by sunlight and resting spots on the southwestern facings. From these areas, they'll work their way into homes, buildings or garages through small cracks and crevices and recongregate to hibernate for the winter inside wall voids, attics or other secluded areas. They occasionally become mobile during warm periods during late winter or early spring, but generally they remain inactive until it's time to disperse when the trees begin to leaf out in the spring. They often become disoriented during the premature or normal dispersal periods and wander about inside homes or buildings, which causes alarm, disgust or nuisances for homeowners.

Control – After exclusion techniques such as caulking and weather stripping have been implemented, the beetles can be controlled adequately sometimes by vacuuming or sweeping. Vacuum cleaner bags, or the beetles, should be removed and destroyed because they might survive and emerge from the vacuum cleaner later. Because beetles might continue to emerge from hiding, daily vacuuming and sweeping might be necessary.

Crawling or flying insect aerosol insecticides containing pyrethroids or synergized pyrethrins can be used to kill exposed beetles. These insecticides don't have long residual activity, so frequent treatment might be necessary as beetles continue to emerge from hiding areas.

Treating the exterior surfaces of the home in late fall – when beetles start looking for a place to spend the winter – with a residual insecticide will help prevent beetles from entering the home. Pyrethroid formulations that last the longest include wettable powders, microencapsulated and suspended concentrates. These should be applied to areas where beetles congregate and into cracks, crevices or voids where they might enter the home.

Photo courtesy of, and copyrighted by, Gene White, pmimages@earthlink.net

Centipede.

MILLIPEDES, CENTIPEDES, SOWBUGS AND PILLBUGS

This group of occasional invaders aren't insects but are related closely to insects. They're not harmful, but they're a nuisance and have a frightening appearance. Their preferred habitat is moist, decaying leaf litter or other organic material around structures. Mostly considered beneficial when found outdoors, they're scavengers – except for centipedes, which are predators on small insects and other arthropods – and their diet consists mainly of decaying vegetation. The organisms are found commonly in wooded areas, mulched areas, compost piles and damp basements.

As with most other occasional invaders, this group will leave their natural habitat under adverse conditions, crawl over lawns and sidewalks, and invade homes in large numbers. For example, large amounts of rainfall can trigger mass migration of millipedes from their natural habitat.

Millipedes have two pairs of short legs on each body segment. There are many species of millipedes, but the ones that commonly invade homes are usually 0.5 to one-and-one-twelfths inches long, gray or brown in color, and curl when disturbed. Sowbugs and pillpugs are gray and have flattened bodies and seven pairs of legs. They range

Millipedes.

Photos courtesy of, and copyrighted by, Gene White, pmimages@earthlink.net

in length as long as 0.5 inch. When disturbed, pillbugs can roll themselves into a ball. Sowbugs can't. They generally resemble an armadillo because of their oval shape and overlapping plates on their backs. The house centipede – the most commonly encountered – is longer than 1 inch and has a flattened body and 15 pairs of long, striped legs used to move quickly across floors or walls in damp basements.

Control – Although the heaviest migrations usually come from nearby wooded areas, mowing the lawn helps prevent invasions. It's important to make a home's exterior as unfavorable as possible to reduce the numbers of pests. Caulk or seal cracks and other openings in exterior foundation walls and around doors and ground-level windows by late summer. Remove leaf litter and decaying vegetation from around the foundation because they provide food and shelter for sowbugs and millipedes. A border of bare soil around the building next to the

Sowbug.

foundation also helps to make the area a less-favorable habitat. Trim and thin foundation planting so ventilation permits the soil to dry more quickly near the foundation. Reduce thatch in the lawn to discourage sowbugs and millipedes by dethatching in early fall.

Inside homes, sowbugs, pillbugs and millipedes will die quickly if moisture levels are kept low. The presence of house centipedes suggests an insect food supply is present and needs to be managed. Remove favorable hiding places such as boxes, bags and other clutter. Any of these pests found indoors can be eliminated by hand collecting, vacuuming or sweeping them.

Insecticides can be used to supplement the aforementioned measures. Select an insecticide and formulation labeled for use against this

Sowbug (left) and pillbug.

group of pests. Apply the spray or granular formulation to any infested area outdoors and as a barrier treatment on foundation walls and the soil along the foundation wall. For indoor treatment, select a labeled insecticide for crawling insect control and follow the directions on the label.

SLUGS AND SNAILS

These animals are related to clams and oysters but aren't found in standing water. At times, they gather in large numbers in damp basements or crawl spaces, leaving glistening mucous trails as they move about at night. Basically, they're plant feeders but sometimes deface buildings with fecal matter. They need a large amount of moisture to survive, so they're most active during periods of wet weather, at night and in moist areas.

Snails are recognized easily by their shells. Common land species usually are a shade of gray or brown and 1 to 1.5 inches long. The giant African snail, found in Florida, California and Hawaii, might have a shell as long as 5 inches. Soft-bodied slugs are gray or molted, slimy creatures measuring as long as 4 inches.

Control – All rotting boards, decaying plant material, and debris that provide harborage and breeding sites should be removed. These pests require damp conditions, so anything that can be done to reduce or eliminate moist conditions will be useful to suppress them long term. Pay attention to crawl spaces and basements that have water problems. Overwatering landscape beds, for example, contributes to problems with these pests.

Chemical control is efficient most often with bait formulations of methiocarb (Mesurol) or

Slug.

metaldehyde. The baits should be applied to infested areas, such as in crawlspaces, under shrubs and in mulched areas. They work well under various conditions, and one treatment often is satisfactory.

CRICKETS, EARWIGS AND CHINCH BUGS

Numerous species of crickets, earwigs and chinch bugs will invade homes, entering mainly from grassy, weedy areas. Related to grasshoppers, crickets' antennae are as long or longer than their body, and their large, back legs are used to jump. As with earwigs and chinch bugs, they feed on various live and dead plant material. They're 0.5 to 0.75 of an inch long and are tan to black in color. Adult females have a conspicuous sword-like, egg-laying device extending backwards from the tip of the abdomen. Crickets are famous for their songs – males chirp by rubbing their wings together. They're most active at night. Field crickets and the house cricket are the most common crickets found in buildings.

Field cricket.

Photo courtesy of, and copyrighted by, Gene White, pmimages@earthlink.net

Earwigs are recognized readily by the pinchers or forceps-like appendage at the end of the abdomen. As with crickets and chinch bugs, they can build large numbers around buildings in warm weather and find their way indoors through cracks in poorly fitted doors and windows, as well as cracks in foundations, siding and utility entrances. They're about one inch long and brown to black in color; some species have yellow- to red-colored stripes. Adult earwigs have a short, leathery pair of wings and a second pair of membranous wings folded underneath the first pair. Some species will fly and are attracted to lights at night. They prefer high moisture and migrate

An earwig tending its eggs.

Photo courtesy of, and copyrighted by, Gene White, pmimages@earthlink.net

indoors during periods of prolonged heat and drought to seek cool, moist hiding places.

Chinch bugs also develop outdoors, feeding mainly on grass in lawns, fence rows and open fields, but under adverse conditions, they'll enter homes in large numbers. Several species can be nuisances. They're small – usually less than 0.25 inch long – black and white bugs with wings that extend about half the length of the abdomen when at rest. As an infestation grows, bugs can be seen crawling over sidewalks, sides of buildings and indoors. Chinch bugs, in addition to being a nuisance when they invade structures, also are severe pests of certain common turf grasses.

Control – Crickets, earwigs and chinch bugs can be managed with sanitation measures – keep grass, weeds and other hiding areas under control, and eliminate damp conditions. Reduce outside lighting to avoid attracting these pests; use less attractive yellow lights; and use caulking and weather stripping around doors, windows, pipes and cracks. If small numbers of pests are entering, remove them with a broom, dustpan or vacuum.

Insecticide treatment should be focused outdoors, using a product to treat a 3- to 5-foot band around the perimeter of a structure so the pests are killed before they can get indoors. Spray and granular formulations are available at lawn and garden shops.

BOXELDER BUG, HACKBERRY PSYLLID AND ELM LEAF BEETLE

Many insects that feed on trees will occur often in large numbers; and when faced with adverse conditions, they'll look for a better place to live and end up indoors. Such in the case with these three insects that feed on boxelder, hackberry and elm trees. That's why they're named after the trees on which they feed. As is the case with many occasional invaders, adults, often in large numbers, leave the host tree in the fall to seek a protected harborage to spend the winter.

Adult boxelder bugs are about 0.5 inch long, brown to black in color with distinctive red or orange markings on the area behind the head. The wings are folded over the back of the body and have red lines marking the lateral margins of the wings. The young (nymphs) are bright red and wingless but generally are similar in shape compared to the adults. In the fall, they search for protected areas to spend the

Boxelder bug.

Photo courtesy of, and copyrighted by, Gene White, pmimages@earthlink.net

winter and often end up indoors. They emerge in the spring to seek female boxelder trees (seed-bearing) on which to feed and lay eggs. Some bugs might become trapped indoors, and although they don't harm household furnishings, they can be annoying when they crawl or fly.

Hackberry psyllids are common in areas where hackberry trees are grown. They're small, gnat-like, about one-eighth of an inch long, and when examined closely, resemble a miniature cicada. They develop inside galls that form on hackberry leaves as a response to psyllid feeding. Adults often emerge in large numbers in late summer, looking for protected areas to spend the winter. These small insects are tiny enough to enter a house through ordinary window screens, are attracted to lights at night, are a nuisance, and will prick the skin creating irritation.

The elm leaf beetle is a pest of elm trees, skeletonizing the leaves and causing them to turn brown. Adult beetles are yellow to dull green in

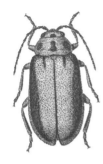

Elm leaf beetle.

color, with a black stripe down each side of either forewing. They are about 0.25 inch long. Adults often spend the winter in structures and becoming a nuisance in the fall when they enter buildings and in the spring when they attempt to leave.

Control – In addition to nonchemical and chemical methods, these three tree-dwelling occasional invaders often can be controlled by spraying the infested trees during mid- to late summer and before the insects leave the trees. Additionally, one or two host trees of no particular value in the landscape can be removed as a means of reducing or eliminating problems.

ROOT WEEVILS AND GROUND BEETLES

Weevils of several species are attracted to buildings as they seek shelter from unfavorable weather conditions. Weevils are small beetles – about 0.25 inch long – characterized by a snout or beak. The larval or grub stage feeds on the root systems of various plants. Adults feed on leaves. When not feeding during the day, adults hide beneath debris or in the soil at the base of the host plants. The strawberry root weevil and black vine weevil are two of the more common root weevils that find their way indoors and create annoyances.

Ground beetle.

Ground beetles also are one of the common groups of beetles. They vary greatly in size (one-eighth of an inch to longer than one inch), shape (generally flattened) and color (black to brilliantly colored). They typically live under leaves, logs, stones and other debris and feed mostly at night as predators. Only a few species can fly or are attracted to lights. They wind up indoors accidently and sometimes are found in hidden, moist areas in the basement or under boxes or other objects on the floor.

Control – Physical removal is the only control necessary for the occasional weevil or ground beetle. If large numbers are present, the aforementioned nonchemical and chemical measures should be used. These are larger insects with hard exterior shells, so it might take longer to kill them with insecticides.

PICNIC BEETLES

Picnic beetles occasionally invade buildings but are better known as those black, hard-shelled intruders that persistently swarm around picnics or barbecues. They drop lazily into food and drink or make themselves a nuisance at outdoor events during the summer. The beetles are about three-sixteenths of an inch to 0.25 inch long and are jet black with four pale yellow spots on their wing covers. They're difficult to control. Even if they're killed in large numbers, they're more likely to enter from untreated areas. Using a bait such as sliced melons to attract the insects away from picnic table might be effective.

Picnic beetles are outdoor scavengers that feed primarily on overripe or damaged fruits and vegetables and, to some extent, decayed portions of bulbs and roots. Anything that can be done to eliminate overripe or damaged fruits and vegetables, in the garden or at picnics and other social gatherings, is helpful to reduce the beetle's presence. They're also attracted to overripe odors, such as the vinegar or mayonnaise in salad dressings, coleslaw and potato salad, as well as beer. Keeping foods sealed before serving and promptly cleaning up debris will reduce their numbers at picnics. Apples, mulberries and other fruits that fall to the ground and decay should be picked up and destroyed.

Residual insecticides applied as sprays or aerosols to grass and vegetation before a picnic also might provide relief.

LIGHT-ATTRACTED PESTS

There are a large number of insects, other than the aforementioned occasional invaders, that are attracted to lights at night. Some of the more important ones are:

* moths
* leafhoppers
* gnats
* midges
* mayflies
* beetles
* stoneflies
* lacewings

Control – The pest management technique that will have the greatest long-term impact on night-flying insects is light manipulation. Indirect lighting and lights away from buildings will guide insects away from buildings. Shade windows so indoor lights won't attract insects. Use yellow light instead of the white light because yellow is less attractive to insects. Sodium vapor or other lighting systems that have a pink, yellow or orange glow will be less attractive than the bright white or blue mercury-vapor or fluorescent lights.

Bug zappers, or backyard insect electrocution traps, will attract and kill some insects, including a few mosquitoes, but they've been shown to attract more insects into an area then they kill, so they're not recommended generally.

Treating outdoor walls and surface areas that are attractive to insects might provide a useful degree of control. Formulations such as wettable powders, suspension concentrates and microencapsulated products will provide the best residual activity on most exterior surfaces.

SILVERFISH AND FIREBRATS

Silverfish and firebrats are nuisance pests primarily, usually causing little damage. However, the potential exists for large, uncontrolled infestations to damage paper, book bindings, wallpaper, cereals, starched fabrics leather, fur and silk. They'll usually be found close to their food source indoors.

Adults are usually about 0.5 inch long with flattened, long and slender bodies that are broad at the front and taper gradually toward the rear. The antennae are long and slender. Three long, slender appendages are found at the rear of the body, which give rise to the common name bristletails. All silverfish and firebrats are wingless. Silverfish are uniformly silver in color, and firebrats are a mottled gray.

They're usually found indoors in areas associated with heat, such as boiler rooms, or moisture, such as near water pipes. They're commonly found in bathtubs where they become trapped while seeking food or moisture. Firebrats and silverfish are most active at night and can run swiftly.

Control – Inspection of an infested home is necessary to determine the source(s) of the problem. Set sticky traps to help determine where silverfish and firebrat numbers are highest. Then control efforts can concentrate on these areas.

If a small number of these pests exists, removal might be all that's needed. Clean up clutter, repair leaks and moisture problems, ventilate closed rooms and remove sources of their food. Caulking cracks and crevices to limit hiding areas often is useful.

Insecticides should be applied thoroughly into all possible cracks, crevices or other hiding places in basements, attics, cupboards and clothes closets, behind baseboards, under bathroom fixtures and wooden partitions, and around steam and water pipes. Dusts are useful for treating wall voids and areas behind baseboards, under commodes and in crawlspaces and attics. Space treatments also might be useful, especially in attics.

SPIDERS

Spiders have a characteristic appearance easily recognized by most people. They have eight legs, lack wings and antennae, and their bodies have only two major regions – cephalothorax (a fused head and thorax) and an abdomen. All spiders have a pair of jaw-like structures called chelicerae. At the end of each is a hollow, claw-like fang. Each fang has a small opening in the end through which venom is injected into its prey. Spinnerets located at the tip end of the abdomen are linked to glands from which silk is spun for web making.

Some people have the idea that all spiders are poisonous or dangerous to handle, but this isn't true. The only spiders capable of inflicting serious injury to humans are the black widow, brown recluse and hobo spiders. These spiders will not bite unless disturbed.

There are more than 400 species of spiders in the U.S. They live almost everywhere, including inside homes and buildings. Most of them spin webs in corners, basements, crawlspaces, etc., in which they catch prey. Spiders feed entirely on living insects or animals small enough for them to catch. They usually lie in wait for their prey. Spiders also use the silk to line their nests, construct egg sacs and make parachutes on which some species travel on wind currents.

Spiders reproduce by laying eggs contained in an egg sac. These sacs, which frequently contain several hundred eggs, are usually ball-shaped

Photo courtesy of, and copyrighted by, Gene White, pmimages@earthlink.net

Black widow spider.

and might be carried by the female wherever she goes. Some species hide their sacs in the web or elsewhere.

Some spiders are associated with moisture and found in basements, crawlspaces and other damp parts of buildings. Others live in warm, dry places such as subfloor air vents, upper corners of rooms and attics. Most species hide in cracks, dark areas or other retreats they construct of silk.

Spiders of most concern – The female black widow is jet black in color. The spherical-shaped abdomen is marked on the underside with a red or yellow hour glass in the female only; and there may be a few red spots on top of the abdomen.

The poison of the black widow affects the nervous system of humans. People bitten might experience various symptoms, such as dizziness, blurred vision, breathing difficulty, nausea and severe pain around the wound. In such instances, a physician should be contacted immediately.

The black window lives in undisturbed locations, such as under rocks and boards, and in and around old buildings. She is active on her irregular web during the day.

The brown recluse spider has a body about three-eighths of an inch long and three-sixteenths of an inch wide. The leg span is about half the size of a half dollar. It's usually light tan to brown in color, with a distinguishing dark brown fiddle-shaped marking on the front half of the back. This mark is why it's known as the fiddle-back spider.

The brown recluse is aptly named because it's a reclusive animal. It's usually found in barns, sheds, garages or even in homes that are dry, littered and contain a supply of insects to serve as food. Favorite hiding places seem to be the arms or legs of garments left hanging undisturbed for some time. People are sometimes bitten while sleeping in beds that have been unoccupied for a long time.

The bite of this venomous spider can cause serious effects. It's especially dangerous to children, the elderly and those in poor physical condition. Contrary to some reports, fatalities from bites of the brown recluse are rare. Reaction to the bite varies considerably and depends on the amount of venom injected and individual sensitivity to it.

Extreme pain might follow almost immediately after the bite, or the bite might not be noticed for an hour or more. The visible sign of recluse poisoning is a small white blister at the site of the bite. The affected area enlarges, becomes inflamed and the tissue is hard to the touch. Eventually, the affected tissue is killed and peals away, leaving a sunken, ulcerating sore as big as a silver dollar.

The healing process is slow, requiring six to eight weeks. Skin grafts might be needed for complete recovery from the ulcerated sore. It's extremely important to get medical attention as soon as possible.

Brown recluse spider.

Photo courtesy of, and copyrighted by, Gene White, pmimages@earthlink.net

Although no specific antidote is available, prompt medical treatment can prevent severe reactions and lessen the long-range effects.

Control – Sanitation is the most practical method of spider control. Clean away all webbing with a vacuum cleaner so eggs and spiders are picked up and destroyed. Ordinary housecleaning with a cloth, dust mop or broom isn't effective. Keep premises free of unneeded, undisturbed clothing, papers and other litter. Many spiders might be excluded from the home by caulking or eliminating cracks and crevices around the foundation of the house and around windows and doors.

Chemical control using a long-lasting residual spray is effective when applied around the outside of the home and in undisturbed locations in the house where spiders are likely to be found. Use only labeled insecticides and formulations – some are designed for outdoor use and others for indoor use.

Outside areas usually needing attention are porches, garages and eaves of the roof. Spiders also might be found in crawl spaces, basements and unexcavated areas beneath the house. All areas where spiders are found should be treated.

11

FABRIC AND PAPER PESTS

SUMMARY: *FABRIC AND PAPER PESTS AND THEIR CONTROL*

Carpet beetles and clothes moth larvae will feed on any type of animal fibers – wool, fur, feathers, hair, bristles, mohair in clothing, carpeting, upholstery and other household furnishings. They feed only incidentally on synthetic fibers, when they're soiled with food stains or body oils. Some of these insects also can be pests in dried food products, such as meat, fish, meal and dried milk products.

CARPET BEETLES

There are several species of carpet beetles, but the most familiar are the black and varied carpet beetle. The brown, hairy, 0.25-inch long larvae or cast skins of carpet beetles are found usually in stored woolens, carpeting, lint accumulations, cracks and corners of closets, dresser drawers, and occasionally in stored food and cupboards. The larvae are active (although slow moving) and might appear almost anywhere in the house. It's probable that every home has some carpet beetles, although finding just a few isn't considered a problem usually. Adult carpet beetles are small (about one-eighth-inch long), oval, black (some species have bright colored scales on their backs) and are pollen feeders; thus, they're not the damaging stage.

CARPET BEETLE PREVENTION

Housekeeping is important. Regular, thorough removal of lint eliminates insect breeding places. Pay particular attention to rugs, carpets (especially next to walls), upholstered furniture, closets, shelves, radiators (and the space under and behind them), registers and ducts, baseboards, moldings, corners and floor cracks. Inspect clothing and storage areas in the fall and spring for potential infestations. Also periodically check that windows and air ducts are properly screened to help prevent the entry of insects.

Dry clean or launder clothing before storing as carpet beetles are more apt to infest soiled material. Store clothing in tight boxes or chests. Generally, it's not advisable to use plastic bags. Although they might not harm clothing during short-term (several months) storage, long-term storage could result in damage to clothing because of moisture problems or potential reactions between the plastic and fabric. Rid or properly store remnants or scraps of wool, fur and fleece.

Place mothballs or crystals of paradichlorobenzene (PDB) with the clothes in storage container (follow label directions). The smell of naphthalene might be difficult to remove from clothing. Dry clean clothing again before wearing to help remove any odor. Cedar chips, although popular as an insect repellent, don't deter carpet beetles effectively.

Fur storage vaults are available in larger cities.

CARPET BEETLE CONTROL

Most pest control specialists provide dependable service for controlling carpet beetles. Because satisfactory prevention and control require a good understanding of these pests and how to use insecticides properly, most homeowners are advised to contact a professional.

CLOTHES MOTHS

The clothes moth larva is a small white caterpillar that lives inside a silken case or web and feeds on wool, hair, fur and feathers. Damage depends on the type of item being fed on and the species of clothes moth involved. The adult is a tiny, buff-colored "miller" that avoids light. Adults don't feed, but their presence indicates a moth infestation.

Likely spots to look for infestations around the home include boxes of old clothing, furs, feather pillows, piano felts, old over-stuffed furniture, carpets, and even lint that collects along baseboards or in

corners. Mothproofing should be done as a precautionary measure
when any of the above items are going into winter or long-term storage,
or when these items won't be routinely cleaned.

CLOTHES MOTH PREVENTION

Each spring and fall, remove all garments from closets, brush them
beneath the folds and hang them outdoors in the sun for several days.
Dry cleaning, or washing and pressing the garments with a hot iron,
also will kill moth larvae and eggs. While the closet is empty, vacuum it
clean and then spray the walls and floors until moist with a household
spray labeled for crawling insect control.

Clothing stored in little-used closets can be further protected
by making the doors at tight-fitting as possible and keeping PDB
(mothballs), crystals or flakes in an open container on the top shelf.
Follow label directions. Never store soiled garments since perspiration
and food stains favor moth development.

Almost any kind of box or bag makes a satisfactory storage
container if it's tight enough (or is taped) to keep out adult moths.
Before storing clothing or blankets, first rid them of any insects by dry
cleaning, washing, pressing with an iron heated to 135°F, or brushing
and sunning. Then place the garments in the storage container, and
add PDB or naphthalene between sheets of white paper laid in with the
articles. The label will instruct you on the amount to use.

CLOTHES MOTH CONTROL

As with carpet-beetle control, a sound understanding of these pests and
how to use insecticides around clothing and bedding is required.

PAPER PESTS

There are numerous pests that will damage paper and paper products.
Termites will eat paper because it contains cellulose, which termites can
digest to meet their nutritional needs. They're discussed extensively in
the termite chapter because of the damage they do to wood and other
cellulose-based building materials.

Silverfish and firebrats occasionally are attracted to paper because
of starch, paste or glue (as in book bindings), or in some cases, because

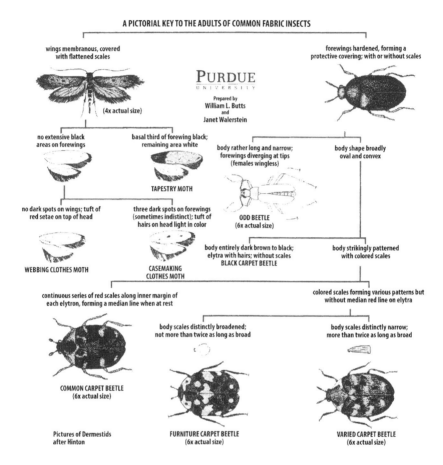

A PICTORIAL KEY TO THE ADULTS OF COMMON FABRIC INSECTS

PURDUE
UNIVERSITY

Prepared by
William L. Butts
and
Janet Walerstein

wings membranous, covered with flattened scales — forewings hardened, forming a protective covering; with or without scales

(4x actual size)

no extensive black areas on forewings — basal third of forewing black; remaining area white

TAPESTRY MOTH

body rather long and narrow; forewings diverging at tips (females wingless) — body shape broadly oval and convex

no dark spots on wings; tuft of red setae on top of head — three dark spots on forewings (sometimes indistinct); tuft of hairs on head light in color

ODD BEETLE
(6x actual size)

WEBBING CLOTHES MOTH — CASEMAKING CLOTHES MOTH

body entirely dark brown to black; elytra with hairs; without scales
BLACK CARPET BEETLE — body strikingly patterned with colored scales

continuous series of red scales along inner margin of each elytron, forming a median line when at rest — colored scales forming various patterns but without median red line on elytra

body scales distinctly broadened; not more than twice as long as broad — body scales distinctly narrow; more than twice as long as broad

COMMON CARPET BEETLE
(6x actual size)

Pictures of Dermestids after Hinton

FURNITURE CARPET BEETLE
(6x actual size)

VARIED CARPET BEETLE
(6x actual size)

of its sizing. For example, the glaze on some paper products will be removed in an irregular fashion, with holes or the edges notched. In libraries, they'll attack book bindings and heavily sized paper and can become significant pests. Paper pests gain entry in cardboard cartons, books and papers, and other household materials. These kinds of materials should be inspected thoroughly before brought indoors.

Some pests will enter paper products (boxes, piles of newspapers, paper bags, books, etc.) as a place to harbor or hide. As they occupy these spaces, they'll chew on products and, if left undisturbed, cause damage. This can be almost any kind of chewing insect. Some of the common ones include cockroaches, crickets, earwigs and ants. This incidental damage isn't limited to paper products. They'll chew on almost any product that's soft (fabrics, leather goods, etc.). In many cases, they damage soft goods simply because they're in the way – for example, carpeting damaged by termites as they emerge from a wood floor.

Control is attained by removing, destroying or cleaning the infested product and using a crawling insect spray in the area of the infestation. Be sure to vacuum and clean the area thoroughly before treating, and follow label directions carefully when treating.

Finding the source of fabric pest infestations and eliminating the source of the pest problem is a challenge to most people, so contact a professional if you need assistance.

FABRIC AND PAPER PESTS

The most important fabric-destroying insects in the United States are two moths and four carpet beetles, although various insect species might cause damage occasionally or be important locally. There seems to have been an increase of carpet beetle and clothes moth problems throughout much of the U.S. The reasons for this resurgence aren't clear. Contributing factors might include a trend of consumer preferences toward garments made of wool, furs or feathers and away from polyesters and other synthetics.

Clothes moths and carpet beetles damage fabric during the larval stage of their life cycle, attacking any type of animal fibers – wool, fur, feathers, hair, leather, horns – found in clothing, carpeting, upholstery, bedding and other household furnishings. Some stored foods – meat, fish meal and dried milk products – also are vulnerable to these pests. All these products and materials contain keratin, a primary structural protein, that can be digested by these fabric pests and used as an energy source.

CARPET BEETLES

The four species of beetles most commonly found infesting fabrics are the black carpet beetle, varied carpet beetle, common carpet beetle and furniture carpet beetle. Together, this group usually is considered more economically important than the clothes moths.

Many other common beetles resemble adult and larval carpet beetles. The hide and cabinet beetles have similar appearances but are associated with animal hides, leather products and stored food products. You'll know the pest by observing the type of infested product.

The larvae of carpet beetles are the only stage that causes damage to fabrics, and all of the adults are small and inconspicuous beetles rarely seen by homeowners. Adults might be found indoors or outdoors and frequently on flowers surrounding a house, where they feed on pollen. Flowering shrubs, such as spirea and pyracantha particularly, are attractive to adult carpet beetles. But other species of flowering plants might be visited. Adult carpet beetles fly readily and actively when indoors and are attracted to windows and lamps or light fixtures, so live or dead specimens often can be found on window ledges or in light fixtures.

Carpet beetle larvae, especially the black carpet beetle, can be found on dead animal carcasses in nature and cause considerable damage indoors to furs, stuffed animals and articles such as hair-bristle brushes. As with the other carpet beetles, lint and hair that collect around the edges of carpet and furniture also are common food sources for the black carpet beetle. However, this beetle larva is less likely than the varied, common and furniture carpet beetles to attack keratin-containing articles. The latter three beetle larvae are found infesting woolen, silk, fur and other animal-based materials more often.

Three species of hide beetles – larder, black larder, and hide or leather beetle – are considered fabric pests because they can be found in tanneries and warehouses that process hides and skins. They also can be found in homes attacking furs, animal skins, feathers, and meats and cheeses, but usually not fabrics per se. These beetles (Dermestids) are found in bird nests, attacking dead bird or mouse carcasses in attics, museum collections of stuffed animals or beehives where dead bees and wax are eaten. The adults and larvae damage materials during feeding.

CLOTHES MOTHS

The webbing clothes, casemaking clothes, and carpet or tapestry moths are called so because of their presence as larvae feeding on woolen clothing. Tapestry moths occur less frequently than the others.

All are small moths, with wingspans of less than 0.5 inch. Their habits are different from most moths because they're rarely seen flying around lights at night. Rather, they prefer dark closets, attics or other areas. They tend to live in dark corners or in folds of fabric.

Newly emerged adults of both sexes fly readily, usually at dusk, or they might fly on the edges of a lighted area occasionally, so they usually remain quite inconspicuous. Once female moths have mated and develop eggs, they'll fly much less and become rather sedentary. They're capable of running and making short, hopping flights to escape disturbance. The females will seek suitable areas for egg-laying, most commonly in quiet, out-of-the-way locations with low light where suitable food materials for development of the larvae are present.

Glue boards or sticky traps can be placed on windowsills to detect and monitor for the presence of these moths indoors. Collections at windows indicate that when clothes moths are flying, they can be attracted to light. Experience shows clothes moths can be captured readily with glue boards that contain no pheromone or other lures, though specialized sex pheromone lures for these species are available.

Clothes moths have a complete metamorphosis. Adults are unable to feed, and it's the larval stages – which are small, cream-colored caterpillars with brown head capsules – that damage fabrics as they feed. In houses, they're most frequently pests of clothing, carpets, rugs, upholstery fabrics, piano felts, brush bristles, blankets, hair from pets, furs, lint and woolens, and any stored wool products, which all contain the animal-derived protein keratin.

Clothes moth larvae can damage other products, such as cotton, linen, synthetic fibers and paper. Such damage is usually incidental, resulting from the larvae damaging such fibers while eating their natural food. Clothes moth larvae are damaging to fabrics stained with materials such as oil from human hair, human sweat, urine, beer, tomato juice, milk or soft drinks. The caterpillars require a certain balance of nutrients in their diet to develop properly. They need vitamin B especially. First instar (stage) larvae can't survive on clean wool but require the nutritional supplements found in soilage, such as body oils from a garment wearer.

CLOTHES MOTH AND CARPET BEETLE CONTROL

Inspection, prevention and control of fabric pests require a good understanding of these insects and how to use insecticides properly. Most homeowners or renters would be advised to contact a professional if they suspect an infestation or have valuable woolen, silk, fur or other animal-based articles they want to protect.

INSPECTION

It's important to remember the adult insects don't feed on woolens or on any of the other materials that might be attacked by the larvae. The presence of adults in an area doesn't necessarily mean larvae are, or will be, in the same area because the adults might have laid their eggs in some other room already and be moving around at random or orienting toward bright sunlight shining through windows because they want to disperse outdoors.

Clothes moth and carpet beetle larvae are found feeding in secluded and protected places most commonly. When searching for them, a flashlight, knife, nail file or small spatula are essential. Larvae usually will be found in dark clothes closets or on furs, taxidermy, bristle brushes, hair padding, woolens, bits of carpeting or other such materials in storage. They're also found in lint, especially under baseboards and around door casings, under the edges of carpeting, in and under wool-upholstered furniture, in collections of animal hair, in air ducts, and anywhere else where suitable food material containing keratin might be available.

When inspecting for carpet beetle larvae, be careful to examine under baseboards, around the bottoms of door casings, under the edges of carpeting and in closets. Use the knife blade or other implement to bring out bits of lint that usually are found in these areas, and examine them closely for live larvae or cast skins, which are sometimes more numerous than live larvae, but they resemble live larvae so closely they can be used for identification purposes.

Roll the edges of the carpet back several inches if possible, and inspect the backing and floor or on both sides of the pad. If eggs have been laid along the edge, the larvae will hatch out and feed (damage) usually for only a few inches in from the edge, and then the larvae will migrate back to the edge for pupation and adult emergence. The infestation and damage doesn't often extend too far away from the perimeter of the carpet or from other areas, such as under seldom moved furniture, where the infestation originated and is focused. Use a flashlight when examining dark closets and other similar places.

In addition to the aforementioned sources, it's important that certain natural sources of infestation be considered. Look for articles of woolen clothing that might have been stored and neglected. Check the premises for old furniture and rugs that might be a source of continuing infestation.

Other important reservoirs that shouldn't be overlooked include sites that represent the natural habitat of these insects. Sparrow, starling or other bird nests, inside or outside of the premises, are common points of origin or continuation for fabric pest infestations. Yellowjacket, mud dauber, hornet, and bumble or honey bee nests found under eaves and in attics, wall voids or crawlspaces also are common sources of carpet beetle infestations. Moth or beetle larvae feed on the remainders of dead insects fed to the wasp larvae, on cast wasp larval skins and sometimes on the living wasp larvae. Paper wasp nests are unlikely to contain larvae of fabric pest species because the nest cells open downward and typically don't provide an accumulation of cast skins or dead insect prey.

The presence of pets, which shed a lot of hair that might provide an important reservoir of food material for carpet beetle and clothes moth larvae, should be considered. Shed hair might accumulate in heating ducts, beneath furniture, in crevices between floorboards, or in hard-to-clean corners. These loose tangles of hair might be sufficient to sustain a small population of fabric pests for a long time, even in places where all wool products have been treated.

SANITATION AND PREVENTION

The prevention and correction of fabric pest infestations require special skills and extensive knowledge about the insects and the problems they create. Preventive measures should be practiced whenever possible because once a hole is made in a piece of fabric, the damage is done and might not be repairable. Preventive procedures include sanitation and exclusion, usually by bagging or packaging susceptible items in tightly sealed containers, and related chemical measures. Furs commonly are stored in specialized cold storage facilities. There also are methods of mothproofing garments or fabrics.

Many fabric pest problems can be prevented and controlled without insecticide use through household cleanliness, including thorough and frequent cleaning of carpet and upholstery with a vacuum cleaner and brushing, airing and dry cleaning susceptible clothing or other articles.

When carpets are cleaned in place, a nozzle-type cleaner, which includes nozzles directed at the edge of the carpet, will be important for control because many of the eggs and damaging larval stages will be at the edges of the carpet. Uprights machines that don't reach the edges of carpet might not help control many of these fabric pest life stages at the key edge locations of carpet. Whenever possible, infested carpet should be rolled back several inches to a foot to vacuum or clean the underside to remove or kill all eggs or larvae present.

Avoid prolonged storage of discarded garments, bedding, fur or animal pelts (unprotected taxidermy) and old wool rugs or furniture upholstered with vulnerable fabrics. A clean environment isn't conducive to fabric-destroying insect activity. It's not necessary the item support fabric insect development. Soiled articles of otherwise indigestible materials and garments of wool-blend fabrics can be attacked.

In all moth and carpet beetle control work, it's essential to eliminate as many potential breeding places as possible. Old pieces of woolen fabric, cut-off pieces of carpeting, old feather pillows, dried insects in collections, and other similar sources of fabric insect food should be destroyed.

Areas under baseboards, behind door casings, under heat radiators, and inside furnace or air-conditioning registers should be cleaned thoroughly with a vacuum cleaner to remove as much lint as possible. A strong-suctioning vacuum cleaner is a useful piece of equipment in such operations. Routine attention to such sanitation procedures by homeowners is a key to limiting fabric-insect problems.

Items in storage that might be subject to attack can be protected if placed within tightly sealed, heavy-gauge plastic bags or other tight and insect-resistant containers. Adult clothes moths have no mouthparts, so they can't chew through anything, and adult carpet beetles are unlikely to chew through thick plastic bags or other tight, heavy-gauge containers that have no indication of a favorable larval food source on the outside. So the careful bagging of or containing uninfested items generally will be effective and reliable.

Other preventive approaches can be used in close association with these sanitation procedures, though their limitations should be recognized and some are falling out of favor because of safety. The most commonly used chemical for preventive control in storage situations has been paradichlorobenzene (PDB), which acts as a repellent and continuous fumigant, though it might not control carpet beetle larvae effectively, except at high concentrations and if tightly contained. Follow label directions carefully when using PDB.

Cedar closets and most cedar chests might have repellency but generally are ineffective for killing or controlling the various life stages of these pests, especially carpet beetles, primarily because a sufficiently tight seal rarely is maintained. Garment storage in cold vaults is an effective preventive measure and is used commonly for very valuable furs or other susceptible garments.

MOTHPROOFING

Various mothproofers will give protection from moth and carpet beetle damage. These chemicals depend on killing larvae after a light feeding or brief contact before feeding occurs. Many fabrics treated with a mothproofing solution at the time of manufacture are safe from damage until the chemicals are removed by washing, dry cleaning or degradation. When homeowners desire to have clothes treated, it's usually best to recommend treatment be made during dry cleaning, if such treatment is available. Such mothproofing of clothes usually is effective during the length of time between cleanings or for storage during the summer.

Certain pyrethroid insecticides such as permethrin, and formulations of nonresidual insecticides, such as pyrethrins or other pyrethroids, are labeled for general mothproofing applications to other articles besides clothing, such as carpets, area rugs, tapestries and drapes. Generally, these are applied after these items have been removed and dry cleaned, if possible, and while located in a convenient place that facilitates a thorough application. Fine sprays should be applied carefully to obtain thorough coverage, but only after possible staining problems have been considered and testing to ensure such problems won't arise.

CONTROLLING EXISTING INFESTATIONS

Complete control of all stages of fabric pests can be achieved if the infested article can be sealed tightly in a polyethylene bag, from which as much air as possible has been removed – which will prevent condensation within the bag after freezing and potential water damage to the article – and placed in a deep freezer for three days at -20°F. The entire article must be chilled down to this temperature, so it may take longer than three days to complete this treatment with certain bulky articles.

When large, bulky items must be stored in commercial freezers, which typically maintain -5 to 0°F, professionals usually do so for at least two weeks. In other cases, vault fumigation might be the chosen method for controlling an infestation on or within specific articles. Neither freezing nor fumigation will leave any effective residual insecticidal protection on the article, but in some cases, this can be achieved by applying an inorganic desiccating dust, such as Drione or Tri-Die, to the article.

Clothing items that haven't been damaged beyond repair can be cleared of an infestation by laundering them in hot, soapy water and drying them using the hot cycle. More delicate fabrics and furs can be dry cleaned to eliminate infestations. However, the entire closet or room in which infested clothing has been kept is likely to be infested. Spray or dust applications of residual pyrethroid insecticides and various nonresidual materials (synergized pyrethrins or other nonresidual pyrethroids) are recommended for spot treatment or general applications as necessary. Desiccating dusts, such as silica aerogel and diatomaceous earth, will be effective against carpet beetle larvae in wall, floor or roof voids. Residual sprays generally are applied with a compressed-air sprayer, using a fine-fan spray nozzle. Some pressurized aerosol formulations also are available.

Critical areas of infestation identified during the inspection process should receive special attention. In carpets, this typically will be around baseboard areas and under furniture. Roll the carpet back several inches to a foot from its edges wherever possible and treat the underside of infested areas. On furniture, apply the insecticide around seams, buttons, cracks and crevices, and padding areas. Void areas within furniture, such as under seating or seat backs, because they can be dusted with a residual insecticide. Any of the aforementioned insecticides can be used alone, but some are available in prepared or ready-to-use combinations. Follow all label directions related to insecticide use. The directions will vary depending on the surface type and the circumstances surrounding the infestation. Regardless of the insecticide, keep everyone, especially children and pets, away from treated bedding, furniture and carpet until they're thoroughly dry.

These residual chemicals will be removed to some extent by subsequent washing, vacuuming and dry cleaning. The insecticide manufacturer's recommendations about length of control and retreatment intervals always should be observed.

If furniture is infested, it might be necessary to open cushions or remove the covering from the bottom of sofas or chairs so padding is exposed. Give special attention to padding inside upholstered furniture, which might be composed of feathers or horsehair – especially in antique furniture – and is susceptible to insect damage.

Low temperature can be an effective treatment for cushions, seat covers, curtains, rolled carpets and other readily portable items that fit into the freezer. If large commercial deep-freezing chambers are available, entire chairs, sofas and mattresses can be treated this way. Items that can withstand elevated temperatures – use caution – can be treated in one hour at 140°F, though bulky items might require longer so insects within will be exposed to that level for at least one hour.

Exposed padding can be treated with sprays that won't harm it, or it can be dusted thoroughly with a suitable insecticidal dust. Dust applications generally are preferred for this situation because no drying time is required and dusts usually give long residual control. Dusts shouldn't be used where subsequent contact with skin or clothing can be expected, so exposed upholstery surfaces or carpeted areas on which people or pets will sit shouldn't be dusted.